KIND AND
USUAL PUNISHMENT

Jessica Mitford

KIND AND USUAL

PUNISHMENT

The Prison Business

Alfred A. Knopf   New York

1975

THIS IS A BORZOI BOOK
PUBLISHED BY ALFRED A. KNOPF, INC.

Portions of this book originally appeared in *McCall's, Harper's,* and *The
Atlantic Monthly.*

Library of Congress Cataloging in Publication Data

Mitford, Hon. Jessica.   Kind and usual punishment.

1. Prisons—United States.   2. Corrections—United States.   I. Title.
HV9471.M58   1973   365'.973   73–7263
ISBN 0–394–47602–6

Manufactured in the United States of America
Published September 17, 1970
Reprinted Twice
Fourth Printing, October 1975

CONTENTS

ACKNOWLEDGMENTS

First and foremost, my most profound gratitude goes to over a hundred prisoners in penitentiaries across the country who, at great risk and cost to themselves, have corresponded with me for the past three years, furnishing information I could not possibly have obtained otherwise. For obvious reasons I cannot thank any of them by name. Taken together, their letters convey as nothing else could the quality of prison life. They are of great variety. Some are intellectual treatises on the criminal justice system, some are factual descriptions of prison routines and procedures, some are full of despair, others witty or sardonic—one writer starts each letter, "Hello out there, Jessica!" These letters sustained me through the often nightmarish task of preparing this book.

There is something deeply disquieting about corresponding with people behind bars. One knows that to buy an 8¢ stamp a convict earning prison wages of 2¢ an hour must work for four hours. One knows that each letter is scrutinized by the prison censor, possibly Xeroxed and put in the prisoner's file for the attention of the parole board, and that as a consequence of making injudicious observations about prison conditions the writer may well find himself or herself in deep trouble with the authorities, even risking extra months or years of confinement.

Frequently my answers would be returned with the malevolent words "Refused by the Censor" stamped on the envelope. I found this totally infuriating, for my correspondent would likely have assumed I had not bothered to answer. There was nothing I could do to correct this impression. There is no recourse from prison censorship, no way of communicating with those inside once the authorities have decided not to permit it. Thus finding oneself suddenly subject to the arbitrary, iron rule of prison discipline one begins to share the prisoner's sense of frustration and helplessness.

I am much indebted to unknown, anonymous collaborators who sent me in plain envelopes all sorts of otherwise unobtainable documents that afford rare glimpses into the workings of the Correctional mind: the minutes of the California wardens' meeting, the memorandum from Senior Statistician Vida Ryan to Director of Corrections Raymond Procunier, Superintendent Fudge's memo about George Jackson, Mr. Procunier's proposal to conduct brain surgery on unruly convicts, the incomparable *Grapevine*, house organ of the American Association of Wardens and Superintendents—all these, and more, arrived in this fashion. Were the senders trustees in some warden's office? Disillusioned employees of the prison? I shall probably never know.

During my three-year odyssey of American prisons literally dozens of people gave me support, encouragement, information, criticism. I can never hope to thank them all adequately, and can only trust that to some small degree I have justified the time and help they have so generously given. Among them: Eason Monroe of the American Civil Liberties Union, who set me on the road; Dr. Robert Coles of the Harvard medical school, Dr. Bernard Diamond of the University of California school of criminology, Tom Murton, former warden of the Arkansas penitentiary, and Professor Alan M. Dershowitz of Harvard University, who urged me forward; Douglas Rigg, David Fogel, and Richard Korn, the trio who invited me to the D.C. Corrections Workshop; John P. Conrad and Judge David L. Bazelon, who got me thinking about criminal types and types of crime.

For research assistance I am indebted to Peter Sussman, who assembled much of the original material; Aileen le Protti, who spent hours finding things in the library; James O. Robison, who prepared the budget information and statistics in Chapters 10 and 11, and who steered me on to many aspects of prison that I should otherwise have missed; Joe Kagan, Roney Nunes, and James R. Williamson, who helped unravel the mysteries of the Inmate Welfare Fund and Prison Industries; Robin Lamson, who plied me with information from the California Assembly Office of Research; Pam Fredericks, who secured my invitation to the 101st Congress of the American Correctional Association; Marion Bromley and Ysabel Rennie of Ohio, for information about Lucasville and related matters; Rosemarie Scherman, who over many months clipped the New York papers for prison news; reporters David Burnham and Walter Rugaber of *The New York Times,* Bob Williams of the Sacramento *Bee,* Morton Mintz of the Washington *Post,* Kitsi Burkhart of the Philadelphia *Inquirer* and author of *Women in Prison,* Robert Patterson of the San Francisco *Examiner,* for much "inside dope"; the Prison Law Project of Oakland, California, which opened up its voluminous files and shared its vast store of knowledge; and the Guggenheim Foundation and the Fund for Investigative Journalism for their generous financial support.

Lawyers all over the country were incredibly generous in sending me transcripts, pleadings, court opinions in prison cases they were involved in. My thanks to Stanley Bass, Alice Daniels, and William B. Turner of the NAACP Legal Defense Fund; Paul Halvonik, Philip Hirschkop, and Herman Schwartz of the ACLU; Malcolm Burnstein, Benjamin Dreyfus, Ronald Goldfarb, Linda Singer, John Hill, Robert L. Segar, E. Barrett Prettyman, Jr., Fay Stender, Michael Keating, Jim Smith, Victor Rabinowitz, Julian Tepper, Paul Albert, Peter Barton Hutt, John Bowers, Laurent Frantz, Charles Garry, Gordon Lapides, Leigh Athearn, Salle Solladay, William vanden Heuvel.

Numerous criminologists, lawyers, ex-convicts, and others were kind enough to read bits of the manuscript at various stages and to offer valuable criticisms and suggestions, among them Aryeh Neier, director of the ACLU; Professor Fred Cohen, Professor Caleb Foote, Professor John Irwin, Professor Anthony Platt, Dr. Sheldon Margen, Dr. Ephraim Kahn; Erik Wright, author of *The Politics of Punishment;* Andrew von Hirsch of the Committee for the Study of Incarceration; Eve Pell of the Prison Law Collective; Mark Dowie of *Transitions;* Willie Holder of the Prisoners Union; writers Maya Angelou and Bettina Aptheker; students Alexander Meiklejohn Frantz and Gerda Ray; my daughter Constancia Romilly; lunching companions Barbara Kahn, Marion Conrad, Pele de Lappe.

The manuscript was typed and retyped with skill and care by Evelyn Mitchell, Dorothy York, and Linda Lippman.

Mrs. Lippman also took charge of compiling the list of organizations in the appendix, prepared the chapter notes, and helped with the index. Sally Mannell managed brilliantly to bring order into a chaotic household. My husband, Robert Treuhaft, endured three years of virtually nonstop prison conversation and was immensely helpful in sorting out the legal material.

My special thanks to Robert Gottlieb, long-suffering and always magnificent editor (who says he sometimes feels he lives in a carefully prepared biting cage, see page 165), and to Nina Bourne of Alfred A. Knopf for their many excellent suggestions.

Lastly, three people made a very special contribution in guiding the direction of this book: Benjamin Dreyfus, who read it at all stages and hammered away at its many shortcomings; Al Richmond, who gave invaluable advice about the organization of the manuscript and who helped prepare the last chapter; and above all Marge Frantz, researcher, critic, and loyal friend, who stuck with it from beginning to end and without whose consistent, painstaking, brilliant help I could never have completed it.

J.M., *March 1973*

KIND AND
USUAL PUNISHMENT

1

THE KEEPERS
AND THE KEPT

My involvement with prisons came about almost by accident.
Early in 1970 I was asked by the American Civil Liberties
Union if I would prepare an article on prisoners' rights to be
published in a national magazine as part of the ACLU's
fiftieth anniversary program. ("That's an easy assignment,"
observed a criminologist with whom I discussed the project.
"Just turn in a sheaf of blank papers—they *haven't* any
rights.") The proposal sounded straightforward enough: there
was a goodly trickle of litigation in the area of prisoners' rights
(since risen in some parts of the country to flood proportions);

one could analyze some of these lawsuits, talk to some lawyers, interview prisoners to find out their major grievances—and prison administrators to get their side of the story . . .

It did not work out that way. I soon discovered that "constitutional rights" (or the lack of them) do not exist in a vacuum but have to be considered in the whole context of the theory and practice of locking people up in cages. And once having stepped into this terrain you do not easily extricate yourself. I found I had plenty of company, people who had wandered into prisondom and had become totally mired in it: lawyers (mostly young) who, having taken on one or two prisoners' cases, eventually wound up spending full time on prison litigation; ex-convicts who, far from shaking the prison dust from their shoes, have dedicated themselves to the cause of their fellows still behind bars; a woman historian in Columbus, Ohio, who, having become curious about the causes of the 1968 riots in the nearby penitentiary, almost single-handedly toppled some of the more hideous abuses in that prison; a Proper Virginian who wrote to me after an outbreak in her hometown jail, "We had a very successful riot here the other day. The prisoners took several hostages, including the director of Corrections."

Early on in my inquiry, a reporter who has for many years covered the prison beat in California forecast some of the difficulties I should encounter. He said, "One thing to understand about prisons: there *is* no truth, you have blending, shifting situations. If you were writing about, say, the Navy, you could soon master the basic facts, but in the penal field the facts all turn into contradictions. Prison is a world unto itself, like a game of Monopoly where the players don't understand the rules."

In pursuit of the elusive "truth" I have dipped into the vast literature on prisons, much of it, alas, as forbidding as the jailhouse itself, couched in the mind-glazing language of sociology: ". . . the prison is a formal or complex organization, a large-scale, multigroup organization characterized by a task orientation, functional specialization, and role-reciprocity," as one writer puts it. I have accumulated court opinions, briefs, government reports, departmental rules and regulations, handbooks for personnel, the ghostwritten memoirs of kindly old wardens, accounts of prison life by convicts and ex-convicts, reams of largely contradictory statistics from various sources. I have met with criminologists, prison administrators, ex-convicts, legislators, lawyers. I have been warned by prison officials not to believe what convicts will tell you, and by convicts not to believe their keepers.

How to find a focus in this shifting, arcane world of some 1.33 million souls, with its complex of juvenile detention homes, city and county jails, federal and state penitentiaries? Years before the Attica uprising and the San Quentin disturbances, the public and the judiciary were well aware of horrible goings-on in some parts of the country—mass graves of murdered convicts in Arkansas, gang rapes of young prisoners in Philadelphia, appalling conditions on southern road gangs—for these and similar stories have appeared with sickening regularity in the press. There are the local jails, as distinct from federal and state prisons, for short-term prisoners. In these, men and women awaiting trial, unable to make bail, are lodged for months on end with convicted offenders serving sentences of less than one year. The jails have no apologists, they are universally recognized to be hellish places.

I decided to forego these pockets of iniquity* and instead to travel the broad highway of prison reform, to look mainly at those large, well-ordered, highly financed prison systems that have incorporated as their stated policy reforms fought for over the decades: rehabilitation as opposed to punishment, utilization of the latest scientific therapy techniques, classification of prisoners based on their performance in prison, a chance

* The exception: an account of my sojourn in the D.C. women's jail, Chapter 2.

for every offender to return to the community as soon as he is
ready.

To find one's way around the modern prison system one
must first master the new terminology. Notable advances have
recently been made in this area. The authors of the Attica
Commission Report, evaluating the work of a special committee appointed by the governor in 1965 to study the treatment of prisoners, concluded that the committee's major ac-
complishment after five years of labor was to change the names
of all the state's maximum security prisons: "Effective July 8,
1970 . . . there were no more prisons; in their places, instead,
stood six maximum security 'correctional facilities.' The prison
wardens became 'institutional superintendents' . . . and the
old-line prison guards awakened that morning to find themselves suddenly 'correctional officers.' No one's job or essential
duties changed, only his title. Certainly the institutions themselves did not change . . . To a man spending 14 to 16 hours
a day in a cell being 'rehabilitated,' it was scarcely any comfort
and no reassurance to learn that he was suddenly 'an inmate in
a correctional facility' instead of a convict in a prison." In the
same spirit some prisons are now called "therapeutic correctional communities," convicts are "clients of the correctional
system," solitary confinement and punishment cells have become "adjustment centers," "seclusion," or, in Virginia, "meditation."

The uninitiated are prone to take the new nomenclature at
its face value. A young friend of mine with a college degree
in social work, seeking a job in San Francisco, came across
an advertisement in the *Chronicle*'s Help Wanted columns for
"Correctional Officers" at San Quentin. It sounded, he said,
like "really constructive, humanitarian work"; on applying, he
was amazed to find that the openings were for prison guards. A
clue as to what his correctional duties would have been was
supplied when he was rejected as "too short" and because he
wears glasses.

There are various schools of thought about prisoners. To their keepers, they are a sort of subspecies of the human race. The viewpoint of many an old-time guard was vividly evoked by Edward F. Roberts, former correctional officer at Raiford State Prison, Florida, in his testimony before the Congressional Select Committee on Crime: "Shortly after I arrived at Raiford, a supervisor told me, 'Mr. Roberts, before you are here one year you'll hate a convict worse than anything on earth.' An officer at Raiford is expected to feel that a convict is the lowest thing on earth."

The up-to-date prison administrator would never be caught uttering such thoughts. He is fond of saying, "Prisoners are people." But as Mr. James Park, associate warden of San Quentin, explained to me, they are also "immature," "have an inability to relate to others," "suffer from retarded mental growth." Thus they are not *quite* people—diminished, inferior people at best.

Then there are those who think prisoners are the salt of the earth, exemplified by attorney Fay Stender in her preface to *Maximum Security*: "I certainly feel that, person for person, prisoners are better human beings than you would find in any random group of people. They are more loving. They have more concern for each other. They have more creative human potential." In a word, they are superior to the rest of us.

From my extensive correspondence with prisoners and acquaintance with ex-convicts, I am not inclined to subscribe to any of the above, but rather concur with Eugene Debs, who, after doing time in three county jails and two penitentiaries, wrote: "The inmates of prisons are not the irretrievable, vicious and depraved element they are commonly believed to be, but upon the average they are like ourselves, and it is more often their misfortune than their crime that is responsible for their plight . . . a prison is a cross-section of society in which every human strain is clearly revealed. An average prison, and its inmates, in point of character, intelligence, and habits, will compare favorably with any similar number of persons outside of prison walls."

Or Bertrand Russell, imprisoned in the First World War for opposing the draft, who writes in his autobiography: "I was rather interested in my fellow prisoners, who seemed to me in no way morally inferior to the rest of the population . . ." And further, in letters to his family: ". . . Life here is just like life on an ocean liner; one is cooped up with a number of average human beings . . . Being here in these conditions is not in the same world of horror as the year and a half I spent at a crammer's. The young men there were almost all going into the Army or the Church, so they were at a much lower moral level than the average."

Debs also takes account of the dehumanizing effect of prison on all who enter the gates: "The guard and the inmate cease to be human beings when they meet in prison. The one becomes a domineering petty official and the other a cowering convict. The rules enforce this relation and absolutely forbid any intimacy with the human touch in it between them. The guard looks down upon the convict he now has at his mercy, who has ceased to be a man and is known only by his number, while, little as the guard may suspect it, the prisoner looks down upon him as being even lower than an inmate."

The character and mentality of the keepers may be of more importance in understanding prisons than the character and mentality of the kept. Would that the hordes of researchers who now invade the prisons would turn their attention to these—explore their childhood traumas, flip inkblots to find out what their Rorschach tests reveal, generally try to discover what makes them tick and what made them choose this occupation in the first place. For after all, if we were to ask a small boy, "What do you want to be when you grow up?" and he were to answer, "A prison guard," should we not find that a trifle worrying—cause, perhaps, to take him off to a child guidance clinic for observation and therapy?

Having researched the literature and found a dearth of information on characteristics of prison guards, Dr. Allan Berman of the University of Rhode Island psychology department administered a series of psychological tests to a number of correctional officer candidates and prison inmates with a view to determining the "violence potential" of each group. He found the profiles "almost identical," with the inmates on the whole coming off slightly better than the guards. The test results, says Dr. Berman, "imply that the officer group actually has the potential for even more unexplained lashing out than does the inmate group." His conclusion: ". . . the officer candidates are as likely as the inmates to engage in assaultive behavior. This would carry along the correlative implication that the reasons why one group is behind bars and the other group is guarding them may be due to incidental factors . . ."

The "incidental factors" which determine the respective roles leap to the eye from every statistical study. Those who become prison inmates are predominantly black, young, unemployed, from large cities. Those who become guards are overwhelmingly white, middle-aged, from small rural towns. This process of natural selection is reinforced and perpetuated by prison geography. Most prisons are located in isolated areas where they often become the economic mainstay of the surrounding countryside,* drawing on the local population for

* In December 1972, when the California Department of Corrections announced it would shortly close down the nine-year-old Susanville Prison, the newspapers ran touching stories about what this would mean to the guards, their families, real estate values, school subsidies, and small businesses in this little community of 6,000. Under the headline "A Mountain Town Battles To Keep Its Grip On Life," the San Francisco *Examiner* reported that residents were up in arms over the threatened loss of the prison; the local radio station manager had urged all listeners to send Christmas cards to Governor Reagan with the message, "Remember Susanville!" Apparently the governor heeded this outpouring of Yuletide sentiment, for the following February the Sacramento *Press Journal* reported that the prison would not be closed after all, but would instead be remodeled at an estimated cost of $4,635,000.

their personnel; some are near Army bases, and in these the guards are almost all ex-servicemen.

Thus many become guards because they have no other choice of livelihood. Their pay is low, the civil service standards are minimal, they are generally considered to be at the bottom of the law-enforcement barrel. A reading of recent congressional hearings on prison conditions reveals, not unexpectedly, that beyond those men and women who become guards because they have no alternative, this occupation appeals to those who like to wield power over the powerless and to persons of sadistic bent.

From prison regulations we can infer that the guard mentality as described by Edward F. Roberts and Eugene Debs is not only a natural outcome of the job but a prerequisite for it. San Quentin's "orientation booklet" for new prison employees (a classified document, hard to come by) reads like instructions for entering a cage of wild animals: "Remember, CUSTODY is always first in order of importance." "Always imply that you expect the correct attitude." "Be constantly on the lookout for contraband, especially weapons of any kind." "Never show the slightest uncertainty as to the course of your action. You must be a leader in the strongest sense of the word; must know and show your authority." "Do not fraternize with any inmate or group of inmates. *It could cost you your job.*" (Emphasis in the original.)

An item in the April 1972 *Grapevine*, house organ of the American Association of Wardens and Superintendents, refers to me as "our great 'know-it-all' on prisons Jessica Mitford, who readily admits she acquired her 'vast' knowledge in a scant two years . . ." This is unkind of the wardens, and I hasten to disclaim any such pretensions. I am sure I shall never know as much as the wardens and superintendents about what they do. Nor did I find them particularly anxious to share their secrets—I soon discovered that prison walls are meant

not only to keep convicts in, but to keep the would-be investigator out. Perhaps understandably, the prison administrator is extremely loath to open up his operation to public
scrutiny. My efforts to penetrate the walls were met with varying success; since the warden has traditionally regarded himself as unchallenged ruler of his domain, his decision whether
or not to admit outsiders (and if so, which outsiders) depends
entirely on his own whim.

A standard reason given for refusing permission to go into
the prison is that it is "too dangerous" for the civilian, and
particularly for a woman, untrained in the ways of convicts,
to enter those precincts. I encountered a variety of other
official explanations for excluding reporters.

In February 1971, a group of prisoners in McNeil Island
Federal Penitentiary smuggled out a letter urgently asking
me to come and see them—the penitentiary was shut down
tight in a full-scale strike against intolerable conditions, they
said. Many strike leaders had been thrown in the hole; some
who were seriously ill had been denied medical attention.
They wanted their story given to the outside world. After the
warden flatly turned down my request to visit the prisoners, I
telephoned the federal Bureau of Prisons in Washington,
D.C., and was told by their press relations man that there is
a "long-standing rule, enacted in 1930 when the bureau was
first established, against allowing reporters to interview prisoners." Why is that? "To protect the prisoners' right of privacy,"
said Press Relations, smoothly. I had not realized that prisons
were noted for their respect for the right to privacy, I answered.
But in any case, had not the prisoners waived this right when
they invited me to come and talk with them? "It might create
a logistical problem for the warden." What sort of logistical
problem?—the warden is there, the prisoners are there, I can
be there. "The warden has decided against it."

In Massachusetts I was told by a lawyer for the Department of Corrections that it would "not be in the best interests

of the institution or the inmate" for me to visit one Dan Nolan, a prison militant who had been locked up in a punishment cell in Walpole Prison for several months for the offense of writing to the editor of the Boston *Globe*, and who had asked me to come and see him. Pressed as to why, the lawyer explained that "the inmate might make defamatory remarks about the institution."

The Principal Keeper (his actual title) of Trenton Prison, New Jersey, admitted a group of us from the Committee for Public Justice to look over the premises—with the proviso that we were not to have any conversation with the prisoners. Why? "Because I won't have it!" Which is roughly the same answer I got from a number of other wardens in both state and federal jurisdictions. As a result, I have left a trail of lawsuits in my wake, brought on my behalf by law firms engaged in "pro bono publico" work, the ACLU, the NAACP Legal Defense Fund and the Prison Law Project, against numerous Departments of Corrections and the federal Bureau of Prisons, in an effort to pry open those closed doors via the courts. (This route is, however, long and tortuous; as this book goes to press none of the cases has been decided.)

Some of the more go-ahead prisons offer guided tours for interested parties, and I could have gone on one of these at San Quentin. But after I read this directive to prisoners in the Director's Rule Book, I decided not to bother: "When visitors are present do not try to attract attention or talk with a visitor unless given permission by an employee. If you are asked a question by a visitor, answer politely but briefly and to the point." Prisoners, it seems, like good children, are to be seen and not heard.

In my travels around the country I found but one Department of Corrections that had a fairly open policy toward admitting outsiders, that of the District of Columbia. It was under their auspices that I spent a day and night in the Women's Detention Center. The department also permitted a day-long conference at Lorton Prison, the D.C. equivalent of Sing Sing or San Quentin, sponsored by the "Lorton Lifers," a group of 60 men under life sentence. About the same number of "free world" men and women came to this gathering—judges, lawyers, social workers, relatives of the convicts. After the plenary session, we broke up into panels, each chaired by a Lifer, and lunched together in the cafeteria. While the content of the meeting was not great ("there were too many judges around, so we couldn't speak freely," said one Lifer), the fact that it took place at all was significant, negating as it did all the official reasons I had been given for not permitting outsiders in other prisons. If one could spend a day freely mingling with the Lorton Lifers, why not with inmates of McNeil Island, Walpole, San Quentin?

No doubt prison administrators sense that to permit the media and the public access to their domain would result in stripping away a major justification for their existence: that they are confining depraved, brutal creatures. As *The New Yorker's* Talk of the Town column put it, "During the Attica uprising, millions of Americans were brought face to face with convicted criminals for the first time. Most of us were wholly unprepared for what we saw . . . The crowd we saw on television was not a mob but a purposeful gathering, and the men we saw were not brutalized, although they may have suffered brutality—they were unmistakably whole men. We saw men acting with dignity, not men stripped of their pride . . . The reformers among us had believed that what in effect were crimes committed by society against the prisoners had brutalized them, or rendered them less than fully human. The hard-liners among us had believed that the crimes committed by these prisoners against society had branded them as less than fully human forever. The prisoners paid with their lives to prove to all of us the truth of what they had explicitly told us: 'We are not beasts. We are men.' "

2

WOMEN IN CAGES

There were nine of us in the paddy wagon. We were all handcuffed and some were also shackled at the ankles, depending on the "crime" we had chosen to be booked for at the police station. Those who had opted for "prostitution" or "shoplifting" wore handcuffs only, while the "murderess" in our midst was draped with chains. There were uneasy giggles as the wagon roared off through the Washington traffic with siren at full blast. An earnest young criminology student spoke up reprovingly: "It's nothing to laugh at, we're supposed to *feel* this, to put ourselves in the place of women who are really going through it."

Easier said than done, for this was, after all, largely an exercise in play-acting, part of an extraordinary eight-day conference, the District of Columbia Crime and Corrections Workshop, held in Shenandoah College, Virginia, under the sponsorship of the National College of State Trial Judges. Participants, a cross-section of the D.C. criminal justice system, included judges, prosecutors, policemen and -women, defense lawyers, prison officials of all ranks—and eighteen prisoners who, accompanied by their guards, arrived in buses each morning and stayed through the dinner hour. There were six men from Lorton, the rough, tough men's penitentiary for convicts serving long sentences, six juvenile offenders, six inmates from the D.C. Women's Detention Center. The "Con-Sultants," they called themselves.

Halfway through the workshop, all "free-world" conferees were required to spend a day and night behind bars as prisoners. The judges were sent to Lorton (to the applause of inmates of that institution, many of whom had been sentenced by these same judges), the younger men to the juvenile correctional facility, the women to the D.C. Women's Detention Center.

Our group in the paddy wagon included a black policewoman, a black former inmate presently working in a drug clinic, a lawyer, a social worker. The rest were observers for whom this was a first introduction to the world of prisons: two students, a reporter from the Washington *Post*, a young woman from the Junior League, a member of the Maryland legislature, and myself, on assignment for the American Civil Liberties Union.

As we raced toward our destination I wondered whether anything could really be accomplished by this voluntary subjection to brief confinement. The prison population knew we were coming (the Con-Sultants having briefed them), the authorities from director to guards on duty were expecting visitors. At best, I thought, we would experience a sanitized version of prison life and should not be able to "feel" the pains of imprisonment in any real sense.

Yet when it was all over, I concluded there were advantages to our special status. Perhaps one is better off "feeling" less and observing more. Had I been a real prisoner, caught up in the net of the criminal justice system, I would have been far too preoccupied with my own predicament to afford the luxury of pondering the purpose of it all, nor would I be likely to have the opportunity to question the director of the prison about policy, purposes, and philosophy of prison administration.

The Women's Detention Center is a gloomy pile of masonry at the edge of the ghetto, formerly used by the police department as a temporary lock-up for people taken into custody. Since 1966 it has been used for detention of women awaiting trial and as a reformatory for sentenced women. Once inside, we were taken in charge by several women guards, symbolically clanking real keys.

The first step for the newly arrested is called "Reception," although it was unlike any reception I have ever attended. The handcuffs now dispensed with, we were assembled in a large room; our handbags emptied on a counter and the contents catalogued, we were photographed and fingerprinted. Ordered to strip, we were searched for narcotics: "Bend over, spread cheeks." Our heads were examined for lice. From a bin of prison dresses in brightly patterned cottons with unfinished hem and sleeves we chose for approximate fit. (I learned later that these bizarre garments were ordered by Mr. Kenneth Hardy, director of D.C. Corrections, a benign administrator who told me he thought they would restore "a sense of individuality" to women formerly required to wear prison gray.) Cigarettes, lipsticks, paperback books were scrutinized for contraband and then returned to us.

From the recesses of the building we heard a disturbing muffled, rhythmic wail. Was it the sound of mechanical equipment, an air-conditioner gone slightly out of kilter? I asked a guard. "Oh, that's just Viola, she's in Adjustment for her nerves."

"It doesn't seem to be doing her nerves much good."

"Her trouble is she's mental, always bothering the other inmates. So we keep her in Adjustment."

Living quarters at the Detention Center are on two floors, each accommodating some 45 women. About half the women confined there have not been convicted of any crime. Their sole offense: inability to make bail, for which they are imprisoned, often for months on end, waiting for their cases to come to trial. (A recent census report reveals that 52 percent of the nation's jail population are "confined for reasons other than being convicted of a crime," or, to put it more bluntly, because they are too poor to pay the bail bond broker.) Unlike most jails, where the "presumed innocent" are herded in with the guilty, the Detention Center segregates those awaiting trial from the convicted offenders.

We were placed with the latter group. Our fellow-inmates were mostly "misdemeanants" serving sentences of less than one year (three months is the average term here), but there were also women sentenced for felonies—robbery, murder, aggravated assault—awaiting transfer to a federal women's penitentiary. More than 90 percent of both inmates and staff of this prison are black, as is 71 percent of the general population of the District. A ghetto within a ghetto.

Our domicile was a short and narrow corridor on one side of which are the cells, at the far end a dining room with television set. Women were standing in desultory knots in the corridor, sitting in their cells, or watching TV. The overall impression: a combination of college dorm (silly jokes, putdowns, occasional manifestations of friendliness), lunatic asylum (underlying sense of desolate futility), a scene from *The Threepenny Opera* (graffiti on the walls: "Welcome to the Whores' Paradise!"). I was struck by the number of little-girl faces, kids who except for their funny-looking clothes could be part of a high-school class, and by one or two sad, vacant old faces. The median age here is twenty-five.

As we entered, our names were called out, we were handed sheets and led to our assigned cells, tiny cubicles with two beds, a dresser, and a clothesline for hanging coats and dresses (the prison, like most, is fearfully overcrowded and now holds more than twice its intended capacity). My cell-mate was a pleasant-faced black woman in her early thirties, named Della. She welcomed me like a good hostess, helped me make my bed, and apologized for the stale, dead smell compounded of people, food, and disinfectant that pervaded our quarters: "We used to have at least some breeze, but they've cut off the air. There's a new rule against opening the corridor window because they claim the inmates were letting down rope to haul up contraband brought by their boyfriends. Now, does that make any sense? With the officers watching you like a hawk every minute of the day and night?"

From Della I learned that, as I had suspected, we had been let off lightly at "Reception." The usual routine, she told me, includes a vaginal examination as part of the search for con-traband and a Lysol spraying of the head. She had found the experience horrifying, totally degrading. Furthermore some of the guards "get their kicks" from scaring the neophyte in-mate by horrendous hints of what to expect from the "bull-daggers" (prison slang for lesbians). Is there actually much homosexuality, I asked? A certain amount, but not as much as the administration seems to think. "They are really hipped on the subject," she said. "They have bed checks all hours of the night, they come around flashing their bright lights, it's hard to get any sleep."

Della had been in the section for unsentenced prisoners for nine weeks waiting for her trial. In all that time she never saw her court-appointed lawyer, and her letters to him were un-answered. She met him for the first and only time in court on

the day of her trial, where he advised her to plead guilty:
"But he never asked me anything about my case, said he didn't
want to hear. Said if we tried to fight it, the judge would be
hard on me. But I don't see how he could have been any
harder—six months for one count of soliciting!"

We wandered out into the crowded corridor to join the
others. Because of the visitors, Della told me, everyone was
on good behavior: "We *scrubbed* this place, girl!" And clean,
though dreary, it certainly was.

Our group was there to learn, so we started asking questions. The Maryland legislator inquired about recreation
facilities. "Re-cre-ation!" an inmate hooted derisively. "Come
here, girls, I'll show you." She led us to one of the barred
windows, through which we could barely descry a small concrete quadrangle entirely hemmed in by the building. On fine
days, she explained, the entire population is sometimes taken
down there for an hour or so if the correctional officers have
time. Vocational training programs? "There's eight old broken-
down typewriters somewhere in the building. I don't know
if anybody ever uses them, though. Or you can go down to
group therapy, but who wants it? A bunch of us bullshitting
about our deprived lives?"

We had been told the authorities had arranged for the
visitors to sample various aspects of prison life, that some
would spend the night in sickbay, others would be brought before a disciplinary committee, accused of breaking the rules.
To fortify myself against the latter eventuality I asked for a
copy of the prison rule book. "No inmate shall engage in loud
or boisterous talk, laughter, whistling or other vocal expression," it said in part. "Talking is permitted at all times except
in church and in school, but talking must be conducted in
a normal voice except on the recreation fields." One of the
prisoners, a vivacious young black woman, confided to me
that she was due to be disciplined that day for laughing too
loud but had been reprieved because of our visit: "It's a dumb

thing anyway to be punished for laughing. When you come to think of it, sometimes it's sort of a release to laugh out loud."

As in hospitals, food is served at unexpected times. At four thirty we went into the dining room to collect our trays of dinner. The food wasn't bad, but like most institutional cooking it was dull and starchy with a touch of wilted green. We ate tuna casserole, Jell-O, a choice of weak coffee or a puce-colored synthetic fruit drink. One of the few white prisoners came and sat beside me, a romantic-looking blonde in her early twenties; she reminded me vaguely of prison movies I had seen. Convicted of possession of heroin, she described her first days in the Detention Center as absolute torture: "You come down cold-turkey, they're not equipped here to treat addicts." She proved to be a discriminating connoisseur of the nation's prisons, and twinkled quite merrily as she rated them for me, one-star, two-star, as in a motel guide. "This joint's by no means the worst, but it's not the best, either." Her goal is to be admitted into one of the treatment centers for narcotics addicts, but so far she has been blocked because they are all full up. She has no idea when, or if, there will ever be an opening for her. What does she do all day? "I work some in the kitchen, just to keep from going crazy. There *isn't* anything to do here." Housekeeping jobs, she explained, are available on our floor but not for the unsentenced women on the floor below: "In some ways they're punished worse than we are, although they haven't even been found guilty of anything." Pay ranges from $5 a month to a top of $13, the higher rate being awarded on the basis of performance and "attitude"; there is no compensation for working part of a month.

"Jessica . . . Mitford . . . to the third . . . floor." The voice over the intercom was tinny and disembodied. I started to the door of our corridor and was at once intercepted by a correctional officer. "No, no, you can't go down by yourself," she said, shocked, and, seizing my arm, led me to the elevator. "You're wanted by the disciplinary committee," she said severely. Lock, double-lock all the way, from our fourth-floor abode to the elevator and down. A third-floor guard took over and led me to the small office where I was to be tried.

My prosecutors, jury, and judges (for the disciplinary committee incorporates all three functions) were the prison psychologist and two correctional officers. They were trying to look suitably stern, to make it all as "real" as possible. One of the officers read off the charges: "At 17.05 hours, Officer Smith opened the door to your cell and found you locked in a passionate embrace with Maureen [the reporter from the Washington *Post*]. As you know, this is an extremely serious offense. What have you to say?"

What, indeed. I could of course deny all (insist she wasn't my type?), but, mindful of my assignment for the ACLU, I decided to go another route. What if I challenged the whole legality of this "trial"? I took a deep breath.

"First, I should like to draw your attention to the prison rule book." (The trio seemed surprised; the rule book, it seems, is not generally available to prisoners.) "I see you have infractions broken down into two categories: *crimes* such as assault, theft, possession of narcotics, and failure to obey *rules* —wasting food, vulgar conversation, not making one's bed. Homosexual acts between inmates are listed here as a crime. Before I plead guilty or not guilty to the charge, I should like to see a copy of the statute under which homosexuality between consenting females is a crime. I don't believe it is a crime in any jurisdiction. I'm already in here for one crime. If you find me guilty of another, it will go very hard with me when my case comes before the parole board."

My inquisitors exchanged uncertain looks. "It's not a *statute,* it's a rule," said one.

"But as you've listed it as a *crime,* I want a lawyer to represent me. I want to cross-examine the officer who accused me, and to call witnesses who'll verify that I was in the dining room watching TV at 17.05 hours."

Nonplussed, the chief correctional officer said she thought they should send for Mrs. Patricia Taylor, the director of the Detention Center. This was done, and I repeated my request.

"Jessica, you must realize we're only trying to help you," said Mrs. Taylor.

"Well, thanks a lot. But I should still like to assert my right to the same procedural safeguards that should apply to any citizen accused of crime."

"You don't understand, Jessica, you are in an institution now, you're an inmate, you haven't a right to a trial. *We'll* decide who's telling the truth. Now, if Officer Smith hadn't seen that, why would she say she had?"

"But I say she's lying, I'm not guilty and I want a chance to prove it. Why don't you bring her down here so I can question her, and clear myself?"

"Jessica, do you realize what would happen to discipline if we permitted the inmates to cross-examine the officers?"

We went over this a few times; I had made my point, but since it was only a charade (and I knew Maureen was waiting for her turn before the disciplinary committee) I soon gave up, and was duly sentenced to "ten days in Adjustment."

What if the situation had been real, I kept thinking? Instead of making this well-reasoned little speech about my constitutional rights I would have been shouting furiously, perhaps in tears. And instead of listening and answering calmly, would not my captors have responded in kind—put me down as a troublemaker or psycho for asserting my rights, and treated me accordingly? Now I was beginning to "feel." The governessy young criminology student would be proud of me!

Accompanied by the chief correctional officer, who firmly gripped my arm (did she think I might try to escape?), I

traversed several corridors and those eerie wails gradually
came closer. The officer in charge of Adjustment took me
over. Here the stripping of individuality is turned up a notch.
I am given a gray cotton shift in place of the patterned dress
from the bin. Bra, shoes, cigarettes, wristwatch, wedding ring,
paperback books are confiscated. To her chagrin, the officer
discovers that all eight solitary cells are occupied (which
means that about one in ten of the inmates is locked up
there). I will have to double up with a thief who was put in
Adjustment for beating up other women. Not a terribly reassuring thought. The door giving onto the corridor of solitary
cells is immensely thick, opened by my keeper with several
huge keys. Now we hear the screams full force—not just from
Viola, they seem to be coming from several cells. "*Let me
out!*" "*I want out!*" Women are moaning, shrieking, pound-
ing with their fists against their doors. This is "Adjustment"?
To what are they being adjusted?

"You have company," the officer announces tersely to my
cellmate, and she double-locks the door behind us. Mindful
of my companion's alleged infraction I flash her a conciliatory
smile, but she is pleased to see me, makes me welcome, we
sit on the bed (sole furnishing except for an open toilet that
flushes only from the outside) and talk.

The Thief's Tale was well larded with fantasy, or so it
seemed to me. A tall, attractive black woman about thirty
years old, she was essentially "state-raised": orphaned at
the age of eight, in and out of trouble, in and out of juvenile
detention (but mostly in) until her middle twenties. "I tried
to go straight for a spell, but I don't really dig it. On welfare,
with two little kids to raise—what kind of life is that?" She
turned to pickpocketing, a discipline in which she had
received much theoretical instruction during her many years
in reformatories. "The best place is near the Americana Hotel
in New York, that's where lots of businessmen hang out." She
told me she could clear upward of $500 on a good night and

that once she netted $14,000 from the wallet of an unsuspecting passerby. Yet, in view of her expanding needs, she found it slow going: "My boyfriend and I wanted to start a nightclub in Atlantic City, we figured on $100,000 to open it. So I told him leave it to me, I'd raise it." The quickest way, she decided, was to travel around the country from motel to motel cashing bad checks in amounts of $500 to $1,000. She had got up to $40,000 of the needed capital when the feds caught up with her.

Our corridor had all but quieted down after the guard left. Now the screams started up again, coming apparently from the cell directly opposite ours, a terrible outcry of rage and misery, shrieks and obscenities interspersed with deep, racking sobs. We peered through the tiny grill in our door and could dimly see movement behind the opposite grill, hands clawing, head wildly shaking. My cellmate shouted soothing words across the corridor: "Now, honey, hush up, won't you? If you be a good girl and stop all that noise, I'll speak to Mrs. Taylor, and I'll see that she lets you out of there. If I say to let you out, she'll do it."

"Who is she?" I asked.

"She's a juvenile, she's down here because she's too young to go upstairs."

"*Too young*? How old is she?"

"Seventeen."

Of course I didn't believe a word of it. Just another of her delusions, I thought, like the $14,000 wallet, the obliging motel managers who cash $1,000 checks for strangers, her role as confidante and adviser to Mrs. Taylor.

Soon—in an hour and a half, to be exact—my "ten days" were up. For further clarification I sought out Mrs. Taylor, a highly qualified black administrator with a long background in social work and Corrections. No longer an "inmate," I was formally ushered into her office, where we discussed what I had heard and seen that day.

First, as to the general prison scene, what are the women here being punished for? The great majority, about 85 percent, are in for a combination of prostitution and narcotics (as one inmate had told me, "They go together like salt and pepper; once you're hooked on the stuff, you have to hustle to support your habit"). Does Mrs. Taylor think prostitution is a crime? No, she believes many women are driven to it by circumstances outside their control. What about drug addiction? That's not a crime either, it's a sickness and should be treated as such.

Checking Mrs. Taylor's opinions against those of others in authority, from correctional officers to Mr. Kenneth Hardy, director of the department, I found unanimity on these points. *None* believed that prostitution and drug addiction are "crimes." Thus the patently crazy situation in which the keepers themselves, up and down the line, believe their mandate to imprison these women rests on a fundamentally unsound premise. But, they all point out, they are merely doing the job required of them by the courts, the legislature, the public: "We don't choose the inmates, we have to take whoever the judges send us."

In our discussion of the Adjustment setup, this sense of total irrationality deepened.

The case of Viola: she is a diagnosed schizophrenic, Mrs. Taylor explained. Because of a recent court decision, she cannot be transferred to a mental institution without a sanity hearing; but the courts are so clogged with cases that no date for such a hearing has been set. How long will she stay locked away in Adjustment? Nobody knows.

The screaming girl across the corridor? My cellmate was right after all, she really *is* only seventeen, she really *is* there because she is too young to go upstairs—in solitary because of a mistake of the Juvenile Court. Finding that she was incorrigible in the children's prison, the judge sentenced her to Women's Detention. But the law says that juvenile offenders may not mix with the adult prison population, so she was put in Adjustment. At first she was allowed "privileges"—mail, books, cigarettes. After several days of total solitude she set her mattress on fire (perhaps, Mrs. Taylor surmised, "to draw attention to herself?"). Consequently she is now considered a "disciplinary case" and all privileges have been withdrawn. How long will she have to stay there? For about three months, until she turns eighteen.

"Aren't you afraid she'll go completely insane by that time?"

"Well . . . there is that danger . . ."

Why, I wanted to know, is the inmate who is being punished for some infraction denied books, newspapers, games—*anything* that might make solitary confinement more tolerable?

"The idea is to remove her completely from the environment. You heard those women screaming in there. If we'd kept you in there for twenty-four hours, you would have been screaming, too."

"Then—is that your purpose, to destroy my self-control, to reduce me to a helpless, howling infant?"

"That's a risk we have to take," said Mrs. Taylor with a faint smile.

What of homosexuality, recognized by everyone in Corrections as an inevitable consequence of long-term segregation of the sexes? Having driven them to it, why punish for it? "Love affairs" between women inmates, born out of loneliness, longing for human affection, lack of male companionship— does Mrs. Taylor consider this sort of behavior criminal? "No, but if permitted it might lead to jealousy and fights. Besides, I am responsible for their morals while they are in here." *Their* morals? Yet Mrs. Taylor had something there, I thought. Is this not the essence of women's prisons, the punishment of unchaste, unwomanly behavior, a grotesque bow to long-out-moded nineteenth-century notions of feminine morality?

There is, Mrs. Taylor regretfully conceded, barely even the pretense of a useful trade or educational program for the women, most of whom she expects to see back again in her custody shortly after they are let out. They exit and reenter as through a revolving door, three quarters of those who are in now have been here before. Chances of getting a decent job when they leave, slim enough for ghetto women in any circumstances, are almost nonexistent for those with prison records, so inevitably they turn to their old ways when released.

This, then, is an American women's prison of the 1970's —and "not the worst," as my dinner companion said. A life of planned, unrelieved inactivity and boredom . . . no overt brutality but plenty of random, largely unintentional cruelty . . . a pervasive sense of helplessness and frustration engulfing not only the inmates but their keepers, themselves prisoners trapped in the weird complex of paradoxes that is the prison world.

And everyone passes the buck. The administrators protest they are merely carrying out the orders of the courts, in a setting they have inherited and are powerless to alter. The judges say they have no choice but to enforce the laws as given to them by the legislature. The lawmakers? With one eye on reelection they bow readily to mindless demands for ever "tougher measures" as a panacea for the nation's ills.

The day after our stay in the Detention Center the workshop reconvened at Shenandoah College to exchange prison experiences. Gone was the calm, deliberative atmosphere one associates with professional conferences. Outraged speaker after speaker rose to denounce angrily what he or she had experienced as senseless, dehumanizing, uncivilized. A judge of the Court of General Sessions, known heretofore for his harsh and punitive sentences ("He hands out years like they were Easter lilies," said a Con-sultant), declared in shaken tones, "We wouldn't stand for having the bears in the zoo treated as we treat the men in Lorton."

In retrospect, it seems to me that the really stunning achievement of the conference—at least in terms of my own response —was this breakthrough into the secret world of prisons, a world traditionally sealed off from judicial and public scrutiny. If the experiment could be repeated on a vast scale, if judges, prosecutors, public officials, and just plain citizens could be required to spend a few days in the archaic conditions to which they so readily condemn their fellows—then perhaps the buck might stop somewhere.

One inescapable conclusion of our experience was that the vast bureaucracies that run the prisons are static, mired in the past, incapable of moving unless pushed. They are impervious to learning even from the history of their own vocation. For example, it has been well known for two centuries that prolonged solitary confinement can drive people insane. Yet today solitary confinement is still the routine punishment for the unruly or "difficult" inmate in every prison in the country. Changing the name of this misbegotten game to Adjustment has not altered its hideous consequences.

The defensive administrator will nonetheless point to progress. Time was, and not so many years ago (he will tell you), that women were flogged, locked in sweat boxes, sexually abused by sadistic male personnel—he will fill you up with horror stories. The women in the Detention Center have many privileges formerly denied prisoners: they are allowed to keep a few personal effects, makeup, photos of their children, books and newspapers, their food is adequate and nourishing, their quarters clean and vermin-free. Certainly he will admit, there are many deficiencies: inadequate recreation space, lack of rehabilitative programs, insufficient therapy, etc. This old building should be torn down, better accommodations should be provided, more personnel . . . the traditional cry of bureaucrat and reformer alike is for bigger budgets, shinier and more modern prisons.

Yet is this not begging the larger question? The purpose of these stagnant human backwaters is unfathomable. Nobody can explain it, because it defies rational explanation. Are the streets of Washington safer because some ninety-plus young women are locked away behind bars? Are these women "improved" or "reformed" by the experience? Above all, what of the "morals" of those who confine them?

Mort Sahl (describing an interview by Dave Garroway
with the warden of Ohio State Prison): "Garroway
asked him what motivates a man to devote 40 years
of his life to prison work? And the warden replied,
with characteristic modesty, 'I guess I like people, Dave.' "
— THE FUTURE LIES AHEAD, L.P. RECORD

3

101 YEARS
OF PRISON REFORM

It is surprising to learn that prison as a place of confinement
for the ordinary lawbreaker is less than 200 years old, an
institution of purely American origin, conceived by its inven-
tors as a noble humanitarian reform befitting an Age of En-
lightenment in the aftermath of a revolution against ancient
tyrannies. There had, of course, been prisons and dungeons
of sorts for centuries; but these were reserved for persons of
quality, state prisoners, the prince, queen, statesmen who
had fallen afoul of the reigning monarch, the philosopher,
mathematician, religious heretic suspected of harboring dan-

gerous or subversive ideas. Lowlier offenders were detained in
prison only while awaiting trial. In colonial America, as in
Europe, the standard punishment for the pickpocket, the
thief, the highwayman was hanging; for lesser offenders
mutilation, the stocks, public brandings and floggings.

Shortly after the Revolution a group of high-minded Pennsylvania Quakers set about the abolition of these barbarities
from the New World. As a result of their efforts the first
penitentiary (their word), the Walnut Street Jail in Philadelphia, was established in 1790. Under Pennsylvania state
law, only murder remained a capital offense. The basic feature
of the penitentiary was total isolation of the offender from his
fellow-miscreants, to the end that he would be sheltered from
their contaminating influence and, serving out his sentence
in solitude with only the Bible for company, would in the
course of time be brought to penitence for his sins and thus
to eternal salvation.

Unfortunately for the good intentions of the Quakers, things
began to go wrong from the very beginning. So many convicts went mad or died as a consequence of the solitary regime
that by the mid-nineteenth century it was generally abandoned,
to be supplanted by the more profitable "congregate hard
labor" system. Not only did their penitentiaries make men insane rather than penitent, but the very corporal punishments
the Quakers had sought to replace flourished and proliferated
behind the walls as prison management devised ever more in-
genious tortures to enforce discipline and control their charges:
sweat boxes, the water cure, iron yokes.

The movement for prison reform developed almost simultaneously with the prison itself. Appalled by these atrocities,
nourished by a missionary zeal to reclaim errant souls,
spurred on by emerging techniques for people-changing, reformers rallied to this cause. The prisoner, fortunate object of
all this Christian solicitude, was to be transformed into a
paragon of industry and virtue—according to one mid-nine-

teenth-century prison enthusiast, everybody could profit from a stretch in the penitentiary: "Could we all be put on prison fare for the space of two or three generations, the world would ultimately be better for it," declared the Reverend James B. Finley, chaplain of the Ohio Penitentiary. It would be a salutary experience, he said, "should society change places with the prisoners . . . taking to itself the regularity and temperance and sobriety of a good prison . . . As it is, taking this world and the next together . . . the prisoner has the advantage."

Elam Lynds, nineteenth-century warden of Sing Sing, once observed: "In order to reform a criminal you must first break his spirit." This twin objective, I discovered, is essentially what both prison administrators and a host of well-intentioned reformers have pursued from that day to this, albeit they do not express it in Warden Lynds' forthright fashion, and over the years methods of achieving it have changed.

More than a century after Lynds' observation that to be mended a spirit must first be broken, I received a letter of invitation to the 101st Congress of the American Correctional Association from E. Preston Sharp, Ph.D., executive secretary, which read in part: "Unfortunately many of the articles and television programs indicate that the only people interested in changes for improvement are either ex-offenders or individuals who have been caught with the reform spirit. Many conscientious correctional administrators have been working in the vineyards for years attempting to make changes and we are hopeful now that with the aroused public interest and intelligent understanding progress can be made."

To get some notion of the background of this organization I plunged into its published literature, beginning with the bulky proceedings of the first Congress of the (then) National Prison Association held in Cincinnati in 1870. From this volume one gathers the meeting was marked by an atmosphere of near-euphoria. As described by a participant, Zebulon R.

Brockway, a leading penologist of his day, the experience was "similar to that of the disciples on the Mount of Transfiguration." Hard-headed wardens, caught with the reform spirit, joined in prayer, song, and enthusiasm with clergymen, progressive penologists, and philanthropists to announce the dawning of a new day for the transgressors in their custody.

The Honorable A. T. Goshorn of Ohio, keynote speaker, set the tone: "Granite walls and iron bars, although they deprive the criminal of his liberty and inflict a just physical punishment, do not work that reformation in the soul of the man that will restore him to society regenerated and reformed. . . . It is left to the philanthropic and Christian sentiment of the age to devise ways and means to elevate the unfortunate and wayward to the true dignity of manhood."

In pursuit of these lofty goals the congress passed a remarkable and innovative Declaration of Principles: the objective of "moral regeneration" of the prisoner as opposed to "infliction of vindictive suffering"; classification of criminals "based on character" as determined by their progress in prison; and the indeterminate sentence under which the offender would be released as soon as "the moral cure" had been effected and "satisfactory proof of reformation" obtained.

After the customary thanks to the Cincinnati hosts for their "graceful hospitality, commodious hall, extended drive through the charming suburban regions adjacent to this noble metropolis," and to the "quartette club of ladies and gentlemen who kindly volunteered their services," the Reverend Mr. F. H. Wines summed up: "My heart is almost too full for utterance. We have all, I am sure, caught the inspiration of this great occasion. Let us, then, go down from these heights of social, intellectual, and spiritual enjoyment, to toil faithfully, resolutely, persistently in our respective fields of labor, and so fulfill the high mission assigned us by Providence—the regeneration and redemption of fallen humanity." Following his address, the congress joined in singing the song "Where do you journey, my brother?"; the doxology was chanted, the benediction pronounced, and the congress adjourned.

Thereafter the association met annually, and has preserved the record of its proceedings in a series of bound volumes. Except for a subtle change in terminology, these read strangely like carbon copies of each other. One can pick a volume at random—1890, 1905, 1922, 1936, 1953—and find therein that a crime wave of staggering proportions is engulfing the United States (lyrically described in the 1870 proceedings as "the sweeping and swelling tide of crime"); that juvenile institutions, county jails, and local lock-ups are breeding grounds for crime; that, in contrast, the prisons are doing well but could do better, if only they had better trained personnel at higher salaries, and more money for rehabilitative programs.

Each year the speakers ardently reaffirm the great reform principles enunciated by the founders and each year they stand on new thresholds, face fresh horizons, welcome the winds of change as the penological millennium draws nearer. They look back with pride and forward with confidence. "It is impossible for an American to touch the subject of prisons without pardonable pride!" declared a speaker at the 1916 Congress. An 1874 speaker: "There is no doubt that good work is done at the penitentiary of Michigan City. It only remains to go on unto perfection . . ." Of course there are shortcomings, obstacles to be overcome, some attributable to the persistent apathy of the public and legislatures and some to the recalcitrance of convicts; as a consequence, prisons are perennially at the crossroads. Yet on the whole these toilers in the vineyards (a recurrent self-descriptive phrase of prison officialdom) are doing a remarkable job, given the low quality of human material they must work with.

An occasional discordant note is struck, as when a guest speaker at the 1964 meeting, Judge John W. Oliver, remarked with some asperity on this complacent repetitiveness: "Must we not, on the basis of the record, place as the first order of discussion the question of how effective this association has been in implementing the ideals to which it long has given lip service? Twenty-four years ago your then president [James V. Bennett] told you that 'like the leaders of 1870 we stand at the end of an era, and like them, we face toward a new day in prison work.' . . . The disturbing thing to me is that what was recommended as a position statement of this association in 1963 was neither new nor was it something that had been recently discovered. We can go back a hundred years before the famous Declaration of Principles in 1870 to find the germs of what has been said over and over again for almost two hundred years."

But two years later they are at it again. Mr. Harold V. Langlois, delivering the 1966 presidential address, describes a new edition of the *Manual of Correctional Standards*: "It permits us to linger, if we will, at the gates of correctional Valhalla—with an abiding pride in the sense of a job superbly done! We may be proud, we may be satisfied, we may be content."

I had the opportunity to observe this Valhalla at first hand in August 1971, at the five-day meeting of the 101st Congress of the American Correctional Association in the Americana Hotel at Miami Beach. (The name of the organization was changed by the prison people in 1952 to the American Correctional Association, as part of the general move to package their product under a more agreeable name and, incidentally, to upgrade their jobs.) The theme of the meeting was "The Truth About Corrections: Finding It, Proving It, Practicing It, Telling It." To receive this truth some 2,000 delegates— up from an attendance of 230 in 1870—converged on the Americana, a genial coterie of wardens, jailers, commissioners of Corrections, and others in the business of locking people up.

A man from Mars dropping into the Americana might be forgiven for concluding that all is serene in the world of Corrections; he would have no way of knowing that an unprecedented, bloodstained upheaval is rocking the prisons from coast to coast. For the most part, our conferees bask in a rosy aura of self-approbation—albeit tinged, one detects, with a certain uneasy defensiveness. Speaker after speaker notes with satisfaction that we are now entering our second hundred years of prisc￼ reform. Offerings listed in the conference program are many and various: plenary sessions, president's cocktail party, ladies' fashion show, and some 90 panel workshops on subjects ranging from "Laying the Correctional Table" to "Practical Liturgical Implementation in the Correctional Setting."

Some congress vignettes:

The delegates' kit, containing a copy of the agenda, a large miscellany of information about Miami nightclubs and other available recreation in the Playground of America, a packet of advertising from the Bacardi rum people, decals of the American flag, and as a fun souvenir of the occasion, a dummy license plate: "ACA Congress, Miami, Florida, 1971," furnished by convict labor in Raiford State Prison.

The exhibits, great halls-full of them, each manned by a concessionaire hawking his wares. They point up the schizophrenia endemic to this field of endeavor. Here a display of educational materials: "WORLD OF WORK," with its acronymic slogans: TEMPO (Training Through Education, Motivation, and Personal Orientation), TOOL (Typing Office Orientation Lab). Next to it, "American Bible Society Serving Correctional Institutions with Holy Scriptures." And next to that, a veritable torture chamber of iron chains with illustrations showing seven different ways to tie a man up ("other uses will readily suggest themselves to officers who become familiar with this equipment"), the Advanced "Han-Ball" Tear Gas Grenade ("It instantly pours out a dense and continuous cloud of CN or CS tear gas right at the place where it will do the most good"), the Stun-Gun Non-Lethal Weapon System ("Hits the target with the immobilizing impact of a heavyweight fighter's knockout punch! Demonstration 5 P.M. today! Meet at this booth."). Nearby, mute reminders of some recent unpleasantnesses, are booths of Super Secure Ware, stainless steel, unbreakable toilets, the Penal Mattress, flame-resistant and knifeproof, of stoutest plastic construction, and the "temperproof" security radiator: "Defies the most violent treatment or abuse."

The all-night cocktail party given by the handcuff people in their penthouse suite, at which wardens, parole officials, and administrators got slowly sloshed, and were heard toward midnight murmuring suggestions of a skinny-dip to various unattached ladies. Could these prison high-ups abide by the total abstinence from liquor and licentious behavior they require of parolees, one wondered?

The memorial meeting on the opening night at which a prayer is offered for wardens and others who passed on this year (although not, it seems, for prisoners who had passed or been caused to pass). The officiating clergyman speaks of love—one cannot, he explains, reform people without loving them. But he moves swiftly from love to the Black Militants, the new breed of political prisoner and their dangerous allies on the outside. He proceeds to draw a moving word-picture of the embattled Corrections administrator who today is forced to spend a third of his time in court defending against accusations of inmates (when presumably he could have spent that time loving them?). Typically, he says, the inmate is represented by the leading legal talent of the community, the courtroom packed with his supporters, while the administrator must make do with some young fellow from the attorney general's office.

Our cordial host, Mr. Louie Wainwright, head of Corrections in the Sunshine State, who according to the program notes has given "life-long dedication" to the work of penal reform. He directs his welcoming speech to the congress theme—The Truth About Corrections. "The first hundred years is the hardest!" he remarks with rueful jocularity. (But he is mum about what happened at Raiford State Prison only six months earlier, when prison guards opened machine-gun fire on unarmed convicts conducting a peaceful hunger strike, wounding 63. For several days thereafter, prisoners, including those wounded in the shooting, had been beaten by guards, gassed, forced to run a gauntlet, kicked in the testicles, and otherwise brutalized. "I gave the order to shoot," Mr. Wainwright told *The New York Times* at the time. "I did it to protect the inmates." He later testified before a congressional committee that he thought the shooting "was in poor taste," but that he did not "think it was a violation of any statute or of any particular regulation.") There is, he says, a social and cultural revolution taking place in the home, the streets, the campuses—it all adds up to a fertile field for delinquency. Yet despite these difficulties, declares Mr. Wainwright, "Corrections has moved forward in the past hundred years, at least in our thinking if not in reality."

The annual banquet, which, like Gala Night on board ship, takes place on the penultimate evening of the congress. Proceedings wind up with presentation of an award to the Jailer of the Year— leading one to speculate whether in times when the death penalty was being enforced, an Executioner of the Year award would have been tendered?

For the first time this year the meeting of the Wardens' Association, formerly closed to all but members, is open to all ACA delegates. The wardens en masse are a rather overwhelming sight, magnificently grizzled, stone-faced, wide of girth—they seem to have stepped straight out of an old Cagney movie. There are exceptions to this prototypical physiognomy, and one of these, Warden Russell E. Lash of Indiana State Penitentiary, rises to address his colleagues in the air-conditioned magnificence of the Floridian Room. At thirty, Warden Lash, spruce, clean-cut, is the youngest of his profession in the country, and, unlike the majority who have risen from the ranks of guards, he is a sociologist by training. "We're proud of you, Russ. You're doing a heck of a fine job," says the chairman. Mr. Lash's topic: The Role of Prison.

"The most fundamental role of prison," says Warden Lash, "is that of an overt, visible sign that laws have been broken. Without the sign of the prison, our free democratic society would be in complete chaos! This raises the question, is prison the best sign? My answer: It is *the* best, proven, demonstrably the best." Turning his attention to critics of prison, he demolishes them with a few well-chosen words: "In recent years a small group of radicals and naïve nincompoops have adopted slogans like 'Tear down the walls! Prisons are a failure!' This is growing to the point where it is permeating even our own correctional literature. I'm amazed at those who say prison is dehumanizing, they never support this contention with facts, because they *have* no facts."

There is a certain amount of levity, as when one of the older wardens, seeking to hold the attention of his audience, prefaces his remarks with this rib-tickler: "Now, I was explaining the other day how you can spot a homosexual: they wriggle in their seats, look over their shoulder at the other fellow, get up and walk around a lot—yes, fellows, I shall be watching you while I give my talk!" And a cautionary word on the necessity for correct parlance; a warden has just declared he is "tough," and another rises to admonish him. "Words like 'tough' are not good. Instead, we should use expressions like 'control.' Also, I prefer to say 'therapeutic segregation'—it's still segregation, of course, but it doesn't sound so bad."

Across the hall some of the Treatment and Research people are in session in a panel of the American Association of Correctional Psychologists Committee on Personnel Standards and Training. Their appearance is in marked contrast to the wardens'—a new and younger breed, fresh-faced, earnest collegiate types, some with hair creeping down almost below the ears. One of them, his theme "The Correctional Officer as Agent of Change," describes a highly successful experiment he conducted at Draper Institute for young male offenders in Alabama. Using several large and impressive charts to illustrate successive stages of his research, he speaks at some length in the polysyllabic language of his calling. Translated and boiled down, his account of the research project is this: prisoners assigned to the clothing factory were constantly showing up late for work, their dismal records in this respect graphically shown in Chart I under the heading "Tardiness"—from the lines we could see that some had indeed been very late. "The median tardiness was one hour," says the young psychologist, pointing with a ruler. The experiment, he explains, consisted of the correctional officer in charge giving warning that in the future late-comers would have to work overtime for two hours in the evening. Presto! The graphs on Chart II show that following this announcement tardiness dropped almost to zero. After a few days the prisoners were told they were being put back on the old system, no penalties for being late. The *dénouement*, on Chart III, clearly shows that following this announcement tardiness was soon back to normal. "Findings such as these show the correctional officer that he can become an agent of change," concludes our speaker, and sits down to applause.

I subsequently received a report from the Alabama Civil Liberties Union on the prisons of that state in which yet another Draper research project is cited: "Correctional Officer Training in Behavior Modification—An Interim Report, May 1971." The project, as described by the researchers:

. . . an officer in charge of a farm squad instituted a program directed towards the reduction of inmate cursing while on the job. Although not a serious problem when first considered, it did "bother" the officer, who commented that "no one likes a foul mouth," and that if he were an employer he would require that the people employed by him either stop their cursing or find a new job.

The officer was provided a wrist counter which, during the first ten recording periods, he carried in his pocket and counted episodes of cursing in such a fashion so as to insure that the members of the squad were not aware of his actions. Examination of Figure 2 indicates that the median curse rate during the first ten days of recording (private) was .57 curses per hour per man. Although not exceedingly high, the officer reported that a small number of men did the majority of cursing, and that rather than single words, they emitted long episodes of cursing. Starting on the eleventh day and continuing through the following 19 days the officer placed the counter on his wrist and recorded publicly, informing the members of the squad of his actions. The median curse rate during these 20 days dropped to .28 which is significant as indicated by the median text ($X^2 = 15.68$ df = 1, p is less than .05)

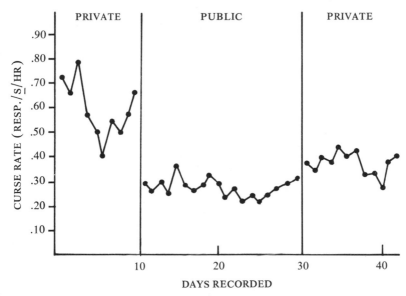

Fig. 2. Rate of cursing per man per hour among inmates working on the institution's farm.

On the 31st day the officer returned to the private recording procedure followed during the first ten days of the project. Although there was a slight but significant increase in curse rate ($X^2 = 14.93$, df = 1, p is less than .05) the median rate of cursing during this period was only .38 lower than those first ten days. Findings such as these point out the potential of the correctional officers as behavior change agents.

If this is the Interim Report, what, one wonders, could the Final Report portend?

An attorney for the Missouri Department of Corrections speaks to the topic of "Coping with the Judiciary," a subject very much on everybody's mind this year. He stresses the urgent need for training more lawyers to defend cases brought by inmates against the prison, and points to some winning techniques he has used. It is important to get "impressive witnesses, people like Maurice Sigler, your president-elect," but the crucial task is to destroy the inmate plaintiff's credibility before the jury: "You are generally dealing with difficult inmates with bad backgrounds, it's not hard to convince a jury they deserve what they're getting—assuming, of course, your institution is abiding by American Correctional Association standards. Once the jury says, 'We don't believe the inmate,' that's the end of the case." The attorney tested out these techniques with signal success in a recent case involving the use of Mace against inmates: "The house chemist for the Mace manufacturer testified for us. The district judge gave us a complete bill of health—he believes the warden, doesn't believe the inmates. That's the way to win a lawsuit. The court ruled that 'judicious use of Mace is not a denial of any federally protected right.' "

Observing the congress in action day by day, listening to the speeches and discussion, hobnobbing with the participants, one got the feeling that there must be more to it than met the eye: surely many of these people in the top echelons of prison work were there because of a genuine desire to help people in distress, to improve conditions, to implement the long-stated goals and principles of their profession? It was extraordinarily difficult to sort out who was who, to distinguish between the man of goodwill and the authoritarian bigot, for the prevailing mood of the congress was one of monolithic unity against dissension from within or criticism from without. Discussion following the scheduled speeches generally consisted of commendation of the speaker for a job well done ("That was a heck of a fine talk, Jim!") and remarks in support of his position; it is apparently not customary at these meetings to dispute or find fault with what is said from the platform.

As the days wore on, one could discern a minority—a very silent minority at that, for they were not among the featured speakers—who were in restive disagreement with the whole tenor of the congress. On the last day, during the report of the Resolutions Committee at the business meeting, one of these, Tom Murton, bid fair to disturb the unruffled good fellowship of the meeting. Debate on his resolution afforded a flash of insight into the correctional mind.

Murton is the prison warden who was brought to Arkansas by Governor Winthrop Rockefeller in 1967 to clean up the penitentiaries of that state. In the course of his brief employment he made public disclosure of conditions as he had found them at Tucker and Cummins prison farms: rampant corruption not only among guards but at the highest levels of the system, the routine use of brutality by whip, and the "Tucker telephone," a fiendish electric torture device, as a means of subjugating prisoners. Furthermore, curious about persistent rumors that some 200 convicts had been murdered over the years and buried about the farmland, he caused portions of the pastures to be dug up—and discovered three decapitated skeletons in shallow graves, whereupon Governor Rockefeller promptly relieved him of his duties. Nor did he win the approbation of his colleagues in Corrections. As Paul W. Keve, then Minnesota commissioner of Corrections, wrote in *Crime and Delinquency*: "Murton felt that past misdeeds were being excused and hushed up. Actually, the governor apparently was not disputing the fact that many inmates had died suspicious deaths in past years; he simply recognized that nothing could be gained by digging up bones except to embarrass and antagonize the legislature. The important job was not to exhume the past, but to build the future." A strange view of law enforcement for a top man in the field, but one that was to be overwhelmingly endorsed by the congress.

Murton's resolution was twelfth, and last, to be acted on. The first eleven passed without a hitch: commendations and appreciation to Louie Wainwright, to the Florida Correctional Association, to the chaplains for their various contributions to a helpful, successful, and spiritually uplifting congress, and so on. Murton's resolution called upon the congress to urge an investigation by Arkansas authorities into the presumed killings of more than 200 missing prisoners, and to reject in principle the "unwarranted use of force in controlling inmates, which often results in their death." The chairman of the Resolutions Committee, Walter Dunbar, assistant commissioner of Corrections in New York, was to achieve worldwide notice a few weeks later when he participated in the decision to send troops into Attica, and told the press the Attica hostages had been mutilated and murdered by convicts, a story that proved to be a lie. Addressing himself to the resolution, he explained mournfully that a no-vote was recommended because "the allegations deal with a subject that properly belongs with law enforcement authorities" and because "the American Correctional Association has for a hundred years enunciated principles of humane treatment of prisoners." Nevertheless somebody had the temerity to move adoption.

Austin MacCormick, grand old man of prison reform, rose to speak against the motion. He himself had been on the scene in Arkansas at the request of Governor Rockefeller, he said, and was well aware of the atrocities. True, things were moving slowly but the prison board, in spite of the fact half of them were against anything Rockefeller did, accepted Mr. MacCormick's report, abolished flogging, endorsed educational programs. Then Tom Murton went before Senator Dodd's committee, filled the caucus room with pictures, brought a fascimile of the "Tucker telephone." "Of all the times to choose! We had a special session of the legislature with key bills sponsored by the department of Corrections before it." Worse yet, Murton opened the graves in a blaze of publicity:

"He knew it was illegal to dig up the bodies without a court order, one of the worst felonies, but he didn't get a court order or have police standing by—no, instead he brought in reporters and television. Arkansas was as mad as could be. We came within an ace of not getting our bills through. I'm unable to analyze Murton's megalomania, he won't stop talking about those things." Springing a surprise, Mr. MacCormick added: "I think many prisoners *were* murdered, although I've never said this publicly before. But the motion shouldn't be passed because it has no basis in truth. I hope it is voted down."

Defending his resolution, Murton responded, "Some people don't like my methods, but I don't know how to deal with murder subtly. I dug up those graves with the permission of Governor Rockefeller who wanted to shock the legislature into action—ten legislators were wiped out in the process, and so for that matter was I. I think we are now in the second hundred years of reform. Why does ACA refuse to condemn murder? When do we start dealing with issues, and cut out the resolutions patting each other on the back?"

Having handily defeated the motion by voice vote, the toilers adjourned to repair to their respective vineyards until next year when the congress would reconvene at Pittsburgh under the thought-provoking slogan "Get to the Point!"

4

THE CRIMINAL TYPE

Time was when most crimes were laid at the door of the Devil. The English indictment used in the last century took note of Old Nick's complicity by accusing the defendant not only of breaking the law but of "being prompted and instigated by the Devil," and the Supreme Court of North Carolina declared in 1862: "To know the right and still the wrong pursue proceeds from a perverse will brought about by the seductions of the Evil One."

With the advent of the new science of criminology toward the end of the nineteenth century, the Devil (possibly to his chagrin) was deposed as primary cause of crime by the hand of an Italian criminologist, one of the first of that calling, Cesare Lombroso. Criminals, Lombroso found, are born that way and bear physical stigmata to show it (which presumably saddles God with the responsibility, since He created them). They are "not a variation from a norm but practically a special species, a subspecies, having distinct physical and mental characteristics. In general all criminals have long, large, projecting ears, abundant hair, thin beard, prominent frontal sinuses, protruding chin, large cheekbones." Furthermore, his studies, consisting of exhaustive examination of live prisoners and the skulls of dead ones, enabled him to classify born criminals according to their offense: "Thieves have mobile hands and face; small, mobile, restless, frequently oblique eyes; thick and closely set eyebrows; flat or twisted nose; thin beard; hair frequently thin." Rapists may be distinguished by "brilliant eyes, delicate faces" and murderers by "cold, glassy eyes; nose always large and frequently aquiline; jaws strong; cheekbones large; hair curly, dark and abundant." Which caused a contemporary French savant to remark that Lombroso's portraits were very similar to the photographs of his friends.

A skeptical Englishman named Charles Goring, physician of His Majesty's Prisons, decided to check up on Lombroso's findings. Around the turn of the century he made a detailed study of the physical characteristics of 3,000 prisoners—but took the precaution of comparing these with a group of English university students, impartially applying his handy measuring tape to noses, ears, eyebrows, chins of convicts and scholars alike over a twelve-year period. His conclusion: "In the present investigation we have exhaustively compared with regard to many physical characteristics different kinds of criminals with each other and criminals as a class with the general population. From these comparisons no evidence has emerged of the existence of a physical criminal type."

As the twentieth century progressed, efforts to pinpoint the criminal type followed the gyrations of scientific fashions of the day with bewildering results. Studies published in the thirties by Gustav Aschaffenburg, a distinguished German criminologist, show that the pyknic type (which means stout, squat, with large abdomen) is more prevalent among occasional offenders, while the asthenic type (of slender build and slight muscular development) is more often found among habitual criminals. In the forties came the gland men, Professor William H. Sheldon of Harvard and his colleagues, who divided the human race into three: endomorphs, soft, round, comfort-loving people; ectomorphs, fragile fellows who complain a lot and shrink from crowds; mesomorphs, muscular types with large trunks who walk assertively, talk noisily, and behave aggressively. Watch out for those.

Yet no sooner were these elaborate findings by top people published than equally illustrious voices were heard in rebuttal. Thus Professor M. F. Ashley Montagu, a noted anthropologist: "I should venture the opinion that not one of the reports on the alleged relationship between glandular dysfunctions and criminality has been carried out in a scientific manner, and that all such reports are glaring examples of the fallacy of *false cause* . . . to resort to that system for an explanation of criminality is merely to attempt to explain the known by the unknown."

Practitioners of the emerging disciplines of psychology and psychiatry turned their attention early on to a study of the causes of criminality. Dr. Henry Goddard, Princeton psychologist, opined in 1920 that "criminals, misdemeanants, delinquents, and other antisocial groups" are in nearly all cases persons of low mentality: "It is no longer to be denied that the greatest single cause of delinquency and crime is low-grade mentality, much of it within the limits of feeble-mindedness." But hard on his heels came the eminent professor Edwin H. Sutherland of Chicago, who in 1934 declared that the test results "are much more likely to reflect the methods of the testers than the intelligence of the criminals" and that "distribution of intelligence scores of delinquents is very similar to the distribution of intelligence scores of the general population . . . Therefore, this analysis shows that the relationship between crime and feeblemindedness is, in general, comparatively slight." In *New Horizons in Criminology,* Harry E. Barnes and Negley K. Teeters go further: "Studies made by clinical psychologists of prison populations demonstrate that those behind bars compare favorably with the general population in intelligence. Since we seldom arrest and convict criminals except the poor, inept, and friendless, we can know very little of the intelligence of the bulk of the criminal world. It is quite possible that it is, by and large, superior."

Coexistent with these theories of the criminal type was one that declares the lawbreaker to be a deviant personality, mentally ill, of which more later.

It may be conjectured that prison people were not entirely pleased by the early explanations of criminality; perhaps they welcomed the rebuttals, for if the malfeasant is that way because of the shape of his ears, or because of malfunctioning glands, or because he is dim-witted—none of which he can help—why punish? In this context, George Bernard Shaw points out, "As the obvious conclusion was that criminals were not morally responsible for their actions, and therefore should not be punished for them, the prison authorities saw their occupation threatened, and denied that there was any criminal type. The criminal type was off." The perverse old soul added that he knows what the criminal type is—it is manufactured in prison by the prison system: "If you keep one [man] in penal servitude and another in the House of Lords for ten years, the one will shew the stigmata of a typical convict, and the other of a typical peer." Eugene V. Debs expressed the same thought: "I have heard people refer to the 'criminal countenance.' I never saw one. Any man or woman looks like a criminal behind bars."

Skull shape, glands, IQ, and deviant personality aside, to get a more pragmatic view of the criminal type one merely has to look at the composition of the prison population. Today the prisons are filled with the young, the poor white, the black, the Chicano, the Puerto Rican. Yesterday they were filled with the young, the poor native American, the Irish or Italian immigrant.

Discussing the importance of identifying the dangerous classes of 1870, a speaker at the American Prison Congress said: "The quality of being that constitutes a criminal cannot be clearly known, until observed as belonging to the class from which criminals come . . . A true prison system should take cognizance of criminal classes as such." His examination of 15 prison populations showed that 53,101 were born in foreign countries, 47,957 were native-born, and of these, "full 50 percent were born of foreign parents, making over 76 percent of the whole number whose tastes and habits were those of such foreigners as emigrate to this country."

At the same meeting, J. B. Bittinger of Pennsylvania described the tastes and habits of these dissolute aliens: "First comes *rum,* to keep up spirits and energy for night work; then three fourths of their salaries are spent in *theaters* and *bar-rooms* . . . many go to *low concert saloons* only to kill time . . . they play *billiards* for *drinks,* go to the *opera,* to the *theater, oyster suppers* and *worse* . . . they have their peculiar literature: dime novels, sporting papers, illustrated papers, obscene prints and photographs." Commenting on the large numbers of foreign-born in prison, he added: "The figures here are so startling in their disproportions as to foster, and apparently justify, a strong prejudice against our foreign population."

The criminal type of yesteryear was further elaborated on in 1907 by J. E. Brown, in an article entitled "The Increase of Crime in the United States": "In the poorer quarters of our great cities may be found huddled together the Italian bandit and the bloodthirsty Spaniard, the bad man from Sicily, the

Hungarian, Croatian and the Pole, the Chinaman and the Negro, the Cockney Englishman, the Russian and the Jew, with all the centuries of hereditary hate back of them."

In 1970 Edward G. Banfield, chairman of President Nixon's task force on the Model Cities Program, updated these descriptions of the lower-class slum-dweller in his book *The Unheavenly City: The Nature and Future of the Urban Crisis*, an influential book that is required reading in innumerable college courses. Since it is reportedly also recommended reading in the White House, presumably it reflects the Administration's conception of the criminal classes as they exist today.

"A slum is not simply a district of low-quality housing," says Mr. Banfield. "Rather it is one in which the style of life is squalid and vicious." The lower-class individual is "incapable of conceptualizing the future or of controlling his impulses and is therefore obliged to live from moment to moment . . . impulse governs his behavior . . . he is therefore radically improvident; whatever he cannot consume immediately he considers valueless. His bodily needs (especially for sex) and his taste for 'action' take precedence over everything else—and certainly over any work routine." Furthermore he "has a feeble, attenuated sense of self . . .

"The lower-class individual lives in the slum and sees little or no reason to complain. He does not care how dirty and dilapidated his housing is either inside or out, nor does he mind the inadequacy of such public facilities as schools, parks, and libraries; indeed, where such things exist, he destroys them by acts of vandalism if he can. Features that make the slum repellent to others actually please him."

Most studies of the causes of crime in this decade, whether contained in sociological texts, high-level governmental commission reports, or best-selling books like Ramsey Clark's *Crime in America*, lament the disproportionately high arrest rate for blacks and poor people and assert with wearying monotony that criminality is a product of slums and poverty.

Mr. Clark invites the reader to mark on his city map the areas where health and education are poorest, where unemployment and poverty are highest, where blacks are concentrated—and he will find these areas also have the highest crime rate.

Hence the myth that the poor, the young, the black, the Chicano are indeed the criminal type of today is perpetuated, whereas in fact crimes are committed, although not necessarily punished, at all levels of society.

There is evidence that a high proportion of people in all walks of life have at some time or other committed what are conventionally called "serious crimes." A study of 1,700 New Yorkers weighted toward the upper income brackets, who had never been arrested for anything, and who were guaranteed anonymity, revealed that 91 percent had committed at least one felony or serious misdemeanor. The mean number of offenses per person was 18. Sixty-four percent of the men and 27 percent of the women had committed at least one felony, for which they could have been sent to the state penitentiary. Thirteen percent of the men admitted to grand larceny, 26 percent to stealing cars, and 17 percent to burglary.

If crimes are committed by people of all classes, why the near-universal equation of criminal type and slum-dweller, why the vastly unequal representation of poor, black, brown in the nation's jails and prisons? When the "Italian bandit, bloodthirsty Spaniard, bad man from Sicily," and the rest of them climbed their way out of the slums and moved to the suburbs, they ceased to figure as an important factor in crime statistics. Yet as succeeding waves of immigrants, and later blacks, moved into the same slum area the rates of reported crime and delinquency remained high there.

No doubt despair and terrible conditions in the slums give rise to one sort of crime, the only kind available to the very poor: theft, robbery, purse-snatching; whereas crimes committed by the former slum-dweller have moved up the scale with his standard of living to those less likely to be detected and punished: embezzlement, sale of fraudulent stock, price-fixing. After all, the bank president is not likely to become a bank robber; nor does the bank robber have the opportunity to embezzle depositors' funds.

Professor Theodore Sarbin suggests the further explanation that police are conditioned to perceive some classes of persons (formerly immigrants, now blacks and browns) as being actually or potentially "dangerous," and go about their work accordingly: "The belief that some classes of persons were 'dangerous' guided the search for suspects . . . Laws are broken by many citizens for many reasons: those suspects who fit the concurrent social type of the criminal are most likely to become objects of police suspicion and of judicial decision-making." The President's Crime Commission comments on the same phenomenon: "A policeman in attempting to solve crimes must employ, in the absence of concrete evidence, circumstantial indicators to link specific crimes with specific people. Thus policemen may stop Negro and Mexican youths in white neighborhoods, may suspect juveniles who act in what the policemen consider an impudent or overly casual manner, and may be influenced by such factors as unusual hair styles or clothes uncommon to the wearer's group or area . . . those who act frightened, penitent, and respectful are more likely to be released, while those who assert their autonomy and act indifferent or resistant run a substantially greater risk of being frisked, interrogated, or even taken into custody."

An experiment conducted in the fall of 1970 by a sociology class at the University of California at Los Angeles bears out these observations. The class undertook to study the differential application of police definitions of criminality by varying one aspect of the "identity" of the prospective criminal subject. They selected a dozen students, black, Chicano, and white, who had blameless driving records free of any moving violations, and asked them to drive to and from school as they normally did, with the addition of a "circumstantial indicator" in the shape of a phosphorescent bumper sticker reading "Black Panther Party." In the first 17 days of the study these students amassed 30 driving citations—failure to signal, improper lane changes, and the like. Two students had to withdraw from the experiment after two days because their licenses were suspended; and the project soon had to be abandoned because the $1,000 appropriation for the experiment had been used up in paying bails and fines of the participants.

The President's Crime Commission Report notes that "the criminal justice process may be viewed as a large-scale screening system. At each stage it tries to sort out the better risks to return to the general population," but the report does not elaborate on *how* these better risks are sorted. Professor Sarbin suggests an answer: "To put the conclusion bluntly, membership in the class 'lawbreakers' is *not* distributed according to economic or social status, but membership in the class 'criminals' *is* distributed according to social or economic status . . . To account for the disproportionate number of lower class and black prisoners, I propose that the agents of law enforcement and justice engage in decision-making against a back-cloth of belief that people can be readily classified into two types, criminal and noncriminal."

This point is underlined by Professor Donald Taft: "Negroes are more likely to be suspected of crime than are whites. They are also more likely to be arrested. If the perpetrator of a crime is known to be a Negro the police may arrest all Negroes who were near the scene—a procedure they would rarely dare to follow with whites. After arrest, Negroes are less likely to secure bail, and so are more liable to be counted in jail statistics. They are more liable than whites to be indicted and less likely to have their cases *nol prossed* or otherwise dismissed. If tried, Negroes are more likely to be convicted. If convicted, they are less likely to be given probation. For this reason they are more likely to be included in the count of prisoners. Negroes are also more liable than whites to be kept in prison for the full terms of their commitments and correspondingly less likely to be paroled."

As anyone versed in the ways of the criminal justice system will tell you, the screening process begins with the policeman on the beat: the young car thief from a "nice home" will be returned to his family with a warning. If he repeats the offense or gets into more serious trouble, the parents may be called in for a conference with the prosecuting authorities. The well-to-do family has a dozen options: they can send their young delinquent to a boarding school, or to stay with relatives in another part of the country, they can hire the professional services of a psychiatrist or counselor—and the authorities will support them in these efforts. The Juvenile Court judge can see at a glance that this boy does not belong in the toils of the criminal justice system, that given a little tolerance and helpful guidance there is every chance he will straighten out by the time he reaches college age.

For the identical crime the ghetto boy will be arrested, imprisoned in the juvenile detention home, and set on the downward path that ends in the penitentiary. The screening process does not end with arrest, it obtains at every stage of the criminal justice system.

To cite one example that any observer of the crime scene—and particularly the black observer—will doubtless be able to match from his own experience: a few years ago a local newspaper reported horrendous goings-on of high school seniors in Piedmont, a wealthy enclave in Alameda County, California, populated by executives, businessmen, rich politicians. The students had gone on a general rampage that included arson, vandalism, breaking and entering, assault, car theft, rape. Following a conference among parents, their lawyers, and prosecuting authorities, it was decided that no formal action should be taken against the miscreants; they were all released to the custody of their families, who promised to subject them to appropriate discipline. In the very same week, a lawyer of my acquaintance told me with tight-lipped fury of the case of a nine-year-old black ghetto dweller in the same county, arrested for stealing a nickel from a white classmate, charged with "extortion and robbery," hauled off to juvenile hall, and, despite the urgent pleas of his distraught mother, there imprisoned for six weeks to wait for his court hearing.

Thus it seems safe to assert that there is indeed a criminal type—but he is not a biological, anatomical, phrenological, or anthropological type; rather, he is a social creation, etched by the dominant class and ethnic prejudices of a given society.

The day may not be far off when the horny-handed policeman on the beat may expect an assist in criminal-type-spotting from practitioners of a new witchcraft: behavior prediction. In 1970, Dr. Arnold Hutschnecker, President Nixon's physician, proposed mass psychological testing of six- to eight-year-old children to determine which were criminally inclined, and the establishment of special camps to house those found to have "violent tendencies." Just where the candidates for the mass testing and the special camps would be sought out was made clear when Dr. Hutschnecker let slip the fact he was proposing this program as an alternative to slum reconstruction. It would be, he said, "a direct, immediate, effective way of attacking the problem at its very origin, by focusing on the criminal mind of the child."

The behavior-predictors would catch the violence-prone *before* he springs, would confine him, possibly treat him, but in any event would certainly not let him out to consummate the hideous deeds of which he is so demonstrably capable. Their recurring refrain: "If only the clearly discernible defects in Oswald's psychological makeup had been detected in his childhood—had he been turned over to us, who have the resources to diagnose such deviant personalities—we would have tried to help him. If we decided he was beyond help, we would have locked him up forever and a major tragedy of this generation could have been averted." They refer, of course, to Lee Harvey Oswald, who allegedly gunned down President Kennedy, not to Russell G. Oswald, the New York commissioner of Corrections who ordered the troops into Attica, as a result of which 43 perished by gunfire.

5

WHAT COUNTS AS CRIME?

Press statement prepared by J. Edgar Hoover:

For release Monday P.M., June 22, 1970—According to figures made available through the FBI's Uniform Crime Reports and released by Attorney General John N. Mitchell, serious crime in the U.S. continued its upward trend, recording a 13 percent rise nationally for the first three months in 1970 when compared to the same period in 1969.

Press statement released by the Attorney General:

For release Monday P.M., June 22, 1970—Attorney General John N. Mitchell announced today the FBI's Uniform Crime Reports show that the rate of increase in violent crimes in the first three months of 1970 slowed by 7 percent in the major cities of the nation—and by 3 percent in the nation as a whole.

This falling-out between the purveyors of mathematics for the millions came to light when reporters discovered that for the first time in four decades the attorney general had done a bit of creative copy-editing of the late J. Edgar Hoover's annual crime statistics press release. Traditionally, preparation of the release has been the prerogative of the FBI director, who year after year dangles before an accommodating press his "new all-time high" in the rate of crime increase, thus assuring suitably lurid crime-wave headlines. Well and good for the FBI's purposes (for the higher the crime rate the easier to pry ever-larger appropriations out of Congress), this did not suit an Administration elected largely on a pledge to "make our cities safe from crime"; hence the attorney general's judicious use of the juggler's craft.

While to the statistician the two releases are not necessarily contradictory (for, as the practitioner of that uncanny discipline will explain, a 13 percent *rise* in crime is not incompatible with a 7 percent slowing of the *rate of increase*), the newspapers were understandably muddled. Next day some papers reported crime was rising, others said it was tapering off, and still others, with one foot firmly planted in each camp, quoted Hoover as saying the risk of being a crime victim was rising and Mitchell as saying crime rates were slowing down. Be that as it may, this tug of war between the mastodons of crime-busting is mainly instructive for what it tells us about clever ways with figures. The public opinion polls show most people have long since come to accept the FBI's annual "all-time high" as an article of faith—for example, in a survey conducted by the Joint Commission on Correctional Manpower, 89 percent of those polled said they believe crime rates have increased in recent years.

The Uniform Crime Reports, single most influential and most widely quoted source of crime information, basis for nightmarish popular fears and sweeping legislative crackdowns, are regarded by many criminologists as highly suspect—not only are they subject to cynical manipulation for political purposes but they give a grossly distorted picture of the crime scene.

What, then, lies behind the familiar headline "Major Crimes Up From 4.4 Million In 1968 To 5.6 Million In 1971"?

Crime rates (and crime waves) are based on "Index Crimes," also known as "major crimes" and "serious crimes," that come to the attention of police; most are reported by citizens, some are discovered in the course of police work. The figures are forwarded by local police departments to FBI headquarters and there compiled into what *The New York Times* calls "virtually impenetrable" tables of statistics, the Uniform Crime Reports. These in turn are summarized and presented in vastly simplified form, with suitable interpretation, to the media.

Like Deadly Sins, the Index Crimes are seven in number, listed as follows by the FBI: willful homicide, forcible rape, aggressive assault, robbery, burglary, car theft, larceny over $50. To list them in this order is, it develops, somewhat like listing national population figures beginning with Luxembourg and ending with China, since the eye-catching first two (murder and rape) account for only about 1 percent of the total and the first four (crimes against the person as distinct from property crimes) for about 13 percent. About half of all reported "serious crimes" in the Index consist of larceny and car theft, which includes joy-riding, mere misdemeanors under the laws of many states.

Venturing further into the thicket of figures, it is surprising to learn that the rate of most crimes against persons—presumably everybody's least favorite and most feared of the Index Crimes—has actually declined over the years. According to the President's Crime Commission Report, the rate of Index Crime No. 1—murder—when adjusted to rising population figures, has decreased by about 30 percent from its high in 1933 and the robbery rate by about 15 percent in the same period. In *The Honest Politician's Guide to Crime Control* Norval Morris and Gordon Hawkins say, "Looking further back to the 1870's and the late 1890's it seems clear that rates of murder, non-negligent homicide, rape, and assault have all appreciably declined with the passage of time."

Furthermore the spectre of the marauding stranger conjured up by the FBI figures is largely mythical, for the great majority of murders (88 percent according to one survey quoted in the President's Crime Commission Report) are committed within the family or among acquaintances. The same is true of other crimes of violence: a District of Columbia study showed that two thirds of rape victims were attacked by boyfriends, members of the family, or other acquaintances, and that only 25 percent of aggravated assault victims were unacquainted with their assailant—which prompts the fanciful speculation that one might be safer out alone in the dark city streets than waiting cozily at home for a convivial troop of relatives and neighbors to drop in.

Moving on down the Index to the property crimes— burglary, car theft, larceny over $50—we discover that the alleged soaring rise in the rate of these is not all it seems, either. For one thing the number of police departments that participate in the reporting program is constantly rising: in 1957, 7,000 departments participated, by 1964, 8,000. For another, much depends on the local police chief; thus there was an 83 percent increase in "major crimes known to the police" in Chicago between 1960 and 1961 when a zealous new chief revised reporting procedures. In a study of the 1963 Uniform Crime Reports, Professor Albert D. Biderman of the Bureau of Social Science Research made these observations: "More than half of the rise in the Index in recent years—the basis for the alarm expressed about the 'mounting crime rate' —comes from increases in the reports people make to the police about things being stolen from them . . . To be reflected in the Index, a reported theft has to involve the stealing of an automobile or of something worth $50 or more." Thus in a period of inflation, when things cost more, thefts that would formerly not have made the Index—because the items involved were worth less than $50—now show up to swell the surging crime wave. Affluence, too, is an important factor in reported thefts: not only are there more valuables around to steal (stolen bikes alone accounted for about 20 percent of all reported larcenies) but due to the spectacular rise in comprehensive homeowners' insurance policies, people are far more likely to report thefts than heretofore. While this may add up to more work for police, says Mr. Biderman, it is hardly a useful indicator for measuring how much lawbreaking is occurring. Musing over the problems of the criminal in these times of soaring inflation, Professor Leslie T. Wilkins of the School of Criminal Justice in Albany, points out that, "If the cost of living legally goes up, presumably the cost of illegal living also rises. If persons who live by illegal means increase their productivity proportional to the increase in the cost of living, does this really mean that 'crime' has increased?"

Thus the foregoing authorities—Morris and Hawkins, Albert D. Biderman, and Leslie T. Wilkins—seem inclined to the view that crime may have remained relatively stable over the past several decades, and in some categories may even have decreased. If this is so, why the almost universally held belief that crime has increased dramatically, reaching horrendous proportions? One probable answer is that in the days of which Morris and Hawkins speak, and up until fairly recently, such crimes as purse-snatching, burglary, robbery, and assault were largely confined to slums and ghettos, where they attracted the attention of nobody outside those areas. The police as a matter of policy seldom interfered in the crimes of poor against poor, black against black; nor did the newspapers bother to report such incidents.

I recall a conversation of some twenty years ago with a black newspaperwoman who lived in Harlem. On a sultry summer night she had dozed off for a few seconds while reading in bed. When she opened her eyes, her small bedside radio had vanished—a cat burglar had scaled seven stories to snatch this almost worthless item through her open window. She mildly derided my shock and amazement over this frightening episode, and assured me such incidents and worse were common, everyday experiences of the ghetto-dweller. Today, they are becoming commonplace in Park Avenue, the Loop, Pacific Heights. The middle and upper classes, once insulated from street crime and theft, are now targets of these crimes, which have become a national obsession reflected in myriad dinner party conversations, in the polls, the press, the get-tough platforms of politicians.

In addition to its précis of the Uniform Crime Reports, the FBI releases other crime news when and as the spirit moves it. If certain categories of violent incidents show a decrease, they may mysteriously vanish altogether from the annual report. For example, in recent years the bureau has furnished figures for racial disturbances in American cities, disorders in secondary schools, numbers of police officers killed or injured by members of the Black Panther Party. All were missing from the 1972 release. Asked by reporters to supply the figures, the bureau reluctantly complied (incidents in all three categories were sharply down from the previous year), and a spokesman explained to the press: "One year doesn't compare to another. I don't think you are supposed to take last year's report and compare it with this one. You can't include everything. One of the problems is to keep this in workable length."

In sum, FBI crime-reporting is shrewdly tailored to focus attention on crimes of those perceived by the Establishment as the dangerous classes: poor people, ghetto-dwellers, political dissidents. These are the crimes that make headlines, sell newspapers, frighten and upset people—and create a solid platform for the politician pledged to vote more money for the FBI.

Absent from the Uniform Crime Reports are crimes committed by the rich and powerful against the rest of the population: murder, assault, and theft via violation of health and safety codes by slum landlords, mine owners, construction companies, robbery by the food industry through deceptive packaging, and organized crime that depends on corruption of public officials, to name a few. That these crimes cause infinitely more death, injury, and impoverishment than those listed in the Index is documented in official government reports and in the annals of criminology. Some random examples of such crimes at high levels, culled from recent newspaper accounts: "The Blacksville No. 1 coal mine, which has been sealed, making it the tomb of nine miners given up for dead, was cited for 485 safety violations since it opened four years ago . . ." "The Sunshine Mining Co. in Kellogg, Idaho, where 91 silver miners perished in a fire, had been cited for 14 fire and safety violations over the past 21 months . . ." "Lockheed Shipbuilding and Construction Co. was accused by the Department of Labor of willful negligence in the San Fernando Tunnel explosion that killed 17 men on June 24 . . ." It is a safe bet that nobody will go to prison for these deaths.

The annual figure on "aggravated assault" given in the Uniform Crime Reports runs around 200,000. In *New Horizons in Criminology,* Barnes and Teeters say that from 8 to 15 percent of all food consumed in this country is contaminated and that each year more than 3 million people are made "seriously ill" as a result of eating tainted or doctored food. Is this not a form of "aggravated assault" committed by the food industry?

According to the President's Crime Commission Report, corporate and business crime, which goes largely unreported and unprosecuted, is absolutely vast in scope, its depredations far exceeding those of the ordinary thief. As George Bernard

Shaw put it, "We may take it, then, that the thief who is in prison is not necessarily more dishonest than his fellows at large . . . He snatches a loaf from the baker's counter and is promptly run into gaol. Another man snatches bread from the tables of hundreds of widows and orphans and simple credulous souls who do not know the ways of company promoters; and, as likely as not, he is run into Parliament." The commission estimates that price-fixing by 29 electrical equipment companies alone probably cost utilities, and therefore the public, more money than all the burglaries put together in a year.

As to white-collar crime in general, the commission says it is "committed in the course of their work by persons of high status and social repute," who are thus differentiated from "low status or disreputable persons" and who are "rarely dealt with through the full force of criminal sanctions." I was afforded a glimpse into why this is so by a friend who owns a chain of restaurants. To her extreme annoyance, she discovered one day that her bookkeeper had embezzled $50,000 of the company's money. I asked her if she intended to prosecute. "Heavens, no! What good would he be to me behind bars? I want him to pay my money back." She added that she was most anxious that word of the bookkeeper's dereliction should not leak out, as she was actively seeking a job for him among her business acquaintances. "I think I'll try to get him placed in a bank," she said reflectively. "That should provide the necessary scope for his particular talents."

Quite naturally, since FBI statistics are compiled from "crimes known to police," crimes committed *by* police figure nowhere in the computations, and the extent of police crime has hitherto been largely unknowable. The public was asked to make an educated guess about this in an opinion survey conducted for the President's Crime Commission. The question: "Do you think the police around your neighborhood are almost all honest, mostly honest, with a few who are corrupt, or are they almost all corrupt?" Difference of response by race

was, the commission found, "more than striking. It was startling." Sixty-three percent of whites and only 30 percent of
nonwhites thought police were "almost all honest." One percent
of whites and 10 percent of nonwhites thought the police were
"almost all corrupt." Polls cited by the Kerner Commission
showed that nationwide 35 percent of black men thought there
was police brutality in their areas, while 7 percent of white
men thought so. (In urban ghettos the percentage of black
men who believed there was police brutality was far higher;
79 percent in Watts, 82 percent in Detroit.)

That the blacks had the better grasp of reality in these matters can be inferred by subsequent disclosures from three
sources: Professor Albert J. Reiss, Jr., and his team of police
observers, the Knapp Commission hearings in New York, and
Professor Paul Takagi's study of civilian killings by police.

At the request of the President's Crime Commission Professor Reiss assembled and trained 36 observers whose task it
was, seven days a week for seven weeks, to accompany policemen in patrol cars and monitor booking procedures in "high
crime" precincts of Boston, Chicago, and Washington, D.C.
Their staggering findings*: although the policemen were fully
aware that their every action was being scrutinized and recorded, one out of every five was "observed in criminal violation of the law." Among the crimes reported: stealing from

* Apparently the President's Crime Commission feared the consequences
of making these astonishing revelations public, for although the commission
had ordered and paid for the survey, none of the findings appear in its
report, "The Challenge of Crime in a Free Society." To the contrary, the
Commission says it "believes that the corruption at all levels and the
widespread use of physical coercion that prevailed in many police departments during the era of Prohibition is largely a thing of the past." According to John P. MacKenzie of the Washington *Post*, Commission Chairman Nicholas deB. Katzenbach dismissed reports that the study had found
evidence of widespread police corruption, physical abuse, and discourtesy
as "inaccurate" and "misleading" (*The New York Times*, November 28,
1971). Professor Reiss eventually published his findings in a sociology text-
book, *The Sociology of Punishment and Correction.*

drunks and "deviants," taking bribes in cash and merchandise in return for not giving traffic tickets or for altering sworn testimony, looting establishments that had been burglarized. The observers also found that 4 out of every 10 policemen routinely violated such departmental regulations as those against drinking or sleeping on the job and falsification of reports.

The observers reported 44 instances of police assault against citizens, 37 of them unprovoked; 13 assaults took place in the station house when at least 4 other policemen were present. "The lock-up was the scene of some of the most severe applications of force," writes Professor Reiss. "Two of the three cases requiring hospitalization came about when an offender was 'worked over' in the lock-up."

Some of the scenes described by the observers:

A white traffic violation suspect had been handcuffed and brought to the station— ". . . the policemen began to beat the man. They jumped him, knocked him down and beat his head against the concrete floor. He required emergency treatment at a nearby hospital."

"One man brought into the lock-up for threatening a policeman with a pistol was so severely beaten by this policeman that he required hospitalization. During the beating, some fellow policemen propped the man up while others shouted encouragement."

Two black teen-agers, arrested at gunpoint on suspicion of refusing to pay their bus fares, were handcuffed and beaten in an interrogation room. "One of the boys hollered, 'You can't beat me like this! I'm only a kid, and my hands are tied.' Later one of the policemen commented to the observer, 'On the street you can't beat them. But when you get to the station, you can instil some respect in them.' "

Although during their rounds in the patrol cars the observers noted a substantial number of police contacts with middle- and upper-class citizens, some of them offenders, none of these was the victim of excessive force or of verbal abuse; on the contrary, they were treated with considerable politeness and respect. Without exception, says Professor Reiss, the victims of assault, both white and black, were "from the lower class."

Beating heads and breaking bones is, it seems, perfectly safe and sound procedure from a police standpoint. In only one of the 37 instances of brutality witnessed by the observers did the victim file a formal complaint. Nor would the victims have been likely to get any satisfaction from the higher-ups, for the reaction of police administrators with whom Professor Reiss discussed his findings was mainly one of annoyance that their patrolmen should have done these things while they knew they were being watched. As one said, "Any officer who is stupid enough to behave in that way in the presence of outsiders deserves to be fired." Speculating on why his observers were able to see as much police crime as they did, Professor Reiss suggests that people do not easily change their habitual conduct in the presence of others, may easily forget they are being observed and continue to behave as they normally do. He adds, "But should one cling to the notion that most policemen modify their behavior in the presence of outsiders, one is left with the uncomfortable conclusion that our cases represent a minimal picture of actual behavior."

The findings of Professor Reiss should go far to dispel the popular myth, assiduously fostered by law enforcement people everywhere, that police misconduct involves only the "occasional rotten apple in the barrel." David Burnham of *The New York Times,* a leading authority on police work whose series on police corruption triggered the Knapp Commission investigation of the New York police department in 1971, told me he estimates that between 75 percent and 80 percent of police accept some sort of graft and that virtually all those charged with enforcing gambling laws get payoffs. Among the Knapp Commission's revelations: construction costs in New York are increased by 5 percent because of bribes paid by contractors to police. In Harlem, the average take from addicts and pushers by one crime-prevention squad was $1,500 a month; "heavy scorers" made as much as $3,000 a month. Police regularly furnished addicts with lists of cigarettes, liquor, and other merchandise they wanted stolen in return for "laying off." In the course of their daily rounds, the police themselves become pushers, doling out daily fixes to their addict informants from their immense stores of confiscated heroin.

The great police funeral, replete with honor guards of law enforcement men massed in tribute to their fallen comrade, is becoming commonplace in large American cities. So are front-page newspaper stories about the alarming increase in police killings, and presidential pledges of tougher measures to safeguard police lives.

What is the converse of this picture? Occasionally killings of civilians by police break into the headlines (as in the Chicago armed raid of Panther headquarters), but the run-of-the-mill "suspect shot while fleeing arrest" gets little newspaper attention and, since his death is almost invariably labeled "justifiable homicide," he does not appear in the statistics of crime victims.

Curious about reported police killings by citizens and unreported killings of citizens by police, Professor Paul Takagi of the University of California and Philip Buell, public health department statistician, did some detective work in the archives of government statistics. Their inquiry disclosed that, contrary to popular belief and official dictum, the *rate* of police killings, while it fluctuates from year to year, has hardly changed since 1963. For, while FBI reports show the numbers of such homicides rose from 55 in 1963 to 86 in 1969, during that period there was an increase of nearly 50 percent in the number of full-time police officers.*

* According to *The New York Times* (August 22, 1971) the rate of police killings by civilians in New York fell from 5.4 policemen killed for every 10,000 in 1930 to 1.9 for every 10,000 in 1970.

Finding out about civilian deaths at the hands of police proved more complicated. Professor Takagi discovered that these are recorded on death certificates as "Justifiable Homicide by Legal Intervention of Police." After disappearing into the maw of the computer, these records eventually surface as "Cause of Death Number 984" in the annually published official volumes of Vital Statistics. From this obscure source he learned that between 1963 and 1968, police killed 1,805 men and 21 women; about half were black. In the same period, 362 policemen were killed by civilians. The rate of civilian killings by police, says Professor Takagi, is rising throughout the nation: in California it increased two and a half times between 1962 and 1969. The California totals, 1961–69: 59 policemen killed by civilians, 363 civilians (of whom 3 were women) killed by police, for a ratio of 6 to 1.

David Burnham tells me he believes these official figures may grossly understate the actual numbers of civilians killed by police. "The New York Police Department, for example, in 1971 told me that their men killed 50 persons," he said. "The medical examiner for the city reported only 16 such deaths, the state 17. Presumably, when Vital Statistics gets around to publishing the figures, New York will show up as 16½ killings."

Surveys in other areas would indicate that ratios similar to those cited by Takagi and Buell obtain throughout: 54 New Yorkers were killed by city police in 1970, during which year 8 policemen were reported "killed in the line of duty." Californians and New Yorkers can take comfort from the fact that despite these shocking figures they are still safer from police gunfire than residents of Chicago, which leads the nation in police killings of civilians. The Chicago Law Enforcement Study Group found that more persons were killed by police in that city than in any other: in 1969–70, 79 persons, of whom 59 were black, perished at the hands of police. To this disclosure the Chicago Patrolmen's Association responded that one reason for the figures was "aggressive police work, responsible for Chicago's low crime rate."

When is conduct a crime, and when is a crime not a crime? When Somebody Up There—a monarch, a dictator, a pope, a legislature—so decrees. If one were to extend Ramsey Clark's imaginary map of high-crime areas into the adjacent suburbs, one might find manufacturers of unsafe cars which in the next year will have caused thousands to perish in flaming highway wrecks, absentee landlords who charge extortionist rents for rat-infested slum apartments, Madison Avenue copywriters whose job it is to manipulate the gullible into buying shoddy merchandise, doctors getting rich off Medicare who process their elderly patients like so many cattle being driven to the slaughterhouse, manufacturers of napalm and other genocidal weapons—all operating on the safe side of the law, since none of these activities is in violation of any criminal statute. Criminal law is essentially a reflection of the values, and a codification of the self-interest, and a method of control, of the dominant class in any given society. (One might suppose that some conduct, such as murder, is universally considered a horrendous crime and punished as such. Not so. Professor Laura Nader, an anthropologist, tells me that in some primitive communal societies murder is considered a relatively trivial matter, involving as it generally does merely a quarrel between two individuals; whereas polluting the river, which affects the whole community, is on the order of high treason.)

History is replete with examples of acts which at one time or another have been subject to criminal sanctions. In Europe between the fifteenth and eighteenth centuries, when the Church was supreme, some quarter of a million people were executed for the crime of witchcraft. In Henry VIII's reign it was a crime to predict the death of the king. With the rise of the Industrial Revolution, statutes embodying new needs of the emerging capitalist class proliferated; in the United States, the number of statutory crimes under federal law alone rose from 33 in 1790 to almost 600 by the mid-twentieth century. Barnes and Teeters say that at least three quarters of American prisoners could not have been incarcerated fifty years ago, since the acts for which they were convicted were not then criminal violations.

As the legislature conjures crimes into being, so too can it will them away. Thus public insobriety, first made a criminal offense in England by a 1606 law entitled "An Act for Repressing the Odious and Loathsome Sin of Drunkenness," has been illegal in this country since the Puritans first came over. But in 1967 the President's Crime Commission discovered that the business of processing drunks through the criminal justice system was wildly inefficient, had become an intolerable burden on police, courts, and jails. One third of all arrests in the United States, the commission found, were for drunkenness; in the District of Columbia, more than half the arrests were for this offense. In some places drunks occupied over 90 percent of the available space in local lock-ups, regrettable in the commission's view because as a consequence "resources are diverted from serious offenders." Taking account of these pragmatic considerations, the commission put its seal of approval on what medical men have been saying for generations: alcoholism is an illness, should be treated as such, should be removed from the inappropriate ministrations of judiciary and jailers, and placed under the jurisdiction of public health workers. District of Columbia skid-rogues may now stand up and cheer, for shortly after the commission pronounced these self-evident facts Congress ordained that henceforth drunkenness is no longer a crime in the District. State legislatures are beginning to follow suit: in the past five years Maryland, Florida, North Dakota, Connecticut, and Massachusetts have all enacted new legislation eliminating public drunkenness from the criminal statutes.

While they were at it, why did not the commissioners take the further step of proposing repeal of the laws against such victimless crimes as homosexuality, prostitution, adultery, gambling, narcotics, and a host of other forms of behavior now legally proscribed thanks to the baleful influence of latter-day Puritans? One answer is suggested by Peter Barton Hutt, a consultant to the commission, in an analysis of the task force report on drunkenness. "I have not conducted any research into their personal habits or private lives, and I would not suggest that I or anyone else do so," he writes. "Nevertheless, a few generalizations can properly be made. First, it is likely that almost every member of the commission consumes alcoholic beverages. It is virtually certain that they have friends and relatives who have drinking problems and may even be alcoholics. . . . They live in a society that condones drinking and tolerates even excessive drinking. Current social mores therefore preconditioned them to acceptance of the position that drunkenness should be handled as a public health problem rather than as a criminal problem. In contrast, I think it fair to assume that something less than a majority of the commission members smoke marijuana or have performed an abortion or have engaged in prostitution . . ."

Had the President chosen to appoint nineteen college students instead of these representatives of the Bourbon Generation, Mr. Hutt thinks the commission might have taken a different tack and would have been more inclined to recommend repeal of the marijuana laws than repeal of drunkenness statutes.

Within the general framework of laws established to preserve the system from subversion, protect property, and enforce the Puritan ethic so dear to the hearts of our lawmakers, there is wild disparity in statutory sanctions imposed at various times by various state legislatures and the federal government. Violation of the Smith Act (advocating overthrow of the government by force and violence, the federal statute under which scores of Communists and other radicals were prosecuted at the height of the McCarthy repression) is punishable by five years in prison. Under the Texas "Communist Control Law," the maximum penalty is twenty years. Texas also authorizes imprisonment of up to twenty-five years for offenses labeled "Insult to United States Flag," "Disloyalty in Writing," "Possessing Flag of Enemy," and "Disloyal Language."

For rape, minimum sentences vary from one year in six states to death in four. Often no distinction is made between forcible rape and sexual intercourse with a consenting underage female. The minimum penalty for armed robbery is one year in ten states, five years in twelve, and death in two.*

California has a maximum prison sentence of fifty years for the crime of incest; in Virginia the same offense is considered a misdemeanor with a one-year maximum sentence. At one time California punished indecent exposure as a misdemeanor, with a sentence of up to one year, no matter how often a person was convicted of it. But in 1952, following a wave of public hysteria about sex crimes, the legislature imposed a statutory penalty of one year to life in state prison for a second conviction for this offense. In Nebraska the penalty for possession of up to one pound of marijuana is seven days in jail. In Texas, possession of a single marijuana cigarette carries a sentence of two years to life.

If statutory penalties are the products of the whims and biases of legislators, their application to convicted defendants reflects the quirks and caprice of judges. Prison literature by authors on both sides of the bars abounds with grotesque examples of disparate sentences imposed on defendants charged

---

* The death penalty for these crimes was nullified by the 1972 U.S. Supreme Court ruling on capital punishment.

with the same offense: in *I Chose Prison,* James V. Bennett, former chief of the U.S. Bureau of Prisons, tells of the disposition in the same year by two federal judges of similar crimes of forgery committed by men in almost identical circumstances, both honorably discharged veterans, unemployed, fathers of young children. One, who had no prior police record, got fifteen years imprisonment. The other, who had previously served time for drunken driving and failure to support his family, was given thirty days in jail. In *An Eye for an Eye,* a convict writer relates the outcome of two armed robberies in Wyoming. A thief in the northern part of the state who stole $7.50 was given a twelve-year sentence, another in the southern section drew three years for stealing $124.

That sentencing is in the nature of a dice game is shown by figures furnished by the federal Bureau of Prisons on penalties imposed by federal courts in New York State for the crime of transporting stolen cars. Defendants sentenced to prison from Brooklyn Federal Court in 1970 for this offense received an average sentence of 51 months. Those sentenced in Manhattan Federal Court for the same crime were given an average of 30.7 months; in the Federal District Courts for Northern New York, the average was 20.9 months.

One maxim about the sentencing process urged on judges by the modern penologist is to fit the punishment to the criminal, not the crime. The evidence is overwhelming that judges do just that, for the criminal justice system functions not only to put some lawbreakers behind bars but to keep others out. The white middle-class offender, social equal of the judge, will be let off lightly: "Most judges justify the minimal sentences they give to businessmen-criminals—fines, probation, or exceedingly short jail terms—on the ground that when such a man is convicted, he generally loses his job, his standing in the community, and his family's respect," reports Lesley Oelsner of *The New York Times.* The poorer and darker the convicted defendant, the more onerous will be his punishment. His job, his standing in the community, his family's respect weigh lightly in the scales of justice as manipulated by the judges.

Just how the dice are loaded, and against whom, is documented in Oelsner's detailed survey of current sentencing practices. Noting that "crimes that tend to be committed by the poor get tougher sentences than those committed by the well-to-do," she cites these examples: 71 percent of people convicted of car theft in 1970–71 went to prison for an average term of three years. In the same year the average penalty imposed for violation of elevator safety regulations in Manhattan was an $18 fine. In at least two such cases the elevators went unrepaired after the owners were prosecuted, and subsequently caused fatal accidents.

Defendants who, unable to afford a lawyer, must make do with court-appointed counsel are sentenced nearly twice as severely as those with private counsel, says Oelsner. Nonwhites serve much longer sentences than whites convicted of the same crime. Federal Bureau of Prisons records show that in 1970 the average sentence for whites was 42.9 months, compared to 57.5 months for nonwhites. Whites convicted of income tax evasion were committed for an average of 12.8 months and nonwhites for 28.6 months. In drug cases, the average for whites was 61.1 months and for nonwhites, 81.1.

Those who have the temerity to proclaim their innocence of the crime with which they are charged and to demand a trial will, if convicted, serve more than twice as long a sentence as those who "cop a plea" of guilty, says Oelsner. Over 90 percent of all criminal cases are dealt out through the plea-bargaining process; judges say that if every accused or even a majority were granted a trial, the criminal courts would become so hopelessly clogged they would soon grind to a halt.

Until a few years ago this pervasive practice, which consists of an accused agreeing to plead guilty to a lesser crime than the one for which he was charged in return for a promise of lighter sentence, was not officially sanctioned or recognized by the courts, since a guilty plea obtained under promise of leniency was an illegally entered plea. It was one of those "secrets" that everybody involved knew about—judge, prosecutor, defense lawyer—but nobody openly acknowledged. The better to preserve the fiction, a standard question was asked of the defendant under oath by his lawyer: "Has any promise been made to you which has caused you to plead guilty?" To which the defendant, coached in advance, would primly and perjuriously answer, "No."

By 1969 the U.S. Supreme Court had rendered this bit of play-acting unnecessary by putting its seal of approval on plea-bargaining, providing it is done with "full understanding of what the plea connotes and of its consequences," and that the judge assembles an "affirmative record" of the proceedings, meaning that the agreement must be officially recorded and is not, as heretofore, an under-the-table deal between defense lawyer and prosecutor.

As characterized by one public defender, plea-bargaining is "trial by trick and deceit." In a typical plea-bargaining situation the prosecutor will pile on felony charges, regardless of whether he has evidence to support them, in order to pose the threat of long years in the penitentiary should the accused put the state to the expense and trouble of a trial and be found guilty. The defendant who, unable to raise bail, has already spent months in jail under atrocious conditions, will be delighted to plead guilty to one of the many offenses he is charged with, even if he is in fact innocent of *any* crime, in exchange for a promise of probation or a short sentence with credit for time served. (According to Gregory J. Hobbs, Jr., writing in the *California Law Review,* conditions in one California jail condemned by Federal District Judge Alphonzo J. Zirpoli as "barbaric" and "cruel and unusual punishment for man or beast" are deliberately kept that way as an extra coercive lever to make those awaiting trial more amenable to plea-bargaining.)

Since trial judges have made such a notorious hash of dispensing justice, some crime watchers reason, the sentencing power should be removed from their erratic ministrations and placed in the hands of an independent body of experts. In *The Honest Politician's Guide to Crime Control,* Norval Morris and Gordon Hawkins go so far as to propose that the length of time served by the convicted lawbreaker should be determined by the prison administration: ". . . within the limits set by prescribed maximum and minimum, the correctional administration should be free to decide how long the prisoners ought to be held beyond the minimum. The correctional administration is in the best position to judge when the release of the prisoner will be safe, and here it can take advantage of any improved methods developed by the behavioral sciences for predicting behavior and identifying dangerous offenders." Which is a pretty good description of what does happen in those jurisdictions that have adopted the indeterminate sentence system.

6

THE INDETERMINATE SENTENCE

"Let prisons and prison systems be lighted by this law of love. Let us leave, for the present, the thought of inflicting punishment upon prisoners to satisfy so-called justice, and turn toward the two grand divisions of our subject, the real objects of the system; viz., the protection of society by the prevention of crime, and reformation of criminals." Thus Zebulon R. Brockway, warden of the Detroit House of Correction and later of Elmira Reformatory, spoke in support of the indeterminate sentence at the 1870 Prison Congress.

The indeterminate sentence was then, as it is now, regarded

by many penologists and outside reformers as integral to the
task of reforming the lawbreaker. Briefly stated, it works like
this: the legislature sets a minimum and maximum term for
each offense within broad limits (for example, in California
burglary second degree carries a sentence of one to fifteen
years; rape, one to fifty; robbery, five years to life; sale of
marijuana, five years to life), and the judge, instead of sentencing the defendant to a specific number of years, simply
remands him to the state prison "for the term prescribed by
law." Thereafter the prisoner is under the jurisdiction of the
parole board, which will consider his case, fix an individualized
term for him based on his prison record, and set a date for his
release on parole.

The idea is to remove the sentencing power from a possibly
prejudiced and vindictive trial judge and place it in the hands
of skilled experts in human behavior. These experts would look
at the man rather than his crime, take into account all circumstances that may have driven him to break the law, keep
close track of his progress in prison, and release him when he
has demonstrated by his behavior that he is ready to return to
the community. Ideally, say some of the more ardent enthusiasts
of this system, indeterminacy should be absolute and all crimes
should carry a sentence of one day to life.

As adopted unanimously by the 1870 Congress, the resolution on the indeterminate sentence reads: "Peremptory sentences ought to be replaced by those of indeterminate duration;
sentences limited only by satisfactory proof of reformation
should be substituted for those measured by mere lapse of time.
The abstract justness of this principle is obvious; the difficulty
lies in its practical application. But this difficulty will vanish
when the administration of our prisons is made permanent and
placed in competent hands. With men of ability and experience
at the head of our penal establishments, holding their offices
during good behavior, we believe that it will be little, if at all,

more difficult to judge correctly as to the moral cure of a criminal, than it is of the mental cure of a lunatic."

And as paraphrased a hundred years later by Ramsey Clark, in *Crime in America*: "If rehabilitation is the goal, only the indeterminate sentence will be used. Such a sentence sets an outer limit beyond which the state may no longer restrain the individual . . . [it] contemplates a rehabilitation program specially designed for each individual convicted. Professionally trained correctional authorities can then carefully observe a prisoner and release him at the earliest time within the limits fixed which his personal situation indicates . . ."

Put this way, the argument for the indeterminate sentence sounds most persuasive: a demonstrably just, humane, enlightened method of dealing with the offender, holding out to every convict the promise that he will be helped, treated as a self-respecting individual, and freed from his bondage as soon as he proves he can function as a law-abiding citizen. Why, then, is it denounced by the supposed beneficiaries—prisoners and parolees—from coast to coast, its abolition one of the focal demands of the current prison rebellion? And why is it coming under increasing attack from those criminologists, sociologists, lawyers, legislators who have taken the trouble to look closely at the prison scene and have informed themselves at first hand about the day-to-day realities of prison life?

Because there is another side to this coin. While ardently proclaiming the humanitarian aims of this system, prison administrators never lost sight of its punitive value. It develops that in his impassioned advocacy of the indeterminate sentence Warden Brockway (who was eventually relieved of his post for overuse of corporal punishment) had other things on his mind besides lighting the prisons with the law of love. In *The American Reformatory System* he writes: "The indeterminateness of the sentence breeds discontent, breeds purposefulness, and prompts to a new exertion. Captivity, always irksome, is now increasingly so because of the uncertainty of its duration; because the duty and responsibility of shortening it and of modifying any undesirable present condition of it devolves upon the prisoner himself, and again, by the active exactions of the standards and criterion to which he must attain."

In short, Brockway rightly saw the indeterminate sentence as a potent psychological instrument for inmate manipulation and control, the "uncertainty" ever nagging at the prisoner's mind a far more effective weapon than cruder ones then in vogue: the club, the starvation regime, the iron shackle. (The fact that today it harmoniously coexists with these earlier disciplinary methods will not be lost on the observer who has followed accounts of how prisoners from Attica to California are dealt with by those in authority over them.)

The enthusiastic acceptance of the indeterminate sentence as the penal panacea by prison administrators from 1870 to the present time is further understandable when one considers that it endows them with total, unfettered power over the prisoners consigned to their charge. It is the perfect prescription for at once securing compliance and crushing defiance, because the prisoner is in for the *maximum* term and it is theoretically up to him to shorten the time served.

The manipulative value of the indeterminate sentence was candidly set forth by the New York commissioner of Corrections in his remarks at the 1930 Prison Congress: "[The prisoner's] knowledge that he may be restrained only for a definite period is in many instances the rock on which our plans split. 'The judge gave me ten years. I can do that standing on my head,' a prisoner once said to me. But if the judge had been able to say not less than ten years and as much longer as seems necessary, we should have witnessed a different reaction on his part."

In effect the message conveyed to the prisoner is: "Keep this joint running smoothly and we'll let you out sooner." Conversely, the really "dangerous" criminal can be confined almost indefinitely, and the decision as to who fits this definition rests, of course, with the correctional authorities. This category is elastic enough to embrace the political nonconformist, the malcontent, the inmate leader of an ethnic group, the persistent writ-writer, the psychotic, the troublemaker. Any one of these may at the pleasure of his keepers serve years beyond the normal term for his crime; if his sentence carries a "life top," he may never get out. As one convict put it to me, "From the vindictive guard who sets out to build a record against some individual to the parole board, the indeterminate sentence grants Corrections the power to play God with the lives of prisoners."

While the indeterminate sentence seems to imply a policy of early release for the rehabilitated offender, it is actually a means of assuring much longer sentences for most prisoners than would normally be imposed by judges; the theme that under the determinate, or "flat time," sentence miscreants are let out too soon recurs in the writings of nineteenth-century penologists. The indeterminate sentence reassures the public on both counts: by promising the reform-minded a benevolent prison system wherein the criminal will be dealt with as fairly as his fallen state deserves, and by offering law-and-order hard-liners assurance that he can be kept in almost indefinitely.

That the indeterminate sentence would inevitably result in longer prison terms was a prospect envisaged by the 1870 Prison Congress. "The supreme aim of prison discipline," said a speaker, "is reestablishing moral harmony in the soul of the criminal himself, and effecting, as far as possible, his regeneration"—which could be a lengthy process, as the congress recognized in its formal resolution on the subject: "It is the judgment of this congress that repeated short sentences for minor criminals are worse than useless . . . Reformation is the work of time; and a benevolent regard to the good of the criminal himself, as well as to the protection of society, requires that his sentence be long enough for reformatory processes to take effect."

As state after state adopted the indeterminate sentence, or some modification thereof, length of time served by convicts rose steadily. Amos W. Butler of Indiana, where the indeterminate sentence law was enacted before the turn of the century, was able to report to the 1915 Congress of the American Prison Association: "Under the definite sentence, our courts measured out so much punishment for so much crime. Having served his time, the prisoner was free to go. Under the present system of indeterminate sentence with parole, accompanied as it is with efforts at reformation, the average length of sentence is markedly longer." And he cited a study made at the Indiana State Prison to prove it: men committed to prison in 1900 under the indeterminate sentence served an average of six months and twenty-three days longer than those committed in 1890, for identical crimes, with definite sentences. By 1906 time served for these same crimes had lengthened by one year, two months, and five days. The reason for this was partially clarified in the discussion following Mr. Butler's remarks. Asked the question: "Is the prisoner eligible to parole when he has served his minimum sentence?" he replied, "No, sir; because many of those persons, while they may have a good prison record and while they may have served their minimum, may at the same time not have gained the confidence of the board."

Nathaniel Cantor, professor of criminology at Buffalo, underscored Mr. Butler's point at the 1937 Congress. Arguing for the ideal, or absolute, indeterminate sentence, he noted that "there is evidence to show that the average period of imprisonment under the minimum-maximum sentence is decidedly longer than under the determinate sentence. It is extremely probable that under an absolute indeterminate sentence periods of confinement will be longer." And, he noted with approval,

"The deterrent effects of an absolute indeterminate sentence upon potential offenders would certainly be as great if not more effective than the present definite or minimum-maximum sentences."

Most states today have some form of the indeterminate sentence. There are various adaptations: in some jurisdictions the degree of indeterminacy is relatively narrow, as in Maine, where a typical minimum-maximum is five to seven years; in others, the range is vast, as in California with its six months to fifteen years, one year to twenty, one to life. Even in "flat sentence" states, a degree of indeterminacy is implied in the rule that allows the prisoner to earn a substantial reduction of his sentence through good behavior, and that conversely permits the authorities to revoke this earned "good time" at whim. In the federal system, for example, a prisoner sentenced to a "flat" term is eligible for parole after serving a third of his sentence, so that in effect a six-year term is a from-two-to-six term, a variation of the indeterminate sentence.

Critics and supporters of the system alike agree that the indeterminate sentence has reached its fullest flowering in California, which boasts the largest and costliest prison empire in the country—some 21,000 incarcerated felons—and maintains a full-time, highly paid parole board, first established as an entity separate from the Department of Corrections in 1944.

The Californian experiment, enviously eyed and often emulated over the years by prison people in other parts of the country, has exerted an enormous influence nationwide on sentencing and paroling policies. In his book *I Chose Prison,* James V. Bennett, for three decades director of the U.S. Bureau of Prisons, relates how impressed he was with the beneficial results of the California system; eventually he succeeded in getting a modified form of the indeterminate sentence enacted into federal law, under which judges now have the option of imposing determinate or indeterminate sentences for most crimes committed by adult offenders. A number of state legislatures are scrutinizing California methods, policies, and procedures with a view to incorporating them into their own correctional apparatus. Therefore it may be worthwhile to take a close look at how these work out in practice.

In California, sentencing and paroling of male convicts are entrusted to a nine-member Adult Authority with an annual budget of close to $1 million; according to its published literature, "it is composed of persons who have demonstrated skills, abilities, and leadership in many fields."

Its members are appointed by the governor for four-year terms. The composition of the present board is not easily squared with its self-appraisal. It is, with the lone exception of a retired dentist, drawn from the ranks of law enforcement and Corrections: former policemen, prosecutors, FBI and prison personnel—"eight cops and a dentist," as the prisoners call them. This board wields total, arbitrary, despotic power over the destinies and liberties of California's state prison population, not only while they are in custody but also after they have been released on parole.

Under cover of the indeterminate sentence, the median term served by California's "felony first releases" had risen from twenty-four months in 1960 to thirty-six months in 1970, highest in the nation and probably the world. According to a publication of the California Youth and Adult Corrections Agency, virtually no adult felons are released at the point of minimum legal eligibility "though the legislature in setting minimum limits presumably expected cases to receive such consideration."

At a meeting of ex-convicts, I asked what they conceived to be the major grievances of the California prison population. There was near-unanimity: surprisingly, the wretched physical conditions of prison life are by no means their major concern. The food, they said, is generally lousy. Medical treatment amounts to criminal neglect in many instances. The highly touted vocational training is a fraud; in San Quentin there are

350 places in the trade programs for a population of over 3,500 (you have to be on a waiting list for eighteen months or more to get in), and even in the minimum-security conservation camps there is little opportunity to learn skills that will be useful on the outside.

But these features of prison existence, disheartening, degrading, and dangerous though they are, pale in importance, say the convicts, beside the total arbitrariness of the bureaucracy that rules every aspect of their existence. One former inmate summed it up: "Don't give us steak and eggs; get rid of the Adult Authority! Don't put in a shiny modern hospital; free us from the tyranny of the indeterminate sentence!"

The crucial moment in the prisoner's life is his hearing before the Adult Authority, which will determine whether or not to set his sentence, whether or not to grant a parole date. If he is serving five years to life, he is legally eligible for parole after twenty months, one third of the minimum term. His first hearing will be eighteen months after he enters prison, and he will come before the board annually thereafter until it is ready to fix an "individualized" maximum term, short of life, and set a date for his release on parole.

The Adult Authority is under no legal obligation to set the term, and in practice it does not do so until it is ready to grant parole. By keeping the prisoner in perpetual suspense, never knowing from year to year what portion of his one-to-twenty or five-to-life sentence he will serve, the Adult Authority maintains maximum control over him for the entire period of his incarceration.*

---

* In early 1972, following a series of prison disturbances protesting this practice, the Adult Authority announced with considerable fanfare and publicity that it would begin setting the term early in the convict's prison career. According to inmates, the announced new policy is not adhered to. The San Francisco *Examiner* (December 6, 1972) reported nearly a year later that "the state Adult Authority quietly has allowed its much-publicized new policy of setting parole dates within six months after inmates enter prison to slip into a hazy limbo."

Assisted by a number of full-time case-hearing representatives, the Adult Authority makes the circuit of the prisons, splitting up into teams of two, to conduct the prisoner interviews. A prison staff member is present to brief the panel on the inmate's record, to make notes on his "attitude" during the hearing and on comments made about him by the panel members after he has left, and to record the panel's decision.

Presumably to ensure a decision uninfluenced by the possible bias of prison authorities, the staff worker is not permitted to make recommendations to the panel. But since he is charged with reporting the institution's evaluation of the prisoner, the outcome is generally predetermined by his written summary.

There are no written guidelines for the conduct of the hearing, and if parole is denied, the prisoner is not entitled to know the reason. No transcript is made of the hearing. The prisoner's family, his counsel, and the press are excluded.

An official version of procedures followed in the prisoner interview is furnished by Mr. Everett M. Porter, former Adult Authority member, in his essay "State Imprisonment and Parole." The interview consists, he says, of "preliminaries intended to put the inmate at his ease" followed by questions designed to reveal "his insights into his behavior, capacities, and goals and his motivation for constructive change." The panel will then ask about "the circumstances of his crime, disciplinary incidents in prison, his participation in particular prison programs . . . In addition to appraising the inmate's personality, the panel tries to help the inmate understand his problems, and to encourage him in constructive approaches. The panel may offer specific suggestions, e.g., that he enroll in Alcoholics Anonymous . . ."

The interview concluded, the panel dismisses the prisoner, makes its decision which will be officially relayed to him a few days later, and calls the next case.

In its official literature, the Adult Authority claims it accords the convicts who come before it an average of a little less than

17 minutes apiece. From many ex-convicts I have learned something about the interview from where the prisoner sits. Typical is the experience of one who has been through it several times (I'll call him Mr. A.); nasty, short, and sometimes brutish, he found it. "Seventeen minutes may be the mathematical average," he said. "In my experience, five to seven minutes was more like it."

The information upon which the panel's decision is based is a mix of what is in the prisoner's central file folder and what the prison staff member (generally a "correctional counselor") has to say about him in his written summary to the board. "A man in prison lives by his central file folder," said Mr. A. "He lives in fear of it and in holy expectation of what good may come from it. Its contents determine everything that will happen to him from his 'custody status' in prison to his eventual chances of making parole."

In this formidable pile of paperwork is contained everything the authorities know, or think they know, about the prisoner: probation officer's report, comments of trial judge and district attorney, evaluations by psychiatrists, psychologists, social workers, reports by guards of infractions of the rules: "a mixture of fact and fiction," said Mr. A.

While his guards are encouraged to familiarize themselves with the contents of the folder, neither the prisoner nor his lawyer is permitted to see it. The rationale: it contains "confidential psychiatric material"—a curious distortion of the privileged doctor–patient relationship, which is supposedly for the patient's benefit and subject to waiver by him. In prison, the privilege is waived not for the "patient" or his counsel, but for policing agencies and the FBI, who are permitted full access to everything concerning him. In fact, according to a California attorney general's opinion the prison psychiatrist's client is the Department of Corrections, not the prisoner.

"Preliminaries intended to put the inmate at his ease" may range, said Mr. A., depending on the mood of the panel, from open taunts ("If you don't have any friends, why don't you get yourself a dog?" "Are your parents as black as you are?" "You're in here for life, and don't forget it.") to an uneasy show of hearty friendliness, "necessarily phony because of the positions of inequality in the situation."

Well aware that his "insights, capacities, and goals" are under scrutiny, the prisoner is at a loss how to respond. "If he lets his true feelings come out and tells the panel: 'You're arbitrary and unjust,' they'll say he's not ready for parole. If he says: 'I've benefited enormously from the rehabilitation programs,' they'll put him down as a smoothie and deny him parole anyway." The important thing is "attitude," Mr. A. continued, "meaning, has the prisoner learned to conform? To get out, you must strike just the right posture of 'sincerity,' repentance, and firm resolve to improve. If the file shows the prisoner refused to submit to 'treatment,' he is in bad trouble."

The man who has pleaded not-guilty at his trial, and who continues to assert his innocence of the crime for which he was sentenced—or even one who refuses to admit guilt for a crime for which he was charged and acquitted—is liable to be in particularly severe trouble. "You've got your 'cop-out sheet' with you, showing what you've done in the past year: vocational training, church attendance, and the like, but you may never have a chance to bring out any of that. The board member asks: 'How do you feel now about the crime you committed?' You answer: 'I'm sorry it happened. I was drunk at the time. I guess I lost my head. But I have a trade now. I've only one beef against me—failure to tuck my shirt in when ordered to do so by an officer.' The member: 'I like the looks of your file, you're handling yourself pretty well. But what about the 1961 burglary?' You protest you were innocent of that. He says that's not what the police said. You get into a hassle— and very soon your few minutes of time are up. There are no further questions, the panel tells you, 'We'll let you know.' "

As for the "constructive approaches" and "specific suggestions" for rehabilitation of the prisoner, these depend on the whim of the individual panel members. Adult Authority policy is to rotate the panels, so that the man whose parole is denied year after year confronts a different duo each time. Nostrums for his rehabilitation vary, said Mr. A., depending on the idiosyncrasies of the individual panel member. "Board Member X may be hipped on religion, so he'll tell you to get with it and go to church every week. But fifty-two Sundays later, you come before Board Member Y: his bag is Alcoholics Anonymous, and even if the prisoner doesn't happen to have an alcohol problem, he'll be told, 'Attend the AA for a year and then we'll see about a parole date.' Yet another may insist you participate in 'group therapy.' This can go on indefinitely, as long as they haven't set his sentence. Meanwhile the prisoner is totally in the dark. He has no way of knowing on what they base these suggestions. Is it any wonder that when he eventually comes out he's bitter and full of revenge?"

While "psyching the board members" is an ongoing prison hobby, no one has ever been able to second-guess them accurately, said Mr. A. "They may talk to you like a dog, you go back and tell everybody, 'I was shot down this time'—and then you'll get a parole date. Or, they may be very sympathetic— even ask about your parole plans—and then deny you. There's a great variety among the board members. For example, there's one member—if you pound the table and yell, he likes that, he thinks that means you can make it! Another would be so mortally offended by that sort of behavior he'd give you two years for it."

The Adult Authority's official orientation bulletin states: "The offense for which a man is committed is only one of the factors that the AA considers when making a decision." Other factors may be (and often are) crimes for which the prisoner was arrested but never brought to trial, or crimes for which he was tried in a court of law and acquitted. The indeterminate sentence law gives the Adult Authority the power to inflict any punishment it deems fit for these unproved crimes, its decision often based on hearsay in the form of letters from prosecutors or police agencies. Lawyers can cite dozens of cases in which a frustrated D.A., unable to secure a conviction, gets his man in the end anyway. Example: an eighteen-year-old black is sentenced to a five-to-life term for a holdup in which no violence occurred and nobody was hurt. He is eligible for parole at the end of twenty months, and, as a first offender with a blameless prison record, has every reason to expect his sentence to be set accordingly. But there is a letter in his file from the district attorney advising the Adult Authority that he is actually a vicious killer. The district attorney had charged him with a double murder (unconnected with the holdup), and although he was unable to get a conviction after three jury trials, he says he knows the prisoner was guilty and will kill again if freed. Year after year the prisoner comes before the Adult Authority, year after year parole is denied and his sentence, unset, remains at life. He has no opportunity to defend himself —he is not even allowed to see the allegations against him in the D.A.'s letter. At age thirty-three, he is released, having served about eight years more than the average time given a convicted first-degree murderer, and fourteen years more than the average sentence for a robbery first offender.

Those prisoners who have foregone a trial and pleaded guilty to a lesser charge, in the belief that under the plea-bargaining system they would serve a correspondingly shorter sentence, may be in for a rude awakening when they come before the Adult Authority. As Gregory J. Hobbs, Jr., puts it in the *California Law Review* for June 1971: "It is known but rarely expressed clearly to defendants that the Adult Authority weighs all the charges that were brought in the prosecution, as well as any prior arrests or convictions, in deciding when to release a prisoner. Thus, a person can serve time in effect for the charges which were dismissed pursuant to the bargain—the

Adult Authority merely holds him beyond the median time served by persons convicted of the charge to which he pleaded guilty." How this works out in practice was described to me by Joseph Spangler, the Adult Authority's administrative officer: "For example, a young woman hears a scratching at her door, opens it, sees a man exposing himself. She screams, the guy flees. Then later he comes back, jimmies the door—she screams again. The neighbors come, catch the fellow, and hold him for the police. His lawyer pleads him to second-degree burglary, which carries a sentence of one to fifteen years. Normally, he would be out in a year or so, but the prison psychiatrists will evaluate him as a sexual psychopath based on the complaining witness's accusation, although he was never convicted of the charge. Officially he's a second-degree burglar, but we evaluate them on an individual basis and set the term accordingly."

Inevitably, a politically appointed lay board such as the Adult Authority is bound to be influenced by changing public attitudes toward crime. Yet another "factor the Adult Authority considers" is newspaper publicity given to certain categories of crime. The luckless prisoner serving time for robbery whose parole hearing comes in the wake of a particularly sensational, violent armed robbery that has made the front pages will find himself caught in the same spotlight, although in his own case no violence was alleged. Robbery having suddenly become the Crime of the Week, the prisoner is punished accordingly—not for his own offense, but for the one currently in the headlines—and his parole is denied.

Summarizing California paroling policies as they have developed in practice, the Progress Report of the Assembly Committee on Criminal Procedure says: "The time that an individual spends in prison seems to depend on three factors: (1) The values and feelings of individual parole board members. (2) The 'mood' of the public. (3) Institution population pressures . . . The parole board operates without a clear and rationally justified policy. Responsibility for decisions involving deep considerations of justice, public safety, and cost is vested in a board legally and scientifically unequipped to justify *any* policy toward less serious offenders. As a result, California general parole policy, reflecting emotion, not facts, has become increasingly conservative, punitive, and expensive."

So much for lighting the prisons with this law of love.

7

TREATMENT

The notion that most lawbreakers are suffering from mental illness—else why should they transgress?—took hold among the prison people at a surprisingly early date, long before psychiatric explanations for all manner of human behavior became fashionable. Thus a speaker at the 1870 Congress of the American Prison Association: "A criminal is a man who has suffered under a disease evinced by the perpetration of a crime, and who may reasonably be held to be under the dominion of such disease until his conduct has afforded very strong presumption not only that he is free from its immediate influence, but that the chances of its recurrence have become exceedingly remote." And another, at the 1874 Congress: "Abolish all time sentences. Treat the criminal as a patient and the crime as a disease."

This theme, reverberating down the century in the works of penologists, has found ready acceptance in the ranks of modern reformers. According to Dr. Karl Menninger, unlawful acts are "signals of distress, signals of failure . . . the spasms and struggles and convulsions of a sub-marginal human being trying to make it in our complex society with inadequate equipment and inadequate preparation." Ramsey Clark writes, "Most people who commit serious crimes have mental health problems." Neither author attempts to document these blanket assertions.*

A contrary view is advanced by Thomas S. Szasz, M.D., a specialist in the interrelationship of law and psychiatry: "The thesis that the criminal is a sick individual in need of treatment—which is promoted today as if it were a recent psychiatric discovery—is false. Indeed it is hardly more than a refurbishing, with new terms, of the main ideas and techniques of the inquisitorial process . . . [the deviant] is first discredited as a self-responsible human being, and then subjected to humiliating punishment defined and disguised as treatment." And the eminent criminologists Harry E. Barnes and Negley K. Teeters assert that lawbreakers are no crazier than the rest of us: "The bulk of our criminals are not emotionally disturbed. In general it would seem reasonable to assume that a cross-section of the criminal world would show no more emotional imbalance than could be found in the general population." (Which is merely to say that there are a lot of kooky people walking around the streets *and* sitting in the jails.)

---

* According to Thomas Shaffer, dean of Notre Dame Law School, the arrest rate among former mental patients is about half that of the general population.

However, the mental illness theory of criminality and its concomitant, individualized treatment for offenders, find instant favor with all sorts of unlikely bedfellows: liberal reformers, prison administrators, judges, prosecutors, law enforcement officers, and those indefatigable experimenters, the "behavior modification" experts. It offers a convenient and scientific-sounding explanation for the difference between Us (the upright white middle-class citizens who run the criminal justice system) and Them (lower-class lawbreakers and other "deviants") who fill the juvenile reformatories, jails, and prisons —for if there *were* no essential difference, how should the former justify doing what they do to the latter? It confers legitimacy on the unchecked discretionary power of captor over captive at all stages of his progression through the criminal justice system from juvenile hall to the penitentiary and beyond that to parole. It assuages the public conscience by replacing imprisonment-for-punishment with the humanitarian alternative of imprisonment-for-therapy. And for the growing army of behavioral scientists it furnishes a stockade of caged human guinea pigs on which to try out ever more exotic techniques of people-changing.

In prison parlance, "treatment" is an umbrella term meaning diagnosis, classification, various forms of therapy, punishment as deemed necessary, and prognosis, or the prediction of the malfeasant's future behavior: will/won't he err again? While the Corrections crowd everywhere talk a good line of "treatment"—phrases like "inadequate personalities," "borderline sociopaths," "weak superegos" come trippingly off the tongue of the latter-day prison warden, having long since replaced the sin-stained souls and fallen men or women with whom his predecessor had to cope—very few prison systems have actually done much about implementing it in practice. Nationwide, only 5 percent of the prison budget goes for services labeled "rehabilitation," and in many states there is not even the pretense of making "therapy" available to the adult offender.

Hence the chronic plaint of the would-be rehabilitator: if the treatment programs have not worked, it is because they have never been given a fair chance due to public apathy and legislative stinginess. Yet thanks to the persistence of some zealous penologists and sociologists, and their supporters in government, there are scattered around the country a few highly financed "treatment-oriented" prisons. Examples are the California state prisons for adult male felons, Patuxent Institution for "defective delinquents" in Maryland, the Draper Experimental-Demonstration Project for youthful offenders in Alabama. It is to these that one must look for answers to the questions: What is the underlying purpose of "treatment" in a prison setting? How does it work in practice? How is it viewed by the "patients"? By the "treaters"? By the prison administration? And, as new theories of psychotherapy, new methods of curing "deviance" evolve, where is treatment headed?

It is widely acknowledged in penological circles that the California prison system lights the way for the rest of the country—and perhaps the world—in its espousal of the treatment philosophy. The state Department of Corrections, in a recent budget report to the legislature, expressed unalloyed self-satisfaction on this score: "The counseling programs available in the Department of Corrections include highly professional and individualized psychiatric treatment, group psychotherapy, individual and group counseling sessions, and group living programs, patterned after the therapeutic community approach used in psychiatric hospitals." Dr. Karl Menninger, in *The Crime of Punishment,* lavishes unstinted praise on these achievements: "The California correctional system . . . has been far out in the lead among the states, with excellent programs of work, education, vocational training, medical services, group counseling, and other rehabilitative activities. A notable feature is the combination of diagnosis, evaluation, treatment, and classification . . . This constitutes a systematic effort along scientific principles to ascertain from collected case history data and from firsthand examination just what the assets and liabilities of the floundering individual are . . ."

Those who have looked beyond the rhetoric and into the realities of this best of all possible correctional worlds— criminologists, legislative researchers, lawyers involved in prison litigation, psychiatrists who have worked in the prisons, and above all the convicts themselves—disagree profoundly with Dr. Menninger's observations. Dr. Bernard L. Diamond, professor of criminology and of law and clinical professor of psychiatry at the University of California, told me, "In 'good' prisons, like those in California, physical degradation is replaced by psychological degradation. I call these 'pastel' prisons; they look good, shiny, sanitary. But inmates will tell you thousands of ways in which they are psychologically degraded." According to many prisoners with whom I have talked, the "combination of diagnosis, evaluation, treatment, and classification" so highly rated by Dr. Menninger is in fact the Catch-22 of modern prison life: "A grand hypocrisy in which custodial concerns, administrative exigencies, and punishment are all disguised as treatment," as John Irwin puts it in *The Felon*.

Yet according to Professor Irwin, himself an ex-convict who did time in San Quentin when the treatment era was first ushered in around 1950, many prisoners responded with a certain enthusiasm. "They were led to believe that they would be able to raise their educational level, to learn a trade, to have physical defects corrected, and would receive help in various individual or group therapy programs in solving their psychological problems," he says. "In effect they were led to believe that if they participated in the prison programs with sincerity and resolve, they would leave prison in better condition than when they entered and would generally be much better equipped to cope with the outside world."

No doubt these hopes were shared by many a missionary

spirit in the echelons of prison administration. A booklet written in the fifties by Norman Fenton, then deputy director in charge of treatment, addressed to the families of California prisoners, positively vibrates with enthusiasm for the new programs. Mr. Fenton describes the daily life of the prisoner (referred to throughout the booklet as "your loved-one") in these glowing terms: "The treatment program for the inmate in the prison is planned in terms of an understanding of him as a person . . . human kindness pervades the things that are done in attempting to help him in the prison . . . with understanding help in an atmosphere of kindness this purpose can best be accomplished . . ." The prisoner's children should be told "their father is there because he needs the help he can receive . . . the prison, the children may be informed, is like a hospital— only the kinds of troubles treated there are not physical illnesses but personal troubles." The family's role is to keep reminding the loved-one of all that is being done for him: "When a person goes to a hospital, he expects treatment. Unfortunately, most men who are sent to prison still expect punishment . . . Nothing which the families can do is more important than to try to change their loved-one's attitudes toward the prisons and to try to accept them as places for treatment not unlike hospitals."

Why the dimming of this bright promise? Some of the built-in contradictions that confound the conscientious therapist who tries to apply the principles of his training in a prison setting are described in an article by Dr. Harvey Powelson, written in collaboration with Reinhard Bendix, entitled "Psychiatry in Prison."

Dr. Powelson was resident psychiatrist at San Quentin in 1950, the Golden Age of California prison reform, when under the benign administration of Richard McGee newly established divisions with benevolent-sounding designations—Guidance Center, Division of Care and Treatment, Medical Division— were assigned the many-faceted task of therapy. Yet Dr. Powelson soon discovered that no matter how assiduously the guiders, carers, treaters, and medics tried to carry out their mission they found themselves frustrated at every turn by the Custody Division (guards) with its "punitive approach to the prisoners" which, in fact, ran the prison, wielding total veto power over the operations of all other divisions.

There is, Dr. Powelson found, "a striking contrast between the custodial and the psychiatric view of the prisoner." The custodial man "regards the prisoner, at least unofficially, as a special form of humanity," and acts on the premise that "each prisoner is a cunning malingerer and that each staff member who is not a guard falls an easy prey to the chicanery of the criminal mind." When staff members complained that prisoners who sought psychiatric treatment were taunted by the guards as "dings" and "queers," the associate warden, who heads the custodial staff, merely replied that the guards did no such thing, "the implication being that the psychiatrists were simply the dupes of malingering prisoners."

In Dr. Powelson's view, only those psychiatrists who become co-opted by the prison and adopt Custody's punitive attitude to the prisoner are likely to remain on the job: "Those who do not fit in will be eliminated and those who do fit in will stay on."

Fitting in has its medical implications: "It is hardly surprising," Dr. Powelson writes, "that psychiatry in the prison consists primarily in therapeutic practices which can have punitive or disciplinary implications: electric shock, insulin shock, fever treatment, hydrotherapy, Amytal and Pentothal interviews, spinals, and cisternals [insertion of needle into spinal cord] and so on—that is, everything except psychotherapy." Treatment, anyone?

To find out more about psychiatry as practiced behind bars, I sought out Dr. Powelson, now head of the psychiatric clinic at the University of California at Berkeley. Among his observations:

Shock treatment was "pretty clearly" used as punishment: "It would take the form of telling the prisoner 'unless your behavior changes you're going to get more of this.' " Another medical procedure visited on the unruly was insulin coma treatment: "It's very dangerous, since fallen into disfavor. You give a large enough dose of insulin to cause coma, the patient stops breathing, is kept on the edge of death. One man did die from this while I was there."

Prison psychiatrists, functioning in their custodial capacity, often sat in on disciplinary hearings in which their findings were used to trap the prisoner into admissions that would result in his reassignment to a tougher "custody status," from minimum to maximum security: "While the reasons for this were couched in psychiatric terms, from the prisoner's point of view the reassignment was punishment, not 'treatment.' " Occasionally Dr. Powelson attended Adult Authority hearings in which board members undertook to interpret the then-popular Rorschach test results in reaching parole decisions. "It's very hard for even a skilled person to interpret these tests," he said. "To use them to predict behavior is about as valid as using a crystal ball. My sense of the situation was that the Adult Authority used the tests for rationalizations for what they'd already decided based on their own intuition. A man had a 'bad' Rorschach test, so they'd say, 'We'll put him over for a year.' It's nightmarish from the prisoner's standpoint— there's no way of knowing how you are doing on a Rorschach test."

There is little wonder that the initial optimism of those on the receiving end of treatment has seeped away over the past two decades. Today, the convicts see themselves trapped in a vise between, as one put it, "the punitive nineteenth-century guard and the 1984 headshrinker." Most prison authorities, while they proclaim allegiance to the treatment philosophy, still regard "protection of the public" and "deterrence" (meaning lock-up and punishment) as the primary functions of the penal system, the traditional privations and rigors of which the prisoner must endure. Overlaid on these are the modern "therapy" and "treatment" goals. The offender must not only pay his debt to society in the old-fashioned way of "doing his time," but in addition he must prove that the modern treatment method has worked, that he is cured, rehabilitated, and ready for parole.

From the convict's point of view, "treatment" is a humiliating game, the rules of which he must try to learn in order to placate his keepers and manipulate the parole board at his annual hearing: "I have gained much insight into my problems during the past year." According to a 1966 study by the Institute for the Study of Crime and Delinquency, "most [inmates] looked upon treatment programs as phony." Seventy percent of inmates polled answered "yes" to the question: Do you believe that therapy and treatment programs are games? The researchers concluded, "Most cons know how to walk that walk, talk that talk, and give the counselor what he wants to hear."

To decline to play can be dangerous indeed. The prisoner who refuses to submit to therapy will find himself "diagnosed" as a troublemaker, and the classification committee will act accordingly by confining him in a maximum-security prison—not, of course, as punishment, but as the next logical step in his treatment. If he continues in his defiance of the treatment staff, the parole board will hear about it, and he will end up serving months or years more than is normal for his offense. An ex-convict told me of an Indian prisoner in San Quentin serving an indeterminate sentence of one to fifteen years for burglary; as a first offender, he would ordinarily have been paroled after a year or so. For eight consecutive years the parole board refused to set a release date because he would not go to group therapy. In the ninth year, he escaped.

From many interviews with ex-convicts—and letters from those still in prison—I have learned something about this humiliating game as it is played today, twenty years after Dr. Powelson's tenure. "Treatment" begins when the newly arrived convict is imprisoned in what the authorities are pleased to call the "Reception and Guidance Center." An ex-convict expressed the views of many about the procedures there: "During the initial six- to twelve-week quarantine period, which each man undergoes when he first enters prison, his manhood and individuality are subtly vitiated. The inmate may have less than a sixth-grade education. Yet he is subjected to a barrage of questionnaires, it's a painful and embarrassing experience. He'll be asked about 'sibling rivalry' although he won't have the faintest idea what that means. And 'Are you obsessed with fears of latent homosexuality?'

"It's vicious, attritional. The whole point of the psychological diagnosis is to get him to go for the fact he's 'sick,' yet the statement he's sick deprives him of his integrity as a person.

"Most prisoners I know would rather be thought bad than mad. They say society may have a right to punish them, but not a hunting license to remold them in its own sick image."

Confirming Dr. Powelson's findings about the attitude of prison psychiatrist to "patient," a black ex-convict told me of a recent session with the chief psychiatrist at San Quentin: "The shrink says, 'Sit down,' so I sit down. He says, 'How are you feeling today?' 'Oh, pretty good I guess.' 'That's rather a negative answer, isn't it?' says the shrink. 'What's *negative* about it?' I say. And the shrink pounces: 'Aha! So *you're* going to ask the questions, are you?' I knew right there I was trapped. And they ask such things as 'How do you feel about your mother?' I said, 'I hate her.' Hell, I *love* my mother, but what could I do? You soon get to know what sort of answers they expect."

Eventually all these bits and snippets of alleged intelligence about the prisoner's psyche as interpreted by the prison psychiatrist are gathered together, made part of his file, and solemnly presented to the parole board for its consideration when deliberating whether to grant him parole. Although the central file folders are kept securely locked away from the public gaze, I got a glimpse into one of them and thus into the quality of "treatment" dispensed and the kind of information on which the California Adult Authority bases its parole decisions. It was the file of a twenty-five-year-old black militant serving a six-month to fifteen-year sentence for burglary. Apparently he successfully held his ground during most of his psychiatric interview, for the psychiatrist observes that "he revealed no peculiar or bizarre mannerisms . . . delusional thinking as such was not elicited . . . he did not appear to be overtly depressed or unduly elated . . ." However, the prisoner foundered on two questions: "Some evidence of impulsiveness was elicited when he was asked what he would do if he were the first to see a fire in a movie theater; he said, 'Leave.' When asked what he would do if he were standing near a railroad track on which a rail was broken and he saw a train coming, he replied, 'I couldn't say.' " The psychiatrist's diagnosis: "Emotionally unstable personality, with paranoid tendencies."

What are the right answers? I asked a prison psychologist for clarification. Should he have said, "I'd save everyone in the theater before leaving"?, and "I'd lay my body on the track to warn the engineer of danger ahead"? "No, that wouldn't do," the psychologist explained. "If he gave those answers, he'd be put down for a Napoleon complex. The correct answer to the first question is: 'I'd quietly notify the manager of the theater about the fire, so as to avoid causing panic in the audience,' and to the second, 'I'd wave a flag to warn the engineer that something is wrong.' "

What of the prison psychiatrist who does not "fit in"? When a psychiatrist who really cares about the prisoners' welfare, and who refuses to knuckle under to "custody," strays into the prison system, he is eagerly sought out by men asking for help. Such was the experience of Dr. Frank Rundle, who was employed as chief psychiatrist at Soledad Prison for a stormy five-month period in 1970–71. His introduction to the work, far from reassuring, consisted mainly of instructions on how to ward off violent attacks ("Always keep a table between you and the inmate, be prepared to shove it hard to pin him against the wall"; "Carry a police whistle at all times") and injunctions not to venture near the "dangerous" prisoners. "My predecessor showed me around," he told me. "We came to a tier of dark, dirty little cages—I couldn't believe my eyes. Some men were rattling their bars and screaming obscenities, others were lying on the cement floor as though in a stupor. I asked, 'What's *that*?' He said, 'It's the Adjustment Center,* don't ever go in there. Those are the most violent inmates in the system.' "

Disregarding this counsel, Dr. Rundle was soon spending most of his time in the Adjustment Center, which he found "filled with the most concentrated human misery to which I have ever been exposed—torturing loneliness and yearning to meet another human being on equal terms, to talk as man to man. Once they knew I wasn't 'custody-minded,' the prisoners urged me to come and see them. They were hungry to be listened to seriously, to be believed, to be respected, to be cared about, to be liked, to be dealt with honestly."

* An account of the origins of the Adjustment Center is set forth in a paper given at the 1955 Congress of the American Correctional Association by three high-ranking California prison administrators: Allen Cook, superintendent of Deuel Vocational Institute; Norman Fenton, Deputy Director of Classification; and Robert A. Heinze, warden of Folsom prison. These authors observe that "Sir Winston Churchill has often been quoted as stating that one measure of a civilization is the way in which captives in its prisons are treated," and they proceed to describe the California plan to measure up: "The term Adjustment Center has been introduced into the nomenclature of the prison system to describe a facility with positive and constructive treatment objectives, a place which is quite the opposite of what in ordinary prison usage is designated usually by some negative and forbidding titles such as 'The Hole,' 'The Shelf,' 'Siberia,' and the like . . . Fundamentally, the experiences in the Adjustment Center are planned for treatment rather than punishment."

Dr. Rundle immediately ran into the conflict described by Dr. Powelson: "Custody runs everything, controls everything, even the conditions of psychiatric treatment." His first open quarrel with the authorities came when the chief medical officer ordered that any inmate identified as a psychiatric patient be locked in a security cell—which meant twenty-four-hour-a-day solitary confinement, no showers, no exercise, no recreation. "I told them I could no longer be responsible for those patients—these are exactly the conditions to drive a man further into a psychosis."

Tension between Dr. Rundle and the rest of the staff rose a notch when he was subpoenaed to give evidence in the case of an inmate accused of killing a guard. Asked about conditions in which the defendant lived, Dr. Rundle described the Adjustment Center as a miserable, filthy place where men went for weeks without a shower, and he told the court of tear-gassings and beatings he had witnessed. On his return from the trial Dr. Rundle was called in by the warden: "It was perfectly clear that he thought it was improper for me to testify as I did, even though my answers were true and I was under oath." After this, he was ordered to have no further contact with any prisoners who might become involved with court proceedings.

The end of Dr. Rundle's career at Soledad came swiftly and dramatically when he refused to turn over to the warden the confidential psychiatric file of a prisoner-patient suspected of killing a prison official. "The warden seemed genuinely surprised when I told him that I would not release the file to anyone unless the inmate requested it," said Dr. Rundle. "To compromise on this issue would be to destroy my position of trust with the inmates—it just wasn't right, legally, morally, or professionally." But the prison has its own way of doing things. Dr. Rundle was cornered and surrounded by some twenty guards who forcibly seized his briefcase containing the confidential file. They strong-armed him into the warden's office, where he was summarily fired. As Dr. Powelson said, "Those who do not fit in will be eliminated."

But, the persistent proponent of treatment might argue, the California experience merely goes to show that the prison authorities, in spite of pious declarations, never really committed themselves wholeheartedly to the treatment philosophy. Had they done so, the professional staff would have been given the upper hand as the decisive, guiding influence and would have had free rein to carry out its therapeutic mission without the noxious interference of Custody.

Visualize, then, a modern institution that houses about 425 convicts, headed not by a warden but by a psychiatrist. Such is Patuxent Institution in Maryland, established in 1955 under the Defective Delinquent Statute as a unique experiment in penal reform, its prime purpose that of a "total treatment facility." According to the state attorney general, Patuxent's staff includes 89 "positions directly related to the welfare of the patients," consisting of:

10 psychiatrists
11 psychologists
17 social workers
9 educational personnel
11 vocational training personnel
4 recreational personnel
12 medical personnel
6 classification personnel
9 dietary staff

Criteria for admission are extremely broad; to qualify, one may have been convicted and sentenced for a felony, or a misdemeanor punishable by imprisonment in the state penitentiary, or a crime of violence, or one of a series of sex crimes. To free the staff from coercive "custody" attitudes and controls, Patuxent Institution was granted full autonomy and functions outside the jurisdiction of the Department of Corrections. The annual expenditure per "patient" (as the staff are required to call the prisoners) is an incredibly lavish $9,600, more than twice that of the Maryland Penitentiary. All commitments to Patuxent are for an absolute indeterminate sentence (meaning, "life top"), the statute specifying that in keeping with the therapeutic purpose of the new institution no inmate should be released until deemed cured. The decision whether or not to release an inmate on parole rests, not with a politically appointed parole board, but with the Institutional Head of Review, headed by the director of Patuxent and composed of practitioners in the disciplines of psychiatry, psychology, sociology, and law. Of Patuxent, Dr. Karl Menninger has said, "I heartily approve. I wish we had an institution like this in our state." " . . . A great idea, it's the only one of its kind. Patuxent is a progressive step forward."

Reformer's dream come true, or nightmarish snake-pit? In 1971 the Montgomery Circuit Court condemned much of the Patuxent operation as cruel and unusual punishment. The court commented with some asperity on the testimony of one of the institution's psychiatrists to the effect that the filthy, roach-infested punishment cells in which prisoners are confined, sometimes for months on end, are "treatment, defined as 'negative reinforcers.' " In fact, said the court, these conditions are "contrary to the rehabilitation of the inmates and serve no therapeutic value of any kind." Other negative reinforcers, the evidence disclosed, are infliction of brutal physical injuries, hosings, beatings, Macings.

Patuxent is organized on a "graded tier level" system in which the "patient" must earn his way from the first to the fourth, and highest, tier level—the quintessence of the carrot-and-club approach, only here the club is no metaphor. He spends at least his first thirty—and more often sixty—days on the bottom tier, where he is deliberately subjected to the unalloyed punishment of solitary lock-up, held virtually incommunicado in a nine-by-six-foot cell for almost twenty-four

hours a day, denied books, letters, visitors, allowed but one
shower a week. His promotion through successive levels is at
the pleasure of the treatment staff, who may also demote him
at whim. The third level is so designed that the inmate can see
into the fourth level and thus glimpse the treats and rewards
that await him there: a comfortable day-room with TV and
magazines, family picnics, the right to paint and decorate his
own cell.

According to Joseph Whitehill, a novelist who has worked
at Patuxent for nine years as volunteer teacher of a Great
Books course, "the basic fatal flaw in the setup there is the
compulsory character of the treatment. To be effective,
therapeutic help must be sought on a voluntary basis and freely
given with no strings attached." Having started out at Patuxent
"with stars in my eyes," Whitehill is today campaigning in
the Maryland legislature for repeal of the Defective Delinquent
Statute and for shutting down the institution.

The decision as to who qualifies for commitment as a "Defective Delinquent" (after initial referral by a court) rests
with the Patuxent staff. Whitehill says that the definition of
this category of lawbreaker is "so loose and impressionistic
that one could remove the entire present population tomorrow,
scan and select from the main body of men in the Maryland
prisons, and come up with 500 *new* 'defective delinquents.' "
In his view, "the evidence is commanding that until very
recently, Patuxent picked for commitment those it thought
it could break. Then came a flood of politicized and radical
prisoners, mostly black, who weren't going to be broken
and weren't going to suck up to white middle-class orthodox
'psychiatry' in order to wheedle their way out, all of which
took Patuxent's administration very much by surprise." Whitehill had long been an advocate of the indeterminate sentence,
which seemed to him logical and humane. "But by the time
I had talked man-to-man with some hundreds of inmates who

were under it, I began to hear what was wrong. Logical or not, the inmate hears 'forever' and despairs. The indeterminate sentence is a frank statement of the naked, absolute power of the state. In this it differs in no significant way from the gas chamber. The man under indeterminate sentence has all the negotiating options of a cornered rat. Rather than subject himself to the emasculating mercies of a white middle-class orthodoxy that hates and fears cultural variance on principle, he elects to commit suicide, either immediately or on the installment plan, dribbling his days away in the punishment cell."

One who refused to commit suicide by either method was Edward Lee McNeil, a black youth described to me by his lawyer as "highly intelligent, steadfast, iron-willed"—qualities that, as his story reveals, may well have saved him from a kind of lifelong purgatory. In 1966 McNeil, then aged nineteen, was convicted without a jury trial of assault on a police officer and assault with intent to rape, charges he consistently denied. He had no prior criminal record. He was a high school graduate, employed at the time, and living with his parents. No evidence of insanity, drug addiction, or drunkenness was offered at his trial. The judge sentenced him to imprisonment for "not more than five years" (under Maryland law, he would have been eligible for parole after serving fifteen months) and, on the advice of a court-appointed medical officer, sent him off to Patuxent for "evaluation and treatment."

McNeil, who was appealing his original conviction, declined to be "evaluated" or "treated" after his first few experiences with the social worker assigned to his case. The record shows that on at least twenty occasions he resisted the blandishments of psychologist, psychiatrist, and social worker alike: "Petitioner refused to become involved in the Achievement Testing program." "Refused to attend staff." "Refused psychiatric examinations: 'I don't want to talk to you, you can go and talk to my lawyer!' " "Refused psychological examination. Petitioner stated that he had court litigation pending and was waiting for the determination."

Consequently he was locked up on the bottom tier for *six years,* and would doubtless have languished there for the rest of his days had he not doggedly persisted in asserting his rights and eventually obtained a hearing by the U.S. Supreme Court. As he said in one of his numerous *pro se* petitions: ". . . it appears that if I do not myself take it upon myself to do something, I will remain here and rot forever." That McNeil's perception of his plight was all too accurate can be inferred from Patuxent statistics furnished to the Supreme Court by his lawyer, E. Barrett Prettyman. The median time served at the institution is ten years. Of 135 inmates paroled from Patuxent from its opening in 1955 until September 1965, 46 percent had served beyond their expired sentences.

Patuxent's view of the matter, as set forth in the attorney general's brief, is that it has both the right and the duty to lock up the noncooperator for life, if necessary: "The state's right to compel cooperation is based upon the state's need for diagnosis. If the state has a right, it cannot be without means of vindicating it. The means chosen—an indeterminate stay in the diagnostic area of Patuxent until cooperation is obtained—is a necessary and proper means to defeat the desire of undiagnosed defective delinquents to evade treatment by sitting out their sentences."

The U.S. Supreme Court thought otherwise. Ordering McNeil's immediate discharge, Mr. Justice Douglas wrote: "The state indeed intends to keep him there indefinitely, as long as he refuses to submit to psychiatric or psychological examinations. McNeil's refusal to submit to that questioning is not quixotic; it is based on his Fifth Amendment right to be silent." Noting that the questioning "is in a setting and has a goal pregnant with both potential and immediate danger," Justice Douglas with restrained indignation identified the underlying purpose of innumerable grillings withstood by the iron-willed McNeil. While his conviction was on appeal and when "concessions or confessions obtained might be useful to the state . . . [he] was repeatedly interrogated not only about the crime for which he was convicted but for many other alleged antisocial incidents going back to his sophomore year in high school. One staff member, after interviewing McNeil, reported: 'He adamantly and vehemently denies, despite the police reports, that he was involved in the offenses'; 'Further questioning revealed that he had stolen some shoes but he insisted that he did not know that they were stolen'; '. . . but in the tenth grade he was caught taking some milk and cookies from the cafeteria'; 'He consistently denies his guilt in all these offenses' " and on and on.

To talk or not to talk? The nature of the trap constructed by Patuxent's treatment staff for the containment of their "patients" is described by Justice Douglas:

"First, the staff refuses to diagnose him . . . unless he talks . . .

"Second, if there is no report on him [because he won't talk] he remains on the receiving tier indefinitely and receives no treatment.

"Third, if he talks and a report is made and he is committed as a 'defective delinquent,' he is no longer confined for any portion of the original sentence [but can be held indefinitely] . . ."

Paraphrasing Justice Douglas's words, McNeil on his release told the Washington *Post* that shortly after he arrived at Patuxent he had asked a social worker to delay an interview temporarily, pending a court decision on his appeal from his conviction. "The social worker got mad, he really got emotional," said McNeil. "He said, 'We don't care, we got enough on you anyway.' So I said in my mind, What is this? What's going on here? From that point on, I decided something wasn't right. I wouldn't let my life be placed in the hands of these people. I've never forgotten that moment. The social worker seemed quite friendly at first, but they all seem that way. They have the appearance of wanting to help and solve your problems, but they're detectives. Their job is to get enough on you to keep you locked up."

Judging by its published literature, the Draper Correctional Center in Alabama is an oasis of rehabilitation in an arid clime, southern prisons in general having long been celebrated in song, story, and film for their unrelieved barbarism. In 1964, Draper was selected for an "Experimental Demonstration Project," financed by the federal government to the tune of $1,800,000, in which youthful offenders committed to state prison would receive intensive educational and vocational training plus treatment designed to modify their behavior: "The behavior-changing process involves the force of the warden's personality and his use of both negative and positive reinforcers," says the Rehabilitation Research Foundation report to the government on the project.

In a frank talk ponderously titled "The Modification of the Subcultures in a Correctional Institution," Warden John C. Watkins, a sociologist, told his colleagues at the 1964 American Correctional Association Congress just how he goes about this.

Early on in his prison work, he discovered that many a convict "will not inform or turn state's evidence, although it could speed release to his wife or girl friend." Noting that "the convict culture is a way incarcerated people have learned to survive," he observes that from the convict's point of view "it is very immoral to inform, or in any way betray the culture to the administration." And within the framework of the convict culture, the prisoner finds "a refuge where he does not have to change, but can do 'good time' without being bothered by the treatment people." The "solid" convicts who live by the convict code "have their own religion: 'thou shalt not tell' . . . they are very moral about their loyalty to the system. If you ask one of them to tell you something, he often puts his hand over his heart and says, 'I know it will help me to tell you, but if I did I couldn't live with myself; I could not look into a mirror or hold my head up.' "

The road to successful "modification of subcultures" lies, it seems, in breaking down this loyalty and converting the young inmates into spies for the administration, a process Dr. Watkins found "exciting." The first step is to identify the solid convict, accomplished via the prison intelligence system: guards may supply clues, or sometimes other prisoners can be persuaded to inform. Dr. Watkins cautions against the apparent "solid" who shows two faces, who "tells the warden or the parole officer how he has changed, how he wants to 'straighten up,' " and then returns to his convict buddies and laughingly tells them how he fooled the free people. Once the solid has been tentatively identified, "find out his attitude about informing. Is informing immoral to him? Is he hostile toward the administration? Does he hate rats?"

After the rat-hating solids have been spotted comes the task of conversion, to "change their loyalty from the convict culture to the representatives of the administration." Such changes are not easy, for the solid "must be taught a way of life that is alien to him." Among the techniques favored by Dr. Watkins is "placing him under stricter custody control, or even telling him that he has been informed on and that you know what he is doing." A judicious use of rewards can be helpful, including assignment to jobs usually performed by "free-world" people: "At Draper, we use inmates as 'dog boys' to capture escapees. Dog boys are able to do this and yet live with the others without incident. In fact, being a dog boy is an important status symbol at Draper." (Dog boys, used throughout the Alabama prison system, are prisoner-trustees who look after trained bloodhounds and use them, when the occasion arises, to track down escaped convicts. According to Allen Tullos, who made a study of the Alabama prisons for the ACLU, they are heartily loathed not only by prisoners but by most of the free-world prison personnel as "the worst kind of stoolpigeon.")

As the treatment begins to take effect, Dr. Watkins continues, the solid gradually moves away from the convict culture. "If he can be persuaded to inform at this stage, deculturization is increased rapidly. I do not, however, press this point with him initially." Success is finally achieved when "he tries to please you rather than the convicts. He will inform and do whatever is necessary for the betterment of the institution . . . informing becomes accepted behavior." The conversion is not, however, without its unpleasant side effects. Dr. Watkins notes in passing that in the process of becoming informers solids "will frequently manifest psychosomatic symptoms such as headaches, nausea, and even dermatitis."

Another view of informers is offered by Eugene Debs: "Every prison is infested with that lowest of mortal creatures—the stoolpigeon. In prison parlance he is known as 'the rat.' The stoolpigeon seems to be a necessary part of a prison under club rule. Human beings ruled by brute force resent and resist and properly so, at every opportunity, and they must be spied upon and watched and betrayed by their fellow prisoners in order to be kept in subjugation. The stoolpigeon is the silent ally of the guard. He . . . finds his reward in immunity from punishment and in promoting his chances for the favorable consideration of his application for pardon, or parole, or commutation . . ."

Which raises the question: Who is "rehabilitated"? The solid who refuses to inform on his fellows or the prison rat who succumbs to Dr. Watkins? An Edward Lee McNeil who manages to hang on to his sanity and fight his way to freedom against incredible odds, or the Patuxent inmate who is eventually pulverized into compliance by the 10 psychiatrists, the 11 psychologists, the 17 social workers, and the rest?

For the prison administrator, whether he be warden, sociol-

ogist, or psychiatrist, "individualized treatment" is primarily
a device for breaking the convict's will to resist and hounding
him into compliance with institution demands, and is thus a
means of exerting maximum control over the convict population. The cure will be deemed effective to the degree that the
poor/young/brown/black captive appears to have capitulated
to his middle-class/white/middle-aged captor, and to have
adopted the virtues of subservience to authority, industry,
cleanliness, docility. Subtle methods are, of course, preferable
if and when they work. If and when they do not, there are
cruder ones in the closet: the club, such products of an advanced chemistry as tear gas and Mace, and, in the last
analysis, the gun.

This is the patent age of new inventions
For killing bodies, and for saving souls,
All propagated with the best intentions.
—LORD BYRON

8

CLOCKWORK ORANGE

Recognition of failure dawns slowly in a bureaucracy, but dawned it has in California prison treatment circles. Prison psychiatrists who are willing to level with reporters admit that they now spend 90 percent of their time on paperwork, writing up reports for the Adult Authority based on perfunctory annual interviews with prisoners, that "treatment" most often takes the form of heavy tranquilization of inmates labeled troublemakers as well as those diagnosed as psychotic. Group therapy, once hailed as an exciting new technique for transforming the "deviant personality," is withering on the

vine. Nor have the treatment programs produced the anticipated docility in the convict population; on the contrary, work
strikes, hunger strikes, and other forms of protest are now
endemic throughout the California prisons.

Some disconcerting conclusions about the efficacy of treatment are set forth in a report to the State Assembly titled "The
California Prison, Parole, and Probation System." It cites an
exhaustive study conducted for the Department of Corrections
in which the researchers observed gloomily, "Thousands of
inmates and hundreds of staff members were participating in
this program at a substantial cost to the Department of Corrections in time, effort, and money. Contrary to the expectations of the treatment theory, there were no significant differences in outcome for those in the various treatment programs or
between the treatment groups and the control group." They
further reported that participation in group counseling did not
lessen adherence to the inmate code, nor did it result in a
decrease in frequency of prison discipline problems.

James O. Robison, author of the report and long-time researcher for the Department of Corrections, traced the course
of disillusionment. "The high mystique of treatment peaked at
the end of the fifties," he told me. "The idea took hold in Corrections that at last, through sophisticated techniques of psychotherapy, we have it in our power to transform the deviant and
to predict with accuracy his future behavior. But in the early
sixties the high priests of Corrections began a sifting of the
entrails. After that, disenchantment and embarrassment set
in—the reason was the quite evident empirical failure of the
treatment programs, as demonstrated by the fact that the
recidivism rate remained constant over the years.

"The rationale for failure was always 'We haven't carried
treatment far enough, there isn't enough of it, it isn't professional enough'—in other words, we need more and better of
same, in spite of the fact we've seen it doesn't work. Even this
reasoning began to break down in the middle sixties, when there

was more attention paid to the fact nothing was happening and more talk of *'Why?'*

"What you are likely to see now is the end of the liberal treatment era—the notion that you can make convicts into converts of the dominant culture 'religion,' the missionary fervor—that's being replaced with 'behavior modification' experiments. The latest reasoning is that it's costly and inappropriate to go the psychotherapy route with these people, to pay high-priced psychiatrists to *talk* them into recognizing the truth of our 'religion'; instead, we'll focus on their deviant behavior and force them to shape up. Of course, this flies in the face of the earlier rhetoric. The Behaviorists say they *are* bad, *not* mad, and we can stop them being bad by utilizing new techniques. This fits in with the law-and-order, no-nonsense conservative viewpoint: henceforth the slogan will be 'they must be *made* to behave.' "

This new trend in Corrections must be highly inspiriting for the behavioral scientists, who have long been eyeing the prisons as convenient reservoirs of human material on which to try out new theories. The shape of things to come was forecast a decade ago at a seminar of prison wardens and psychologists chaired by James V. Bennett, then director of the U.S. Bureau of Prisons. As described in *Corrective Psychiatry & Journal of Social Change,* the seminar provided "provocative fruitful interaction between social scientists and correctional administrators."

Addressing himself to the topic "Man Against Man: Brainwashing," Dr. Edgar H. Schein, associate professor of psychology at MIT, told the assembled wardens: "My basic argument is this: in order to produce marked change of behavior and/or attitude, it is necessary to weaken, undermine, or remove the supports to the old patterns of behavior and the old attitudes," to be accomplished "either by removing the individual physically and preventing any communication with those whom he cares about, or by proving to him that those whom he respects are not worthy of it and, indeed, should be actively mistrusted." Dr. Schein, who said he got most of his ideas from studying brainwashing techniques used by North Korean and Chinese Communists on GI prisoners of war, cautioned his audience not to be put off by this fact: "These same techniques in the service of different goals may be quite acceptable to us . . . I would like to have you think of brainwashing not in terms of politics, ethics, and morals, but in terms of the deliberate changing of human behavior and attitudes by a group of men who have relatively complete control over the environment in which the captive population lives."

Some of the techniques which could usefully be applied in the U.S. prisons: "social disorganization and the creation of mutual mistrust" achieved by "spying on the men and reporting back private material"; "tricking men into written statements" that are then shown to others, the objective being "to convince most men they could trust no one," "undermining ties to home by the systematic withholding of mail." The key factor is change of attitude: "Supports for old attitudes have to be undermined and destroyed if change is to take place . . . Do we not feel it to be legitimate to destroy the emotional ties of one criminal to another, or of a criminal to a sick community?" How to bring about the desired change was explained by Dr. Schein: "If one wants to produce behavior inconsistent with the person's standards of conduct, first disorganize the group which supports those standards, then undermine his other emotional supports, then put him into a new and ambiguous situation for which the standards are unclear, and then put pressure on him. I leave it to you to judge whether there is any similarity between these events and those which occur in prisons when we teach prisoners 'to serve their own time' by moving them around and punishing clandestine group activity not sanctioned by the prison authorities."

The discussion, says the report, ranged from "specific, practical management issues such as 'How shall we manage the

Muslims?', 'Whom should we isolate?'" to more basic questions such as "the use and effectiveness of brainwashing and other means of persuasion." Mr. Bennett recalled that "during the war we struggled with the conscientious objectors—nonviolent coercionists—and believe me, that was really a problem . . . we were always trying to find some way in which we could change or manipulate their environment."

Much attention was focused on what to do about the Black Muslims: "not so much whether you take action against the Muslims as a group," as one speaker put it, "but how can you counteract the effects of the kinds of techniques they use to recruit members and cause general mischief in the prison system?" To which a Dr. Lowry responded, "We found that many of these Negro Muslims were highly intelligent . . . here again, we have to apply the techniques which we heard about in terms of appreciating what the goal of the Muslims is, or of any other group, and then doing some analytic study of the methods that they are using so that we can try to dissipate the forces that are going in the direction that we regard as destructive." On ways of dealing with the unruly, a panelist offered this: "To some extent where we formerly had isolation as a controlling technique, we now have drugs, so that drugs in a sense become a new kind of restraint. The restraint, therefore, is biochemical, but it is restraint nevertheless."

Summarizing the discussion, Mr. Bennett pointed out that the federal prison system, with some 24,000 men in it, presents "a tremendous opportunity to carry on some of the experimenting to which the various panelists have alluded." He added, "What I am hoping is that the audience here will believe that we here in Washington are anxious to have you undertake some of these things: do things perhaps on your own—undertake a little experiment of what you can do with the Muslims, what you can do with some of the sociopath individuals."

That Mr. Bennett's counsel was taken to heart by his subordinates in the federal prison system can be inferred from a report addressed to the United Nations Economic and Social Council, prepared and smuggled out of Marion Federal Penitentiary in July 1972, by the Federal Prisoners' Coalition, a group of convicts housed in the segregation unit for refusing to participate in the behavioral research programs. "In the latter part of 1968 some changes in the U.S. Department of Justice enabled the U.S. Bureau of Prisons to make a quiet beginning at implementing an experimental program at Marion Federal Prison to determine at first hand how effective a weapon brainwashing might be for the U.S. Department of Justice's future use," says the report. It describes how Dr. Martin Groder, prison psychiatrist, applies the proposals outlined in Dr. Schein's paper to "agitators," suspected militants, writ-writers, and other troublemakers. The first step, according to the report, is to sever the inmate's ties with his family by transferring him to some remote prison where they will be unable to visit him. There he is put in isolation, deprived of mail and other privileges, until he agrees to participate in Dr. Groder's Transactional Analysis program. If he succumbs, he will be moved to new living quarters where he will be surrounded by members of Dr. Groder's "prisoner thought-reform team," and subjected to intense group pressure. "His emotional, behavioral, and psychic characteristics are studied by the staff and prisoner paraprofessionals to detect vulnerable points of entry to stage attack-sessions around. During these sessions, on a progressively intensified basis, he is shouted at, his fears played on, his sensitivities ridiculed, and concentrated efforts made to make him feel guilty for real or imagined characteristics or conduct. . . . Every effort is made to heighten his suggestibility and weaken his character structure so that his emotional responses and thought-flow will be brought under group and staff control as totally as possible.

". . . It is also driven in to him that society, in the guise of its authorities, is looking out for his best interests and will help if he will only permit it to do so. Help him be 'reborn'

as a highly probable 'winner in the game of life,' is the way
this comes across in the group's jargon." Once reborn as a
winner, he will be moved into a plush living area equipped
with stereo, tape recorders, typewriters, books. He is now ready
to indoctrinate newcomers into the mysteries of the group "and
like a good attack dog, he is graded and evaluated on his
demonstrated capacity to go for the vulnerable points of any
victim put before him." The entire program is made self-per-
petuating and economically feasible by the participants doing
the work themselves, says the report: "They are taught to police
not only themselves but others, to inform on one another in
acceptable fashion—as bringing out misconduct of another in
a truth-session is not considered informing even if a staff member is present."

Evidently these techniques are finding increasing favor with
the federal prison administration. Scheduled to open early in
1974 near Butner, N.C., is a new federal institution, the Behavioral Research Center, built at a cost of $13.5 million,
which, says a handout from the Bureau of Prisons, will be "a
unique facility in the federal correctional system." Some of the
unique features are spelled out in a confidential operations
memorandum from the bureau to staff, dated October 25,
1972, on the subject of Project START, acronym for Special
Treatment and Rehabilitative Training, already in operation
in Springfield federal penitentiary. The goal, according to the
memorandum, is "to develop behavioral attitudinal changes in
offenders who have not adjusted satisfactorily to institutional
settings" and to provide "care, custody, and correction of the
long-term adult offender in a setting separated from his home
institution." "Selection criteria" include: "Will have shown
repeated inability to adjust to regular institutional programs,"
"will be transferred from the sending institution's segregation
unit," "generally, will have a minimum of two years remaining
on his sentence," "in terms of personality characteristics shall
be aggressive, manipulative, resistive to authority, etc."

Dr. Martin Groder, who will direct the Butner operation, told Tom Wicker of *The New York Times* that he "believes in the possibility of rehabilitating prisoners" because he has done it, at Marion. He does not favor any large-scale return of incarcerated men to community programs, on the contrary he prefers to keep them in his custody: "If we can get a top-notch rehabilitation program within the institution, a prisoner will be better off in it than wandering around the streets." Wicker reports that Dr. Groder is "not precise" about the rehabilitative methods he intends to apply, and that he is "cheerfully aware that the new federal center he will head is suspect in some circles—not least among federal prisoners, who are not anxious to be 'guinea pigs' in behavior research. He is nevertheless pressing ahead . . ."

A further elaboration on the brainwashing theme is furnished by James V. McConnell, professor of psychology at the University of Michigan, in an article in *Psychology Today* titled "Criminals Can Be Brainwashed—Now." It reads like science fiction, the fantasy of a deranged scientist. Yet much of what Dr. McConnell proposes as appropriate therapy for tomorrow's lawbreaker is either already here or in the planning stages in many of the more go-ahead, highly financed prison systems.

Dr. McConnell, who spent many years successfully training flatworms to go in and out of mazes at his bidding by administering a series of painful electric shocks, now proposes to apply similar techniques to convicts: "I believe the day has come when we can combine sensory deprivation with drugs, hypnosis, and astute manipulation of reward and punishment to gain almost absolute control over an individual's behavior . . . We'd assume that a felony was clear evidence that the criminal had somehow acquired full-blown social neurosis and needed to be cured, not punished . . . We'd probably have to restructure his entire personality."

The exciting potential of sensory deprivation as a behavior

modifier was revealed through an experiment in which students were paid $20 a day to live in tiny, solitary cubicles with nothing to do. The experiment was supposed to last at least six weeks, but none of the students could take it for more than a few days: "Many experienced vivid hallucinations—one student in particular insisted that a tiny spaceship had got into the chamber and was buzzing around shooting pellets at him." While they were in this condition, the experimenter fed the students propaganda messages: "No matter how poorly it was presented or how illogical it sounded, the propaganda had a marked effect on the students' attitudes—an effect that lasted for at least a year after they came out of the deprivation chambers."

Noting that "the legal and moral issues raised by such procedures are frighteningly complex," Dr. McConnell nevertheless disposes of them handily: "I don't believe the Constitution of the United States gives you the *right* to commit a crime if you want to; therefore, the Constitution does not guarantee you the right to maintain inviolable the personality forced on you in the first place—if and when the personality manifests strongly antisocial behavior."

The new behavioral control techniques, says Dr. McConnell, "make even the hydrogen bomb look like a child's toy, and, of course, they can be used for good or evil." But it will avail us nothing to "hide our collective heads in the sand and pretend that it can't happen here. Today's behavioral psychologists are the architects and engineers of the Brave New World."

For some convicts in California, those perceived as "dangerous," "revolutionary," or "uncooperative" by the authorities, it *has* happened here, and Dr. McConnell's Brave New World is their reality. Signposts in this bizarre terrain may need translation for the auslander:

Sensory Deprivation: Confinement (often for months or years) in the Adjustment Center, a prison-within-prison.

Stress Assessment: The prisoner lives in an open dormitory where it is expected he will suffer maximum irritation from the lack of privacy. He is assigned to the worst and most menial jobs. In compulsory group therapy sessions staff members deliberately bait the men and try to provoke conflicts among them. The idea is to see how much of this a person can stand without losing his temper.

Chemotherapy: The use of drugs (some still in the experimental stage) as "behavior modifiers," including antitestosterone hormones, which have the effect of chemically castrating the subject, and Prolixin, a form of tranquilizer with extremely unpleasant and often dangerous side effects.

Aversion Therapy: The use of medical procedures that cause pain and fear to bring about the desired "behavior modification."

Neurosurgery: Cutting or burning out those portions of the brain believed to cause "aggressive behavior."

The "behavior modification" programs are for the most part carried out in secret; they are not part of the guided tour for journalists and visitors, nor are outside physicians permitted to witness them. Occasionally word of these procedures leaks out, as in the autumn of 1970 when *Medical World News* ran an article titled "Scaring the Devil Out" about the use of the drug Anectine as "aversion therapy" in the California prisons.

Anectine, a derivative of the South American arrow-tip poison curare, is used medically in small doses as a muscle relaxant, but behavioral researchers discovered that when administered to unruly prisoners in massive amounts—from 20 to 40 milligrams—it causes them to lose all control of voluntary muscles, including those used for breathing.

An unpublished account of the Anectine therapy program at Vacaville, California, by two staff researchers, Arthur L. Mattocks, supervisor of the research unit, and Charles Jew, social research analyst, states that "the conceptual scheme was to develop a strong association between any violent or acting-out behavior and the drug Anectine and its frightful consequences," among which were "cessation of respiration for a period of approximately two minutes' duration." Of those selected to endure these consequences, "nearly all could be characterized as angry young men," say the authors. Some seem to have been made a good deal angrier by the experience, for the report notes that of 64 prisoners in the program "nine persons not only did not decrease but actually exhibited an increase in their overall number of disciplinary infractions."

According to Dr. Arthur Nugent, chief psychiatrist at Vacaville and an enthusiast for the drug, it induces "sensations of suffocation and drowning." The subject experiences feelings of deep horror and terror, "as though he were on the brink of death." While he is in this condition a therapist scolds him for his misdeeds and tells him to shape up or expect more of the same. Candidates for Anectine treatment were selected for a range of offenses: "frequent fights, verbal threatening, deviant sexual behavior, stealing, unresponsiveness to the group therapy programs." Dr. Nugent told the San Francisco *Chronicle,* "Even the toughest inmates have come to fear and hate the drug. I don't blame them, I wouldn't have one treatment myself for the world." Declaring he was anxious to continue the experiment, he added, "I'm at a loss as to why everybody's upset over this."

More upset came a year later, when the press got wind of a letter from Director Raymond Procunier to the California Council on Criminal Justice requesting funding estimated at $48,000 for "neurosurgical treatment of violent inmates." The letter read, in part: "The problem of treating the aggressive, destructive inmate has long been a problem in all correctional systems. During recent years this problem has become particularly acute in the California Department of Corrections institutions . . . This letter of intent is to alert you to the development of a proposal to seek funding for a program involving a complex neurosurgical evaluation and treatment program for the violent inmate . . . surgical and diagnostic procedures would be performed to locate centers in the brain which may have been previously damaged and which could serve as the focus for episodes of violent behavior. If these areas were located and verified that they were indeed the source of aggressive behavior, neurosurgery would be performed . . ." Confronted by reporters with this letter, Dr. Laurence Bennett, head of the Department of Corrections Research Division, explained: "It is not a proposal, it's just an idea-concept." He added wistfully, "It's quite likely that we will not proceed with this, but if we had unlimited funds we would explore every opportunity to help anyone who wants such assistance."

Although the plan for psychosurgery was halted—at least temporarily—by the newspaper uproar that ensued, the authorities have other methods at hand for controlling the unruly, principal among which is forced drugging of prisoners. In widespread use throughout the nation's prisons is the drug Prolixin, a powerful tranquilizer derived from phenothiazine, which, if given in large doses, produces dangerous and often irreversible side effects. A petition addressed to the California Senate Committee on Penal Institutions by La Raza Unida, a group of Chicano prisoners confined in the California Men's Colony, describes these: "The simple fact that a number of prisoners are walking the yard in this institution like somnambulists, robots, and vegetables as a result of this drug should be reason enough to make people apprehensive as to the effect it is having. That no prisoner feels safe because he never knows when he will become a candidate for said drug is another factor in producing tension in this institution."

According to its manufacturer, E. R. Squibb, Prolixin is "a highly potent behavior modifier with a markedly extended duration of effect." Possible adverse side effects listed by Squibb include: the induction of a "catatonic-like state," nausea, loss of appetite, headache, constipation, blurred vision, glaucoma, bladder paralysis, impotency, liver damage, hypotension severe enough to cause fatal cardiac arrest, and cerebral edema. Furthermore, Squibb cautions that "a persistent pseudoparkinsonian [palsy-like] syndrome may develop . . . characterized by rhythmic, stereotyped dyskinetic involuntary movements . . . resembling the facial grimaces of encephalitis . . . The symptoms persist after drug withdrawal, and in some patients appear to be irreversible."

Dr. Philip Shapiro, a San Francisco psychiatrist who has on occasion managed to intrude his presence behind bars to treat prisoner-patients, described the effects of Prolixin on prisoners to a group of San Francisco health workers: "In general, it causes deep depression that may last for weeks." Although the drug is specifically recommended for treatment of schizophrenics, he said, it is dispensed in the prisons to persons who have never been so diagnosed.

The theme of prison as a happy hunting ground for the researcher is very big in current penological literature. In *I Chose Prison,* James V. Bennett poses the question, What will the prisons of 2000 A.D. be like? And answers it: "In my judgment the prison system will increasingly be valued, and used, as a laboratory and workshop of social change." Dr. Karl Menninger echoes this thought in *The Crime of Punishment:* "About all this [causes of crime], we need more information, more research, more experimental data. That research is the basis for scientific progress, no one any more disputes . . . Even our present prisons, bad as many of them are, could be extensively used as laboratories for the study of many of the unsolved problems."

Taking these injunctions to heart, researchers are descending in droves upon the prisons with their prediction tables, expectancy scales, data analysis charts. With all the new money available under federal crime control programs, and the in-

genuity of grant-happy researchers, the scope of the investigations seems limitless. In California some $600,000 of the De-
partment of Corrections budget is earmarked for research, but
this is just the tip of the iceberg, for most of the work is done
under lavish grants from foundations and government agencies
channeled through universities.

Something of the quality of the research, and the bitter irony
of the situation in which the convict-research subject finds
himself, can be learned from the stream of monographs, research reviews, and reports that flow out of the prisons. His
captors having arranged life for the prisoner so that he becomes enraged, perhaps goes mad, and (no matter what his
original sexual preferences) engages in homosexual activity,
they invite researchers to put him under their microscopes and
study the result. A forty-eight-page monograph titled "Homosexuality in Prisons" published in February 1972 by the Law
Enforcement Assistance Administration reports, "in view of
methodological difficulties, the following estimates of male
homosexuality should be viewed with caution," and proceeds
to give them, complete with footnotes referring the luckless
reader to yet other publications on this subject. Estimates of
the incidence of homosexuality given by experts vary, says the
author, from 7 to 90 percent. He concludes, "There is above
all a compelling need for a wide variety of comparative data,"
and proposes to fill the need by conducting "longitudinal or
retrospective studies."

Among the offerings of the California Department of Corrections Research Review for 1971 is "The Self-Esteem Project,"
its aim "to obtain some picture of the effect of incarceration
upon the perception of self-worth," in which the Modified
Coopersmith Self-Esteem Scale is found to be "a useful instrument for measurement." Having subjected the inmate's self-
esteem to the pulverizer of prison, the department proceeds to
measure and tabulate what is left. If the prisoner happens to

be Chicano, he will be eligible for a study entitled "The Consequences of Familial Separation for Chicano Families," its purpose "to study the consequences of separation from family members for Chicano inmates and also for their families in terms of social, psychological, and economic needs and stresses." Thus the precise quantity and quality of suffering, anxiety, impoverishment of families caused by locking up Chicanos can be tidily computed and catalogued for the edification of social scientists. By now the prisoner may well be ready for the Buss Rating Scale of Hostility or the Multiple Affect Adjective Checklist, "a standardized and reliable rating instrument that can be scored for anxiety, depression, and most importantly hostility."

Omitted from the 1971 Research Review is one of the more ambitious experimental projects of that year: establishment of a Maximum Psychiatric Diagnostic Unit (MPDU) designed to hold 84 convicts (a number possibly chosen in subconscious tribute to George Orwell) selected as research subjects from among the 700 inmates of the state's Adjustment Centers. The goal of MPDU, as defined in the department's grant application to the California Council on Criminal Justice, is "to provide highly specialized diagnostic service for Adjustment Center inmates who are violently acting-out and management problem cases within the California prison system . . . and arriving at decisions as to the needed intervention and placement." The budget for this "service" would be approximately $500,000.

Who are the Adjustment Center inmates from whose ranks the 84 would be chosen? What are the conditions of their life? Robert E. Doran, who made a study of California Adjustment Centers under a grant from LEAA for the American Justice Institute, says the inmates are "deviants within a society of deviants," or put another way, rebels who refuse to conform to prison life. They are younger and darker than the prison population as a whole: 61 percent are under 30 compared with 39 percent for the total prison population, 60 to 70 percent are black or Chicano compared with a nonwhite overall prison population of 45 percent. The majority are there for "disrespect for authority," disobeying some disciplinary rule—refusing to work, shave, attend group therapy; a growing number are there because they are suspected of harboring subversive beliefs.

In 1972, 10 inmates of Folsom Prison filed a federal suit (unsuccessful), charging they had been kept in long-term solitary confinement because of their political views, and alleging that the practice is routinely used against prisoners who are outspoken about prison conditions or voice "militant" political views. Department spokesmen strenuously deny that they use lock-up in the Adjustment Center as punishment for political dissidents and leaders of ethnic groups. Mr. Philip Guthrie, press agent for the Department, told the Sacramento *Bee* on March 10, 1972: "We're very careful not to lock a guy up just because of his political views." But in their closed departmental meetings it is a different story. As reported in the confidential minutes of the wardens and superintendents meeting, October 11–12, 1972, under the topic "Inmate Alliances," Director Raymond Procunier "asked the problem be kept in perspective, comparing it to the Muslim situation ten years ago. The director suggested the leaders of the various groups be removed from the general population of the institutions and locked up."

Much has been written about the California Adjustment Centers, for it was in the exercise yard of "O-Wing," Soledad Adjustment Center, that three unarmed black convicts were shot to death by a guard in early 1970, triggering a series of events that culminated in the death of George Jackson, the trial of the surviving Soledad Brothers, and the trial of Angela Davis. From three sources—the Department of Corrections, academic investigation, and congressional testimony—one can learn something about the roots of violence in the Adjustment Centers.

Departmental memoranda to staff in charge of "O-Wing" contain these directives:

Yard Exercise: Two officers (one armed with a Gas Billy and one armed with Mace) will enter the tier to be released and, after subjecting each inmate to an unclothed body search, release him from his cell, by key, directing him to the yard.

All inmates housed in "O-Wing" first tier, when escorted from the security section for any reason, are to be given an unclothed body search while still in their cells . . . The inmate will be given a visual inspection of his body, to include his hair, ears, mouth, private parts and feet . . . The inmate will be handcuffed behind his back and escorted from the section . . .

"O-Wing" Equipment: 1. Gas Billy (blast type). 2. Gas Billy Reload. 3. Triple Chaser Grenade. 4. Aerosol Mace (Mark IV Atomizer) . . .

Any inmate who self-mutilates or attempts to hang himself will be housed in the Hospital Annex cells only on the direction of the medical staff.

Robert E. Doran describes what he learned about the guards' view of assignments to the Adjustment Center. "Those staff who have 'really been there,' experienced the trouble, used the gas, the batons, the weapons, and the muscle, and did so effectively, receive the highest status and deference from other custodial staff. . . . Staff battle ribbons and badges are won or lost within the A/C when trouble takes place. Actually the A/C, much like the general prison situation, has in terms of relative percentage of time, very little trouble. But it is the folklore, the beliefs and the history as passed from one generation of custodial personnel to the next that promulgates the idea that has grown up around the A/C which in effect says, 'This is the front line: here is where the battle is really won or lost for staff who wear the custodial uniform.' "

Testifying in San Francisco before a congressional sub-committee, two lawyers related some exploits of these front-line heroes. Edwin T. Caldwell of San Francisco said, "I will testify for the record that I am a registered Republican from a conservative background. This is such a shocking thing for me I just can't believe it exists." He told the committee his client in Soledad's "O-Wing" had been "viciously attacked" by guards on numerous occasions, and had suffered lacerations requiring six sutures, a fractured tooth, a broken jaw. Fay Stender of Oakland handed the committee chairman a note signed by Lieutenant Flores, Adjustment Center guard, written in response to an inmate who was coughing blood and had asked for help. The note said: "Yell for help when the blood is an inch thick, all over the floor, and don't call before that."

Details of the highly specialized services to be rendered the 84 chosen from this milieu, and the nature of the needed intervention, were discussed at a "think session" called in November 1971, by Mr. Laurence Bennett, head of the Department of Corrections Research Division, to which I was invited by a psychologist who had been told he could bring a "colleague." Participants were some 25 representatives of the healing professions—medicine, psychology, psychiatry—many of them faculty members from nearby universities and medical schools. "They struck me as such agreeable, civilized people," said my psychologist friend ruefully, "until the discussion got under way."

The new unit, said Mr. Max May, program administrator, would be closely modeled after Patuxent Institution in Maryland, with four 21-man cellblocks, "single five-by-seven-foot cells with bars, only we call them barriers." Construction costs would be kept to a minimum since the prisoners were to build their own cages, the work, according to the grant application, consisting "primarily of pouring two concrete floors, erecting wire screen partitions, also a gun tower."

The objective, said Mr. Bennett, is "to develop a basic

knowledge of the causes of aggressive, violent behavior. Our aim is to learn how to identify small groups, how to deal with them more adequately. We hope through psychological management to learn how to lessen their violence potential."

Discussion from the floor, and at the pleasant luncheon gathering in the faculty club dining room, centered on methods by which this might be accomplished: "We need to find the stimulus to which the subject responds. We also need to find out how he thinks *covertly* and to change how he thinks." "We need to dope up many of these men in order to calm them down to the point that they are accessible to treatment." "Those who can't be controlled by drugs are candidates for the implantation of subcortical electrodes" [meaning electrodes plunged deep into the brain].

Dr. Keith Brody of Stanford University, who said he runs a "unit for mood disorders," stressed the importance of "intensive data collection" via spinal taps and other tests: "These tests can lead to therapy decisions. We need to segregate out and dissect out these sub-groups." Other proposals for therapy were to burn out electrically those areas of the brain believed to be the "source of aggressive behavior"—one speaker said he reckoned about 10 percent of the inmates might be candidates for this treatment; the administration of antitestosterone hormones, which have the effect of chemically castrating the subject; the use of pneumoencephalograms (injecting air into the brain cavities, an excruciatingly painful procedure).

Asked whether the Anectine torture "therapy" would be resumed in the new unit, Mr. Bennett did not answer directly but declared with some exasperation, "If it could be shown empirically that hitting an inmate on the head with a hammer would cure him, I'd do it. You talk about his civil rights— civil rights for what? To continue to disrupt society?" Nor would he answer the further questions: "Does not the prison system itself, and particularly the Adjustment Center, generate violence?" and "Would the researchers be directing any part of their inquiry to violence by guards against prisoners?"

As for the compliant participation of the distinguished group of faculty members in this bizarre discussion, one possible explanation was suggested by the lone black psychiatrist present, Dr. Wendell Lipscomb, who had stormed out of the meeting halfway through, declaring he "couldn't take any more of this crap." Later, he told me, "What you were seeing at that meeting were the grant-hunters, hungry for money, willing to eat any shit that's put before them."

9

CHEAPER
THAN CHIMPANZEES

In 1947, 15 German doctors, distinguished medical men at the very top of their profession, were convicted by the Nuremberg war crimes tribunal of criminal responsibility for cruel and frequently murderous "medical experiments" performed on concentration camp inmates.

In their defense the accused doctors cited comparable experiments carried out on prisoners by American physicians: in 1906, a group of Philippine convicts were given "an abundance of cigarettes and also cigars if they desired them" for submitting to infection with plague and induction of beriberi. One died; others suffered paralysis, mental disturbances, and heart damage. In 1915, pellagra was induced in 12 Mississippi convicts, all of whom became seriously ill. They were rewarded by the promise of early parole. In 1944, several hundred Illinois and New Jersey prisoners were infected with malaria so that new cures could be tried out on them. They were paid in dollars. Some became extremely ill with malaria, others suffered horribly from the toxic effects of the experimental "cures."

Of the doctors tried in Nuremberg, seven were sentenced to death by hanging, others to long prison terms. Whatever deterrent effect these stiff sentences might have had elsewhere in the world, they surely have had none in the United States. The Nuremberg tribunal established standards for medical experimentation on humans which, if observed, would end the practice of using prisoners as subjects. Yet in the twenty-six years since the Nuremberg judgment there has been a huge expansion of medical "research programs" in many prisons in the U.S., sanctioned by federal health agencies and state prison administrations who do not choose to recognize these standards as applying to the captives in their custody.

Efforts by international medical societies to prohibit the use of prisoners as subjects have been effectively frustrated by American medical experimenters. The World Medical Association in 1961 proposed that prisoners, "being captive groups, should not be used as the subject of experiments." The recommendation was never formally adopted, largely because of the opposition of American doctors.

"Pertinax," writing in the *British Medical Journal* for January 1963, says: "I am disturbed that the World Medical Association is now hedging on its clause about using criminals as experimental material. The American influence has been at work on its suspension." He adds wistfully, "One of the nicest American scientists I know was heard to say, 'Criminals in our penitentiaries are fine experimental material—and much cheaper than chimpanzees.' I hope the chimpanzees don't come to hear of this."

Behind the nice American scientists lurk a handful of pharmaceutical concerns with huge financial stakes in experimental testing on human subjects. FDA regulations require that all new drugs be tested on humans before being marketed. The testing, after the drug has cleared animal tests, is done in three stages: in Phase I, the new compound is tried out for effectiveness and possible toxic properties on a small group of normal, healthy individuals. If these survive without serious side effects and the drug appears promising, it is passed into Phase II, in which several hundred normal subjects are given the compound and the dosage is gradually increased until the experimenter decides the limit of safety has been reached. Once this is established, the drug is ready for Phase III, in which it is given as medication to patients to test its efficacy as a remedy for illness.

Dr. Robert Batterman, internist and specialist in pharmacology, told me, "Phase I is very big in prisons. FDA prefers Phase I to be on an in-patient basis—the only place available for large-scale toxicity studies is prison. But the vast majority of new drugs—more than 90 percent—never get into medical practice. They prove too toxic and fall by the wayside in Phase II."

There are formidable barriers to inquiries about medical experimentation on human subjects in prison. Yet horror stories crop up in the press with sufficient regularity to give some indication of the scope and nature of the experiments.

In 1963, *Time* magazine reported that the federal government was using prisoner "volunteers" for large-scale research, dispensing rewards ranging from a package of cigarettes to $25 cash plus reduction of sentence; that prisoners in Ohio and Illinois were injected with live cancer cells and blood from leukemia patients to determine whether these diseases could be transmitted; that doctors in Oklahoma were grossing an estimated $300,000 a year from deals with pharmaceutical companies to test out new drugs on prisoners; that the same doctors were paying prisoners $5 a quart for blood which they retailed at $15.

In July 1969, Walter Rugaber of *The New York Times* charged that "the federal government has watched without interference while many people sickened and some died in an extended series of drug tests and blood plasma operations . . . the immediate damage has been done in the penitentiary systems of three states. Hundreds of inmates in voluntary programs have been stricken with serious disease. An undetermined number of the victims have died."

The anti-heroes of Rugaber's story are a physician named Dr. Austin R. Stough, some of the largest pharmaceutical corporations in the country, the Food and Drug Administration, and the Department of Health, Education, and Welfare. Dr. Stough's two-pronged operation consisted of selling blood plasma extracted from prisoners in Alabama, Arkansas, and Oklahoma and subjecting prisoners in these states to experimental drug tests. From 1963 to 1969 he carried out some 130 investigative studies in the prisons of Alabama, Arkansas, and Oklahoma for 37 drug companies, including such giants as Wyeth, Lederle, Bristol-Myers, Squibb, Merck, Sharp & Dohme, Upjohn—concerns that are among the 300 largest corporations in the country. His earnings from these activities were impressive; in a good year he would gross close to $1 million.

HEW, FDA, and the sponsoring drug companies were long aware of the "extremely dangerous" methods employed by Dr. Stough in his drug experiments and plasma collections, writes Rugaber. An executive of Cutter Laboratories who visited the site of the Alabama plasma operation in 1964 pronounced it "appalling," with evidence of "gross contamination"; nevertheless, Cutter remained one of Dr. Stough's biggest customers. Asked why they did not arrange to collect the plasma themselves without using Dr. Stough as middleman, the Cutter spokesman replied that Dr. Stough had contacts at the prison and it was through him that permission to operate the program was obtained from prison officials.

When rampaging epidemics of infectious hepatitis broke out in all the prisons under his ministrations—and instances came to light of prisoners who "died slowly in very painful fashion"—Dr. Stough was barred by the Alabama authorities from further collecting plasma. He was, however, allowed to continue his drug experiments without interruptions until these came under attack from the Montgomery, Alabama, *Advertiser*, which ran a series of exposé stories about the drug studies. The Alabama Medical Association instituted an inquiry and concluded that Dr. Stough's work was "bluntly unacceptable." Throughout all this, the drug companies stood by their man: a spokesman for Lederle pointed out that Dr. Stough's testing operations in the Oklahoma State Penitentiary "had not been criticized publicly by qualified medical observers," and Merck, Sharp & Dohme declared that Dr. Stough's staff, equipment, and procedures were "particularly suited" to the studies they required.

Had the epidemics and deaths occurred in, say, a school, a hospital, an Army base, there would no doubt have been a public hue and cry followed by government intervention and grand jury investigations. But official guardians of the public health at all levels took the position that their writ does not run behind prison walls. Thus Dr. Herbert L. Ley, then commissioner of the Food and Drug Administration: "Our responsibility is not the direct supervision of the drug investigators, it's to evaluate the data that comes in to us. We can't be omnipotent or omniscient." Dr. Roderick Murray, then director of HEW's Division of Biologics Standards: "The conclusion we came to was that the quality of the product was not affected, and therefore we had no backing to tell the drug companies not to use plasma that came from Stough." The division, he said, has "no statutory authority" to promulgate regulations for the protection of prisoner blood donors. A spokesman for the communicable disease center which traced the hepatitis epidemic directly to Dr. Stough's operation: "The center is only a consultant to the states, enforcement is up to the state authorities." And at the end of the line, Dr. Myers, Alabama public health officer: "The State Health Department has no specific jurisdiction in the prisons."

Dr. Stough seems to have taken his money and run; according to Rugaber, he dropped out of sight after the Alabama investigation and has not been heard of since. But the rate of medical experimentation on prisoners continues to rise.

There is something for everybody in the prison research studies. The drug companies, operating through private physicians with access to the prisons, can buy human subjects for a fraction—less than one tenth, according to many medical authorities—of what they would have to pay medical students or other "free-world" volunteers. They can conduct experiments on prisoners that would not be sanctioned for student-subjects at any price because of the degree of risk and pain involved. Guidelines for human experimentation established by HEW and other agencies are easily disregarded behind prison walls.

Since the studies are carried out in the privacy of prison, if a "volunteer" becomes seriously ill, or dies, as a result of the procedures to which he is subjected, it is unlikely this will ever come to anybody's attention. As Rugaber discovered, when trying to trace the number of deaths caused by Dr. Stough's operation, prison medical records that might prove embarrassing to the authorities have a habit of conveniently disappearing. There is minimal risk that subjects disabled by the experiments will bring lawsuits against the drug companies, for the prisoner is usually required as a condition of his participation to sign a waiver releasing everyone in sight from damage claims that may result. Such waivers are fraudulent, worthless, and illegal. They have been held legally invalid as contrary to public policy, and are prohibited by FDA regulations having the force of law, but the prisoner is hardly likely to be aware of such fine points. The psychological effect of signing the waiver, coupled with the general helplessness of prisoners, makes lawsuits a rarity.

For the prisoner, the pittance he gets from the drug company—generally around $1 a day for the more onerous experiments—represents riches when viewed in terms of prison pay scales: $30 a month compared with the $2 to $10 a month he might make if fortunate enough to have been granted a "pay slot" in an ordinary prison job.

Dr. Robert Batterman told me, "The prisoner-subject gets virtually nil." He cited an estimate given him for experimenting on prisoners in Vacaville, California: $15 a month for three months to be *lowered* to $12.50 a month should the experiment run for six months. "We would normally do it the other way around with 'free-world' volunteers. We'd give them more money if the experiment ran longer, because of the added risk involved." Dr. Batterman makes considerable use of student-subjects from a nearby Baptist divinity school. For a comparatively undemanding experiment—one requiring a weekly draw of blood—he would pay a student upward of $100 a month, he said.

The prisoner's view of the largesse dispensed by the drug companies is reflected in a series of interviews conducted in 1969 at Vacaville prison, California, by Martin Miller, a graduate student at the University of California Department of Criminology. Some of the prisoners' comments: "Yeah, I was on research, but I couldn't keep my chow down. Like I lost about 35 pounds my first year in the joint, so I started getting scared. I hated to give it up because it was a good pay test." "Hey, man, I'm making $30 a month on the DMSO thing [chronic topical application of dimethylsulfoxide]. I know a couple of guys had to go to the hospital who were on it—

and the burns were so bad they had to take *everyone* off it for a while. But who gives a shit about that, man? Thirty is a full canteen draw and I wish the thing would go on for years —I'd be lost without it." "I was on DMSO last year. It paid real good and it was better than that plague thing (bubonic plague vaccine immunization study) that fucked with guys last year. There was a lot of bad reactions to DMSO, but I guess that's why it paid so good." Of DMSO, Morton Mintz, staff writer for the Washington *Post*, had written three years earlier: "Human testing has now been severely curbed by FDA because of reports of serious adverse effects."

The participating physician cashes in on the programs in various ways. He may make a direct deal with the drug company for financial backing, out of which he pays the expenses of research and pockets the rest as his fee. An individual research grant might run from $5,000 to upward of $50,000, enabling a doctor with good prison contacts to handily double or triple his regular income. Or if he is, as many are, a faculty member in a medical school, he can route the grant through his university to the acclaim of his colleagues and the tenure committee. His prestige and hence his worth in terms of salary will be greatly enhanced when the results of his research appear in a professional journal. (Whether these publications serve the cause of advancing scientific knowledge is another matter. Dr. Stough published a number of articles on his findings, says Rugaber—on examination, these turned out to be puff pieces for the drug companies, with nary a critical appraisal of the drugs he was testing.) According to Dr. Irwin Feinberg of the University of California Medical Center, "Medical schools in the last two decades have increased their research activities dramatically, and the 'publish or perish' rule of other university departments is now applied relentlessly to the emerging full-time medical faculties."

Some of the vicissitudes the medical researcher may expect to find in his quest for prisoner-subjects are described by Dr.

Robert E. Hodges in the *Journal of the American Medical Association*. In the late forties, Dr. Hodges and his colleagues reached a "verbal working arrangement" with Iowa prison officials enabling them to canvass the prison population for volunteers who would submit to prolonged hospitalization in the University Hospitals as research subjects. "We knew this procedure was not specifically permitted by law," writes Dr. Hodges. "But neither was it specifically prohibited." Eventually the experiments came to the attention of Iowa's attorney general: "In his judgment, it was not legal for us to accept prison volunteers for medical research." There followed two fallow years in which the experiments were perforce halted, but Dr. Hodges, undaunted, put this time to good use: "We sought and obtained enactment of a specific law permitting the use of prisoners for medical research at University Hospitals." The path thus cleared, a total of 224 convicts were in the course of time delivered over to Dr. Hodges and his colleagues at the University Hospitals.

Speculating on the "incentives and motives" that induce prisoners to volunteer for research studies "which are usually somewhat unpleasant and in a few instances involve distinct risks," Dr. Hodges surmises that "for some, it probably represents a new experience which takes them away from the monotony and oppressiveness of prison routine." The relief from monotony: "They have eaten strange diets, swallowed tubes, submitted to repeated venipunctures, and participated in a wide variety of physiological tests . . ."

For some prisoners, "monetary gain may be the incentive, though inmates are paid only $1 daily." Iowa prisoners are not supposed to receive reduction of sentence in return for volunteering, but Dr. Hodges routinely sent a thank-you letter to the warden for each subject: "It is possible that this letter in the prisoner's file may favorably influence the parole board." As for the incentives and motives of researchers, Dr. Hodges reports that more than 80 scientific publications resulted from the Iowa studies on prisoners.

Dr. Hodges becomes almost lyrical in his discussion of the moral and ethical aspects of such experimentation. The prisoner-volunteers, he says, are "our companions in medical science and adventure"; the subject "in whatever degree derelict or forlorn, has sacred rights which the physician must always put ahead of his burning curiosity." Dr. Hodges, without elaborating on what these sacred rights might be, concludes: "A system of voluntary participation firmly based on legal and ethical standards has provided a rich opportunity for clinical investigators who wish to study metabolic, physiologic, pharmacologic, and medical problems. This has been a rewarding experience both for the physicians and for the subjects." (If, as spokesmen for the drug industry and their allies in medicine and government claim, participation in research is a rewarding experience for prisoners, who feel they are expiating their crimes, how much more rewarding might it be for the stockholders in the giant pharmaceutical corporations to volunteer for this noble cause, since they stand to gain financially and could incidentally expiate the many crimes of the companies in which they have invested!)

One such rich opportunity is described by Dr. Hodges in one of these scientific publications: "Clinical Manifestations of Ascorbic Acid Deficiency in Man," in the *American Journal of Clinical Nutrition* of April 1971. The object: "to define the metabolism of this vitamin in the face of severe dietary deficiency." For the study, which consisted of experimentally induced scurvy, five companions in medical science and adventure were recruited from the Iowa State Penitentiary "and their informed consent was obtained." Among the rewarding experiences they encountered: for periods ranging from 84 to 97 days they were fed a liquid formula free of ascorbic acid by stomach tube: "because of the unpalatability of this formula, the men took it thrice daily via polyethylene gastric tube." They were exposed in a cold-climate "control room" to a temperature of 50 degrees for four hours each day. The volume of blood drawn "for laboratory purposes" was large enough to "cause mild anemia in all the men." In a throwaway line, Dr. Hodges observes that "the mineral supplement [recommended by the National Research Council] was inadvertently omitted from the diets during the first 34 days of the depletion period."

The experiment was a great success. It was, in fact, the second of its kind, Dr. Hodges having tried it once before with far less favorable results: "Despite a somewhat shorter period of deprivation in the second scurvy study, the subjects in the second study developed a more severe degree of scurvy . . . although none of the subjects in the first scurvy study developed arthralgia, this was a complaint in four out of five men who participated in the second scurvy study. Joint swelling and pain made themselves evident in Scurvy II, but had not been observed in the subjects participating in Scurvy I."

The gradual onset of scurvy in the five prisoners is traced by Dr. Hodges with the enthusiasm of a young mother recording Baby's first steps. "The first signs of scurvy to appear in both studies were petechial hemorrhage [hemorrhages in the skin]. Coiled hairs were observed in two of the men and first appeared on the forty-second and seventy-fourth days, respectively. The first definite abnormalities of the gums appeared between the forty-third and eighty-fourth days of depletion and progressed after the plasma ascorbic acid levels fell . . . The onset of joint pains began between the sixty-seventh and ninety-sixth days . . . Beginning on the eighty-eighth day of deprivation there was a rapid increase in weight followed by swelling of the legs in the third man, who had the most severe degree of scurvy."

By the time it was all over, Dr. Hodges was able to chalk up these significant accomplishments: all five subjects suffered joint pains, swelling of the legs, dental cavities, recurrent loss of new dental fillings, excessive loss of hair, hemorrhages in the skin and whites of the eyes, excess fluid in the joint spaces, shortness of breath, scaly skin, mental depression, and abnormalities in emotional responses. The youngest, a twenty-six-year-old, "became almost unable to walk as a result of the rapid onset of arthropathy [painful joints] superimposed on bilateral femoral neuropathy [disease in both large nerves to the thighs and legs plus hemorrhage into nerve sheaths]. The onset of scurvy signaled a period of potentially rapid deterioration." Dr. Hodges's anticlimactic conclusion: "Once again our observations are in accord with those of the British Medical Research Council."

To doctors in the business of curing people rather than making them ill, the "ascorbic acid deficiency" study appears a senseless piece of savage cruelty visited on the five volunteers. "This study was totally pointless," Dr. Ephraim Kahn of the California Department of Public Health said of Dr. Hodges's publication. "The cause and cure of scurvy has been well known in the medical profession for generations. Some of the side effects he lists may well be irreversible—the young man who had the most severe case of scurvy may never have recovered. There's a clue here to the degree of competence of these so-called researchers—they 'inadvertently' omitted a mineral supplement from the diets. This no doubt weakened the men and exacerbated the other side effects. It might cause them to go into shock and to suffer severe cardiac abnormalities." Among the effects of the experiment recorded in the publication that could be permanent, Dr. Kahn cited heart damage, loss of hair, damage to teeth, hemorrhage into femoral nerve sheaths—the latter is "terribly painful and could lead to permanent nerve damage."

As seen by top brass in the American medical profession, the overriding "ethical problem" posed by use of prisoners for research is not, as one might have supposed, the trail of death and disease left in the wake of the experiments. Rather it is the danger that prisoner-subjects may be unduly rewarded for the pains of research by inappropriately large sums of cash and/or promise of early release. The reasoning is that the prisoner, not wishing to forego these benefits, may be tempted to conceal symptoms and side effects, thus calling into question the validity of the entire effort. The idea that a $1 a day stipend to a healthy adult can be so overwhelmingly attractive as to invalidate the results of medical research is conceivable only in the irrational world of prison. Yet this is precisely the fear expressed by some spokesmen for the medical profession.

In the late forties, Governor Dwight H. Greene of Illinois appointed a prestigious committee of physicians, including Dr. Morris Fishbein (then editor of the *Journal of the American Medical Association*) to advise the Department of Public Safety on "ethics governing the service of prisoners as subjects in medical experiments." A policy statement on this was needed because of widespread criticism of the wartime malaria experiments at Statesville Penitentiary in which, according to published accounts, subjects suffered severe abdominal pains, nausea, vomiting, transient changes in their electrocardiograms, fever, and a variety of other symptoms.

The committee's report disposes of the Statesville experiments in one line—it pronounced them "ideal because of their conformity with . . . ethical rules"—and turns its attention to the problem of "excessive rewards" in the form of reduction of sentence held out to the prisoner-subjects.

There is, the committee found, "reformative value in serving as a subject in a medical experiment," and in some cases "a reduction of sentence in prison for serving as a subject may be considered favorable to the reformative purposes of imprisonment." But how should this be determined? Apparently the trick is to ferret out the prisoner's *real* reason for volunteering—is he motivated by a lofty desire to serve science and society, or does he just want to get out of prison?—and then reward him or not, accordingly. As the committee explains in this brain-teaser: "If the sole motive of the prisoner is to contribute to human welfare, any reduction in sentence would be a reward. If the sole motive of the prisoner is to obtain a reduction in sentence, an excessive reduction of sentence which would exercise undue influence in obtaining the consent of prisoners to serve as subjects would be inconsistent with the principle of voluntary participation."

After Rugaber's disclosures about the doings of Dr. Stough, the Senate Select Committee on Small Business held hearings on the subject. Dr. Herbert L. Ley, Jr., testifying about the deaths and epidemics attendant on Dr. Stough's prison experiments in Alabama, observed: "The basic problem here, Mr. Chairman, is that the remuneration to the prisoner was too much. This meant that the prisoner had a very strong pressure not to report and not to withdraw from the study. Therefore he would decline to say that he felt any adverse reactions. This is bad for the prisoner in that it exposes him to unnecessary risk, it is bad for our records in that it does not provide us full information." Asked what the going rate was in Alabama for prisoner-volunteers, Dr. Ley replied: ". . . the fee varies depending on the test, and I suspect, as usually is the case, on the number of times the prisoner has to be bled. But an average figure across the board would be somewhere about $1 a day."

I asked Dr. Robert Hodges, now a professor of internal medicine in the University of California Medical School at Davis, how much he had paid the scurvy test volunteers. "I think it was $1 or maybe $2 a day," he replied. "Over the years, when I was in Iowa, as the cost of cigarettes and razor blades went up, we increased prisoners' pay somewhat. It's unethical to pay an amount of money that is too attractive. Oh, we had the money, we could have paid much more, of course—but we weren't just being cheap, we were considering the ethics of the situation. The prisoners got a bit extra for really unpleasant things—if we had to put a tube down their throats for several hours, or take a biopsy of the skin the size of a pencil eraser, we'd give them a few dollars more."

Doctors with whom I have discussed the matter are unanimously agreed that FDA regulations requiring drugs to be tested on humans before being marketed are sound and necessary. They point to the notorious greed and often criminal irresponsibility of the pharmaceutical industry, as evidenced by the thalidomide disaster and the sloppy fashion in which the birth control pill was released for mass consumption with harmful consequences for many women. But human experimentation, they say, must be conducted within a framework of stringent rules for the protection of the human subject.

Hence, one by-product of the enormous proliferation in recent decades of medical research on humans by government agencies and the drug industry is a parallel proliferation of "guiding principles" and "codes of ethics" developed by the medical profession to govern the conduct of the experiments, curb the overzealous researcher, and safeguard the human subjects. An American Medical Association resolution of 1946 on human research was in turn followed by FDA regulations of 1962 and the Helsinki Declaration of 1966.

These are largely repetitive. All affirm that human experiments must be based on prior laboratory work and research on animals, emphasize the grave responsibility of investigator to subject, exhort him to avoid experiments that are of no scientific value or that subject humans to unnecessary pain and risk.

The principle of informed consent is basic to all the codes. As stated in the Nuremberg judgment (and adopted almost verbatim by the Food and Drug Administration), "the voluntary consent of the human subject is absolutely essential. This means the person involved should have legal capacity to give consent; should be so situated as to be able to exercise free power of choice . . . and should have sufficient knowledge and comprehension of the elements of the subject matter involved as to enable him to make an understanding, enlightened decision." Are prisoners, stripped of their civil rights when they enter the gates, subjected for years or decades to the iron compression chamber of the penitentiary, free agents capable of exercising freedom of choice? Are they furnished by the experimenters with "knowledge and comprehension" to enable them to make "understanding and enlightened" decisions? To ask these questions is to answer them.

In 1972 the U.S. Department of Health, Education, and Welfare issued a set of comprehensive and detailed regulations, incorporating principles of the previous codes, entitled "The Institutional Guide to DHEW Policy on Protection of Human Subjects."

The guide expresses a "particular concern" for "subjects in groups with limited civil freedom. These include prisoners . . ." Having uttered this praiseworthy sentiment, HEW has apparently let the matter drop. Dr. D. T. Chalkley, chief of the Institutional Relations Branch, Division of Research Grants, and signer of the guide, tells me that HEW does not even maintain a list of prisons in which HEW-financed research programs are in progress and has "no central source of information" on the scope of medical experiments on prisoners by drug companies—in any event, the regulations set forth in the guide apply only to HEW studies, and not to those sponsored by private industry. "The FDA has some data on prisoner usage by drug houses, but I doubt if this is collated."

What efforts have been made by HEW to enforce its guidelines in HEW-financed medical research behind prison walls? "We do give some grants that involve prisoners. But there's no convenient way of recovering the information as to whether our guidelines are being followed," said Dr. Chalkley. "That responsibility lies with the principal investigator." I asked him about a letter I had received from Dr. Richard B. Hornick, director of the Division of Infectious Diseases, University of Maryland School of Medicine, who is currently conducting cholera, typhoid fever, viral respiratory, and viral diarrhea studies at the Maryland House of Correction under a grant from the National Institutes of Health, a division of HEW. "We can predict how many people will get sick following a particular dose of bacteria," Dr. Hornick wrote. "With cholera or with typhoid we will use a dose of organisms that will produce disease in 25 to 30 percent of the control [unvaccinated] population." He had furnished me with a copy of the consent form that prisoner-subjects in these studies are required to sign, in which the prisoner agrees to "release and forever discharge" the principal investigator and everybody else involved in the experiment "from liability for any injury which may result directly or indirectly from the performance of these investigations." "Oh *damn!*" said Dr. Chalkley. "I was aware of this form two years ago—I thought they said they were going to quit using it. I don't know. Give us hell; I guess we deserve it." Has HEW ever brought any action to enforce its regulations in any prisons anywhere? "None, to date."

Dr. Alan Lisook, of FDA's Office of Scientific Evaluation, said: "We've no list of prisons where drug research is going on. We know it does go on in certain prisons. The way we learn of it is through the IND [Investigational New Drug] submissions by the pharmaceutical companies. It's a touchy area, probably confidential information under the Trade Secrets Act. I suggest you make a written request—say the magic words 'Freedom of Information Act'—and I will get an opinion from counsel as to whether we can compile the information for you." I did so, and in the course of time I obtained a list of prisons. "It is without doubt imperfect since this information is not routinely abstracted in a retrievable form," wrote Dr. Lisook. He was unable to furnish the names of drug companies experimenting in these prisons, or the number of inmates involved.

Missing from Dr. Lisook's imperfect list is Patuxent Institution, Maryland. Phil Stanford, writing in *The New York Times Magazine*, reports that Johns Hopkins, the University of Maryland, and the National Institute of Mental Health are conducting a number of experimental "behavioral control" drug programs in the institution. "It's no sweat getting volunteers because all of these programs pay volunteers," a staff member told him. Stanford cites a Johns Hopkins experiment in which an inmate is getting dosages of a female hormone, "presumably to counteract his 'supermasculinity,'" and quotes the following exchange between Edward Tomlinson, a law professor, and members of Patuxent's professional treatment staff:

TOMLINSON: Does he understand the effects of the drug?

DR. HAROLD M. BOSLOW, DIRECTOR OF PATUXENT: Yes, we explained the whole thing to him. We don't want any misunderstanding.

TOMLINSON: Well, what are the effects?

DR. ARTHUR KANDEL, ASSOCIATE DIRECTOR: We don't know. That's what they're trying to find out.

A forthright explanation of the secrecy surrounding prison research was furnished by the vice-president in charge of research and development at Wyeth Laboratories, who asked me not to use his name. "Almost all our Phase I testing is done in prisons," he said. "The locations of the prisons in which we do research—that's fundamentally confidential information. *Where* we get our clinical work done is just as much a trade secret as *what* we're doing. There are industrial spies everywhere. If we let the names of the prisons out, our competitors could easily get a pipeline to what we're doing, and the secret would be out." Mr. Paul Stessel, public relations man for Lederle Laboratories, advanced a further reason for keeping mum. I asked him whether his company has a policy against

disclosing names of prisons where it does research: "Yes, as
a matter of fact." Why is that? "The prison administrators
might get upset if there was publicity about it."

From my conversations with drug company executives and
physicians involved in research I learned that prisons today
furnish virtually the entire pool of subjects for Phase I testing.
"If the prisons closed down tomorrow, the pharmaceutical
companies would be in one hell of a bind," said one medical
researcher. (The drug houses, are, however, casting eyes in
the direction of the "underdeveloped" nations as potential
reservoirs of human experimental material.) Most pharmaceutical concerns have to queue up for available prison populations
on which to experiment, but two of the biggest—Upjohn and
Parke Davis—are in the enviable position of having acquired
exclusive rights to Michigan's Jackson State Prison. In what
Charles Mangee, public relations spokesman for Upjohn, calls
"a beautiful operation run in a highly ethical fashion," the
two companies maintain fully equipped laboratories built at a
cost of $500,000, complete with hospital bed space for 40
inmate subjects, within the walls. Title to these facilities was
turned over to the State of Michigan in 1963 for a beautiful tax
saving to the companies as a "charitable donation."

Of Jackson's 4,000 convicts, more than 1,200 are in the
research programs at any given time. According to *Business
Week*, "tests at the prison are designed primarily to measure
the toxicity of a drug, rather than its efficacy . . . doses . . . are
built up gradually to the point where adverse reactions occur."

The rehabilitative value of the program, says *Business
Week*, lies in the work performed by inmate technicians and
nurses who staff the laboratories: "Prisoners get a valuable
feeling of self-respect. 'I'm helping other people,' says one
inmate-technician, 'and I've never felt like this in my life.'"

Inmate laboratory workers in the Upjohn-Parke Davis
clinics, who frequently put in a sixteen-hour day, are paid a
wage ranging from 30¢ a day for a nurse to $1.25 a day for a

chief technician. Evidently 34 co-workers of *Business Week*'s unnamed technician did not share his enthusiasm, for in 1968 they brought suit against Upjohn, Parke Davis, and the Department of Corrections, alleging that the drug companies "are obtaining or have obtained hundreds of thousands of dollars worth of labor free by use of the device here involved." (Although the allegations with respect to wage levels were not in dispute, the case was decided in favor of the defendants on other grounds.)

Over the past ten years a brisk traffic in human subjects for drug company experimentation has grown up in the California Medical Facility at Vacaville, a prison specifically designated for men deemed by the authorities to be in need of psychiatric treatment. Vacaville has a population of some 1,500, of whom from 300 to more than 1,000 may be in the "volunteer" medical research program at any given time.

The medical experiments are organized under the aegis of a shadowy outfit called the Solano Institute for Medical and Psychiatric Research (SIMPR) with headquarters in the prison. I discovered that even such prison knowledgeables as faculty members at the School of Criminology in Berkeley and California legislators who have devoted years to studying prison conditions were but dimly aware of the existence of SIMPR and had no idea of the extent and nature of its activities. Unlike the Upjohn-Parke Davis operation, which is financed directly by the two drug companies, SIMPR is set up as a nonprofit corporation under California's charitable trust law. According to its financial statements filed with the Registry of Charitable Trusts, SIMPR's income from "various researchers" rose from $47,000 in 1963, its first year of business, to $266,000 in 1971. I asked Mr. Ralph Urbino, SIMPR administrator, which drug companies had paid over this money. He seemed quite shocked at the question: "We couldn't receive funds from drug companies," he said. "As a nonprofit organization we are barred from receiving money from private business concerns. Our income is derived from the physicians who have been given research grants for the purpose."

The "various researchers," then, for the most part faculty members from neighboring University of California medical schools, are merely a conduit for tax-exempt payments from giant pharmaceutical concerns including Lederle, Wyeth, Dow Chemical, Roche, Abbott, Smith Kline & French. According to a 1972 SIMPR publication addressed to potential customers, "One research team from the University of California has been continuously active since the inception of our program here . . . There have been no deaths or serious sequelae resulting from drug research at this institution . . . the reservoir of volunteer subjects offers investigational possibilities not found elsewhere."

Checking on SIMPR's claim that there have been no deaths or "serious sequelae" is not easy since SIMPR maintains it is not required, under the California Public Records Act, to disclose medical data. But something of the modus operandi of the prison experimenters can be gleaned from records subpoenaed and depositions taken in a lawsuit, eventually settled out of court for $6,000, that arose out of a 1962 experiment. The two principal defendants in that suit are prime operatives in SIMPR today. Dr. William C. Keating, Jr., then superintendent of Vacaville, was a founder of SIMPR and serves on its board of directors; Dr. William L. Epstein, chairman of the dermatology department at the University of California, conducted the experiment in question together with a colleague, Dr. Howard I. Maibach. Drs. Epstein and Maibach are the self-same "continuously active research team" featured in the 1972 SIMPR publication.

The plaintiff, who according to Dr. Keating had been classified as psychotic and sent to Vacaville for "psychiatric programing and treatment," was one of 20 subjects selected to undergo what Dr. Epstein calls "pain tolerance studies" consisting of intramuscular injections of Varidase (fibrinolytic enzymes used as an anti-inflammatory agent), a Lederle Laboratories product. The plaintiff testified in his deposition that he was seized by four prison trusties who forcibly injected the drug in both his arms. Evidence given by independent physicians disclosed that he thereafter suffered an agonizing, near-fatal disease of the muscles, in the course of which his weight dropped from 140 to 75 pounds. He subsequently developed chronic stomach ulcers as a result of being treated for his condition with steroids, a tricky medication that unless used with care can produce very serious side effects.

From the deposition of the doctors in charge it appears that nobody involved knew much about Varidase except that it makes people very ill. The purpose of the experiment, as explained by Dr. Epstcin, was to find out just how ill and learn more about adverse side effects caused by the drug. "The reason we did the experiment was the pain and the fever . . . what we were looking for was pain, discomfort, aching in the arm. We were told [by Lederle] they might also have fever, malaise, and chills." Dr. Keating recalled that the only information on the drug available to him was "a little brochure that comes with the preparation" containing "a list of medical cautions, but at the time I read them . . . this was not a significant concern." Questioned about whether the drug had been "subjected to all the normal procedures required by FDA," Dr. Epstein replied, "I wouldn't know this. I wouldn't be expected to know it." Could the Varidase injections have caused the plaintiff's condition, asked plaintiff's attorney Malcolm Burnstein. "There was the possibility that this could have been due to the drug," said Dr. Epstein. "I think that looking back on it now it is a possibility, a better possibility than I thought initially because I never heard of this thing . . ."

As to his role as principal investigator in overseeing the experiment, Dr. Epstein could not remember if he was present when the subjects were chosen or when the injections were given—they were given by inmate nurses, he said. His visits to Vacaville were infrequent, once a week or once every two weeks. No signed consent was required of the prisoner-subjects, said Dr. Keating. Asked in his deposition whether "the dangers of any of those possible medical problems were mentioned or explained to any of the potential volunteers for this project," he answered, "I don't know. I would think not." A "large fund" was granted by Lederle for the research, said Dr. Epstein. Compensation to the plaintiff for taking part: "He received $4, $3 spendable and $1 to retention funds."

If pain, discomfort, fever, and chills were what Dr. Epstein was looking for, he was not disappointed. In a letter to his sponsors at Lederle he wrote, "I am enclosing a rough copy of the comments from one of the subjects. I thought you might enjoy his description of the symptomatology; it's fairly representative of what all the men experienced." Among the descriptions that Lederle might have enjoyed, given by the 19 subjects who did not sue, and subpoenaed by the plaintiff as part of the record: "Cold chills, sweated, nauseated throughout the night." "Sharp abdominal pains." "I have a headache and my stomach feels terrible." "My body feels weak all over, right arm hurts worse than ever." "My head feels as if it will fall off." "Chilled, feverish, weak and exhausted." "Lost four pounds in three days—Dr. Epstein said it was a natural reaction except it was more severe in my case for some reason but not to worry." (What eventually became of the 19— whether they made a full recovery—history does not relate. That nobody bothers to follow up the subsequent medical history of research subjects in prison can be inferred from Dr. Epstein's testimony: "Since [the plaintiff] cleared the initial experiment, it was forgotten, because like all the other people they were just let go . . . And he came back, I couldn't tell you how soon, complaining of aching . . .").

Thorough researcher that he is, Dr. Epstein was soon at it again. He writes to Lederle a month after the plaintiff was stricken: "We are planning this week to try four more men and I am prepared to give them some steroids when the severe symptomatology starts."

From my discussion with SIMPR administrator Urbino, a genial retired Air Force man who is the institute's only full-time "free-world" employee, I gathered that SIMPR evolved in a somewhat haphazard fashion and is run on highly informal lines. For the first four years of its existence SIMPR lived off the bounty of the prison (and hence the taxpayers), paying no rent or prison personnel wages. "It was a potential time-bomb for the Department of Corrections," said Mr. Urbino. "Besides, they saw SIMPR as a very prosperous operation, they wanted to get their hands on some of that money." In 1966 SIMPR entered into a permit agreement with the department, and since then the gravy has been spooned around a bit: the corporation now pays an annual rent of $1,000 plus "custodial coverage" (guards' wages) of about $14,000 a year, and provides moonlighting jobs for other state employees to the tune of some $17,000.

SIMPR also hires convict labor—technicians, nurses, paramedical, and clerical personnel—for wages in the range of $5 to $8 a month, about one hundredth of what free personnel would command in these positions. (As Ken E. Haden pointed out in a 1963 report on the Vacaville operation to the U.S. National Institute of Mental Health: "Without this reservoir of skilled technicians, laboratory aides, clerical help, medical research could not be more than a token activity in a prison setting.") In SIMPR's first four financial reports this item, between $700 and $800 a year for work worth $70,000 to $80,000 outside the walls, shows up as "inmate salaries." Thereafter it disappears, along with most other cost items, into a general category labeled "cost of goods sold." Could these inmate salaries be another potential time-bomb for the Department of Corrections? The California constitution specifically prohibits the contracting out of convict labor "to any person, co-partnership, company, or corporation," which would seem to cover the SIMPR operation. Mr. Urbino, who is not a lawyer, was unaware of the constitutional prohibition.

Payment to the prisoner-subjects of the experiments is variously recorded in SIMPR's financial statements as "honorarium," "donations," "benefits to recipients under charitable trusts." Why is that? "The word 'honorarium' escapes me," said Mr. Urbino. "It's called 'donations' now. It's not a salary. Maybe it's a tax ploy? Dr. Keating set it up that way." Spiraling upward with the fortunes of SIMPR, these honorariums, donations, or charitable benefits rose from $34,000 in 1963 to $150,000 in 1970. The eight-year total is $787,000. Thus, assuming the drug companies would have had to compensate "free-world" volunteers at ten times what they pay convicts, they obtained some $7.8 million worth of research for their $787,000.

Who establishes the amount of pay for each experiment? "I do," said Mr. Urbino. "Several factors go into it: number of times we bleed the man, number of times he has to report to the lab on any given day." Sample payments range from $15 a month for a two-month study of inflammatory dermatophytosis (fungi described in the protocol as "one of the most prevalent health hazards to military personnel stationed in Southeast Asia") to $30 for one day for Cleocin HFC levels, a Dr. William L. Epstein production in which a gram of muscle tissue is removed. If unusually adverse side effects are anticipated, the pay goes up accordingly. "We're in the middle of one now, conducted by Dr. Howard I. Maibach, a Wyeth safety study, WY-21,743. It pays $60 a month." What side effects might be expected? Mr. Urbino, who is not a medical man, did not know. (I subsequently asked Wyeth's vice-president for Research and Development what mysterious WY-21,743 consists of. His reply: "That's confidential information in the Investigational New Drug file. I wouldn't tell my own mother about it!" Nor would FDA reveal the formula. Dr.

Lisook told me, "The Freedom of Information Act specifically prohibits such disclosure. Our new regulation says 'the very existence of an IND is confidential.'") The highest he ever remembers paying an inmate, said Mr. Urbino, was $100: "The Army had an elaborate study in heart research. It had to do with a treadmill, pressures on the heart. The convict got $100 for one day. It cost us more for the correctional officer and the car! But it was quite a holiday for the guy."

Why does the Department of Corrections tolerate the SIMPR presence—is it because the rent money and payment to guards (who would have to be paid anyway) is a nice financial cushion for the institution? "That's part of it," said Mr. Urbino. "But the main benefit to the department is that the research programs cut down on disciplinary problems. A man has to have a relatively infraction-free record to qualify as a volunteer subject. And the department figures if he has $30 a month to spend on canteen, he'll be a lot cooler." Thus, the ultimate exploitation of the prisoner: systematically impoverished by his keepers, denied a decent wage, he is reduced to bartering his body for cigarette and candy money.

Presumably to insure against any repetition of the 1962 lawsuit, SIMPR now requires each convict-subject to sign a consent form and waiver stating: "I hereby fully and forever release, acquit, and discharge" all state agencies involved, plus SIMPR, "from any and all liability which may accrue" from his participation in the research project.

To my question whether the waiver is not in clear violation of HEW guidelines, I got these answers: Dr. Alan Lisook, who had on behalf of FDA twice inspected the SIMPR operation, was not aware that such a waiver was being used. "Although we require a consent form in all drug experimentation, we do not require that the wording be cleared with us, nor that copies be submitted. It would be very difficult to enforce the prohibition against exculpatory clauses." The vice-president for Research and Development at Wyeth: "The medical monitor of Wyeth is in charge of that." (The name of the medical monitor is, however, confidential, he said.) Mr. Paul Stessel, public relations spokesman for Lederle: "It's the responsibility of the investigator to follow the guidelines and obtain a proper consent form. We don't dictate to the clinician how he runs these things. I'm sure you're aware that the more prestigious the clinician is, the more convinced he is that he knows what he's doing. If you use him, you have little choice but to trust what he says he does." Dr. Howard I. Maibach, principal investigator for many SIMPR experiments: "Yes, I'm familiar with the consent form used at Vacaville. It's in a period of change, a state of flux . . ."

Theoretically, the University of California medical schools exercise considerable control over faculty-member researchers through committees on human experimentation, consisting of medical professors and laymen, established by the president of the university in 1966. These are supposed to review and pass on the protocol for each proposed study under University of California sponsorship—"regardless of funding source"— in the light of HEW and FDA standards.

At a meeting of the University of California Medical Center Committee on Human Experimentation, I was told that few SIMPR protocols had ever been submitted to the committee. "Prison research that comes before this committee is extremely rare," said one member. "The minute a Vacaville study comes in, the red flag goes up!" Although both Dr. Epstein and Dr. Maibach are on the medical center faculty, the committee had never heard of most of the experiments they are currently conducting at Vacaville. Of another team of doctors, listed in SIMPR's 1971 report as faculty members of the medical center and principal investigators in current research studies, I was told that one had been "severed" by the university in 1966 and the other had died in 1968.

In one section of the California Department of Corrections

annual *Research Review,* some 30 experiments conducted under the auspices of SIMPR are set forth in précis form. Since these are couched in the language of pharmacology and medicine, the nature of the experiments is for the most part obscure to the layman. (An exception is the "Aedes mosquito study," in which "freshly grown, unfed female mosquitoes in carefully prepared biting cages are applied to the forearms of volunteers for a period of ten minutes," which seems explicit enough.)

Seeking clarification, I showed a copy of the 1971 *Research Review* to Dr. Sheldon Margen, a physician with wide experience in human research who, as chairman of the Department of Nutritional Sciences at the University of California, uses students and other "free-world" volunteers as experimental subjects. Dr. Margen read with fascination and mounting indignation the experiments described in the *Review.* He translated the procedures for me, interjecting a frequent "Wow!" "Brother!" "God, that kills me!" Some of the studies, he said, are innocuous; others, extremely painful and potentially dangerous.

For example, Dr. Epstein's study of Cleocin HFC levels, for which "10 healthy normal volunteers" were selected; its purpose, "to determine antibiotic levels in various tissues and/or fluids." Each subject gets "150 mg. of Cleocin q.i.d. for a single day," following which he will be relieved of "sebum, 2–4 ml.; sweat, 4–5 ml.; semen, amount of normal ejaculation; and muscle tissue, 1 Gm. In addition, a 15 cc. blood sample will be drawn . . ." "Here's what happens to these 10 guys," said Dr. Margen. "First they make them masturbate to collect semen. Then they cut into the arm or go through the flesh to get the gram of muscle tissue. That's the horrific part. The experiment itself may be totally justified —the drug presents virtually no risk—but this procedure is cockeyed. It would never be approved for student-subjects."

Nor had it ever been approved by the University of California Committee on Human Experimentation; Dr. Lesley Bennett, chairman of the University of California Medical Center committee, told me "there's no evidence this was ever submitted for review."

The "organic phosphates toxicity" study, purpose of which is "to determine the threshold of incipient toxicity in human subjects of organic phosphates currently in wide use as insecticides," involves the use of the most dangerous and poisonous of all pesticides, said Dr. Margen. Would this be approved for experimentation on students? "Are you kidding?" Possible hazards of other experiments described in the *Research Review* include, he said, cardiac failure; total loss of blood flow resulting in neurological damage and loss of fingers; fungous infection; and allergic reactions. He added, "If the researchers really believe these experiments are safe for humans, why do they go to the prison for subjects? Why don't they try them out in their own laboratories on students or other 'free-world' volunteers? Because they know the university would never permit this—and furthermore it would never enter their minds to do these things to people they associate with in daily life. They make a distinction between people they think of as social equals or colleagues and men behind bars, whom they regard as less than human."

Which brings us full circle to the phenomenon of the doctors tried at Nuremberg. After the trial, Andrew C. Ivy, a member of the tribunal, cautioned the medical profession against ascribing the atrocities to "the infamy of a few crazed, psychologically twisted practitioners." It was clear, he said, that several hundred German physicians were aware of what was going on and that the crimes were "only the logical end result of the mythology of racial inequality . . ." Is it then farfetched to perceive a kind of parallel between that mythology and the approach of the American medical experimenters to their "less than human" convict-subjects?

Following is a list of U.S. prisons, furnished by the Food and Drug Administration, where medical experiments are conducted.

ALABAMA: Alabama State Prison System, Montgomery.

ARKANSAS: Arkansas State Prison, Cummins.

CALIFORNIA: California Institution for Women, Chino; California Medical Facility, Vacaville.

CONNECTICUT: Connecticut State Prison, Somers; Connecticut Correctional Institution, Montville.

FLORIDA: Avon Park Correctional Institution, Avon Park; Florida State Prison, Raiford; Glades Correctional Institution, Belle Glades; Lowell Correctional Institution, Lowell; Largo Prison Farm, St. Petersburg.

GEORGIA: U.S. Federal Penitentiary, Atlanta.

ILLINOIS: Joliet Prison, Joliet.

INDIANA: Indiana State Prison, Michigan City; Marion County Jail, Indianapolis.

IOWA: Anamosa State Men's Reformatory, Iowa City.

LOUISIANA: Orleans Parish Prison, New Orleans.

MARYLAND: Maryland House of Correction, Jessup.

MASSACHUSETTS: Massachusetts Correctional Institution, Norfolk.

MICHIGAN: Southern Michigan State Prison, Jackson; Detroit House of Corrections, Plymouth.

MISSOURI: Missouri State Penitentiary, Jefferson City.

MONTANA: Montana State Prison, Deer Lodge.

NEW JERSEY: Essex County Prison, Caldwell.

NEW YORK: Attica State Prison, Attica; Sing Sing Prison, Tarrytown.

OHIO: Cincinnati City Jail, Cincinnati; Ohio Correctional Institution, Lebanon.

OKLAHOMA: Oklahoma State Penitentiary, McAlister.

OREGON: Oregon State Penitentiary, Salem.

PENNSYLVANIA: Bucks County Prison, Doylestown; Lancaster County Prison, Lancaster; Holmesburg Prison, Philadelphia; Philadelphia House of Corrections, Philadelphia; Berks County Prison, Reading; Northampton Prison, Easton; Chester County Farm, Westchester; Delaware County Prison, Thornton; Lebanon County Prison, Lebanon.

RHODE ISLAND: Adult Correctional Institution, Howard.

TEXAS: Texas State Penitentiary, Huntsville.

VERMONT: Vermont State Prison, Windsor.*

VIRGINIA: Virginia State Penitentiary, Richmond; Lorton Reformatory, Lorton.

* Dr. Lisook's diffidence about the accuracy of this list is apparently well-founded: in a letter to *The Atlantic* (May 1973), Kent Stoneman, Vermont Commissioner of Corrections, writes: "Vermont State Prison is listed as one of the institutions where medical experiments are conducted. The last such study, which dealt with the relationship between obesity and diabetes, terminated in June 1971. As a matter of policy, medical experimentation in Vermont correctional institutions has been prohibited since that time."

10

THE PRISON BUSINESS

Riots, work stoppages, hunger strikes in prisons across the nation have opened the eyes of even the most myopic to the shocking and degrading physical conditions to which prisoners are subjected. From Attica we learned that men work for twelve hours a day in temperatures of often more than a hundred degrees, are permitted but one shower a week, one roll of toilet paper every five weeks. We heard the prisoners' vivid descriptions of rotting food, roach-infested cells, gross medical neglect—all ruefully acknowledged by the prison administration and confirmed by subsequent official investigations.

The reflex reaction of the conventional reformer to such revelations is to demand ever bigger appropriations for Corrections, and in this he is heartily seconded by prison officialdom. Facts are marshaled about how much we spend on dispatching astronauts to the moon while men and women prisoners in this, the richest nation in the world, are forced by tightwad legislatures to suffer incredible privations. Ramsey Clark chides us for spending less than $2 billion a year on all Corrections—federal, state, and local—while we squander $9 billion on tobacco and $12.5 billion on liquor. Thus the message from the Corrections men and their reformer-allies to the growing numbers of people who are appalled by the barbarism of prison conditions: in the name of common decency give us a larger slice of the public monies that we may more adequately supply the needs of those in our charge. How best to orchestrate the money pitch, enlisting reformers for the purpose, was explained to a group of us by a public relations man for the American Correctional Association at the 1971 Congress. Discussing the problem of do-gooders who want to go poking about in the prisons, he said: "We shouldn't be afraid of them. We should let them in the prisons, because they can become our best lobbyists for funds. Although they may still go on squawking about all the things they don't like, they are invaluable in getting appropriations out of the legislature."

Instead of climbing on this bandwagon it might be well to take account of the present realities of prison expenditure. At the time of the Attica uprising, Russell G. Oswald, New York commissioner of Corrections, predictably blamed much of the trouble on what he termed "fiscal starvation." The deputy corrections commissioner, Wim van Eekeren, gloomily told *The New York Times* that the department had been "trying to shift to a more nutritional diet, but the effort was slowed by a tight budget."

Yet in 1971 the New York State prison budget was $71.6 million, up from $62.4 million in 1966; in the same period, the convict population dropped from 16,400 to 13,000. Divide $71.6 million by 13,000 and you get a bountiful $5,500 per year per convict. Why then are they denied the most rudimentary necessities of life?

Of the $9.2 million total increase over the five-year period, more than $8 million was accounted for by "salary adjustments." By 1971, staff in the New York prisons numbered 6,306, making the prisoner/employee ratio just over 2 to 1, exclusive of central administration. About 70 percent of this work force was in custody, another 10 percent in maintenance, 7 percent each in clerical and counseling/education, 1 percent professional medical personnel. Commenting on additional funds appropriated in 1971 for New York prisons before Attica erupted, *The New York Times* notes that "much of this year's increase—about $5 million—has gone into administration overhead, including the creation of a number of new top-level and middle-management jobs, and the $200,000 cost of new offices." This, at a time when the food budget was frozen at 72¢ per prisoner per day because of the alleged "fiscal starvation."

So prison money, far from benefiting those at the bottom, floats or is propelled up to the top, there to be converted into jobs for organization men and the latest in office equipment rather than into decent food or sufficient toilet paper for the prisoners. When the inevitable crisis erupts, a cry goes up for additional millions to restore order via more concrete, more hardware, more guards.

Immediately after the Attica uprising, Governor Rockefeller opened up the state coffers and ordered an emergency allocation of $4 million, $3 million of that "to initiate restoration of essential functions for safe and secure operations of the State Correctional Facility at Attica," the balance for investigating committees and purchase of security equipment including, according to *The New York Times*, "the latest things for mob control."

Six months later, Commissioner Oswald reported that a total of 339 new guards had been hired, thousands of gas masks purchased, bidding would shortly begin for "new, diversified metal detectors," sites were being sought for a maxi-maxi security prison (required, he said, "because of the militant tendencies of some inmates")—and under the heading of Inmate Improvements, "an increase in the number of showers permitted, an expanded clothing issue, a better provision of toilet paper." Checking with New York authorities several months later, I learned the prisoners now get *two* showers a week and "toilet paper as requested." For this, 43 men died?

No doubt like schools, old-age homes, mental hospitals, and other closed institutions that house the powerless, prisons afford a very special opportunity to employees at all levels for various kinds of graft and thievery. Convicts will tell you about profitable deals made with local merchants for supplies in which the warden pockets a handsome rakeoff, unexplained shortages in the canteens, the disappearance of large quantities of food from the kitchens. Occasionally scandals break into the press: a prison administrator caught with his hand in the till, the deep-freeze, or the toolbox, pilfering money, meat, or equipment intended for his charges. Yet even these excesses pale beside the legitimate, legislatively sanctioned dissipation of the vast sums appropriated for the prison establishment.

Budgets for tax-supported institutions are tricky territory, whether they be for schools, welfare departments, the Pentagon, your local library, or prisons. Woe to the innocent taxpayer who tries to discover where his money goes; he will find himself in a quagmire of incomprehensible terms and figures. Aware of these perils—and of the danger of generalization—I have endeavored to take a close look at one prison budget, that of California, largest in the nation, in an attempt to get some notion of how prison money circulates and for whose benefit.

Unlike the New York prison administration, the California Department of Corrections does not plead poverty. Mr. L. M. Stutsman, deputy director, told me: "The Department of Corrections has a relationship with the Administration that no other department has. We've got all we asked for, since Reagan took office."

In the nine fiscal years 1964–65 to 1972–73, California's prison budget soared from $61.5 million to a proposed $96.5 million. During this period the prison population dropped from 26,600 to an estimated 20,500; thus the per capita costs more than doubled, from $2,313 to $4,702 per year per inmate.* As Table I shows, there has been considerable fluctuation in the prison population, which reached the all-time high of 28,500 in 1968–69 and thereafter fell precipitously to an estimated 20,500 for 1972–73. Not so the budget, which continued in its inexorable rise.

Robin Lamson, chief researcher for the California State Assembly Office of Research, says that today it costs as much to keep a man in San Quentin as it would to send him to Harvard (which suggests the interesting possibility of exchange scholarships between these two institutions). Where does all the money go? In recent years the California budget has become even more difficult to interpret owing to a changeover in the accounting procedure from "line item" to "program

* These estimates consider only General Fund expenditures and do not include other sources of revenue such as California Correctional Industries and Inmate Welfare Fund. Taken together, the total institution costs for 1972-73 are estimated by the Department of Corrections' Management Services Division at $110.5 million, or $5,239 per capita. Because figures including the Industries and the Inmate Welfare Fund are unavailable for some of the years under consideration, Table I on page 181 is based on budgets exclusive of those categories.

budgeting," a change ordered by Governor Reagan. (This is the same planned program budgeting with which McNamara was going to trim the fat in the Defense Department and obtain "more bang for the buck" in Vietnam.) Costs were formerly expressed in terms of location, by institution, but are now grouped under "program" or "activity" headings: "security," "housekeeping-maintenance," and the like. The new technique, which puts a dollar value on each "program," is supposed to simplify the legislator's task in arriving at intelligent decisions about allocation of funds.

However, a CPA in the state auditor's office told me that while the figure for the year's total expenditures is accurate, the breakdowns by "program" are meaningless because the department does not have an accounting system equipped to handle the new method. "For proper accountability you must have a consistent and rational accounting method of gathering cost information, and that does not exist," he said. "Although they say they do 'program budgeting,' they do not have a program cost-accounting system. They're terribly far off. If you ask how they do it, they can't answer. The figures are a sheer fabrication. That's called fraud where I come from." So the prison administration, adept at obfuscation in all its dealings, has now discovered how to apply this skill where it will yield substantial cash rewards in the dollar-and-cents columns of its annual explanation to the legislature of estimated budgetary needs.

How the conscientious statistician sets about program budgeting in the area of life and death is disclosed in a departmental memorandum from Vida Ryan, senior statistician, to the California director of Corrections, written shortly before the Supreme Court abolished the death penalty. Discussing the budgetary consequences of pending legislation, she writes: "In the computation of costs of 1972 legislative bills involving death penalty, some assumptions must be made or thought be given to the possibility of certain events occurring."

Should the legislature replace the death penalty for first degree murder with a life sentence without possibility of parole, the department must, she points out, expect to find a difference in program costs: "Persons received with a death penalty will spend approximately *three* years in prison before execution. If commuted to life without possibility of parole, the additional cost is based upon a period of seventeen years." Computing the programmed cost of life versus death in prison, Ms. Ryan reports that: "In accordance with basic costs, Mr. Ritter estimated (telephone conversation of 1-18-72) that the additional direct costs are: $4,000 annual cost per man, $750 cost per execution." She adds this postscript: "Bills increasing or adding the death sentence for such selected offenses as robbery, burglary, sex, and destruction of property might result in savings for the Department of Corrections, as the length of time in prison would be less."

Despite the obstacles erected by program budgeting, it is possible, by questioning the men in Sacramento who run the prisons, extrapolating from old "line item" budgets, and enlisting the help of researchers privy to the ways of prison budgets, to penetrate some of the mysteries.

The broad categories are fairly predictable. In the 1972–73 proposed budget far and away the largest chunk of money, $42 million or 38 percent, pays for "Security: effective control of the inmates, prevention of riots, escapes, arson, assault, introduction of contraband, and other incidents," as the department describes it. Nearly all of the Security budget (formerly designated Custody) goes for guards' wages: officers, sergeants, lieutenants, and captains who together comprise well over half of all personnel in the prisons. The remaining expenditure for Security buys weapons, ammunition, tear gas, restraint equipment, chains, handcuffs, flashlights, etc. It develops that the crueler the conditions of custody the more expensive it gets: the department estimates the cost of keeping a man caged in "Adjustment Center" solitary confinement for 23½ to 24 hours a day at $7,000 a year, compared with $1,970 per prisoner in the minimum security conservation camps.

The next largest budget entry is "Inmate Support," 26 percent of the prison dollar, a catch-all category that includes food, clothing, medical-dental services, housekeeping and maintenance. The latter, and largest, item is budgeted for a surprising $10 million, more than is spent for food—especially surprising when, as the department states, "maintenance of the institutions' physical plants is accomplished by inmate workers," supervised by free personnel. (Indeed, the grounds outside San Quentin and Soledad as seen by the visitor are quite lovely—brilliant expanses of flowers and shrubbery bathed in California sunshine. These, of course, are seldom seen by most prisoners, who must make do with the concrete-enclosed bare blacktop of the prison yard.)

Treatment accounts for $14.5 million, or 13 percent. It comprises academic education, counseling and psychiatry, vocational training, religion, recreation. Of these, academic education and vocational training are allotted $2,600,000 apiece, or $10 per month per inmate; however, only one fourth of the population is actually enrolled in academic education and one seventh in vocational training. Psychiatric and counseling services seem, on the face of it, to have been accorded rather a large share: together they draw down $8.25 million. There are in fact 32 full-time psychiatrists and 24 psychologists in the California prison system, the largest group of these in the California Medical Facility at Vacaville. We have already seen something of the modus operandi of the prison psychiatrist. As for the "counseling services," these consist for the most part of writing reports and are in many cases performed by guards whose jobs have been upgraded to "correctional counselor." The remainder of the treatment budget goes for "Leisure-Time Activities," $415,000 or $1.67 per month per inmate, and Religion, $544,000.

Everything seems to come higher in prisondom. Thus in

the 1969 budget "movement processing," meaning busing prisoners from one prison to another, was budgeted at just under $1 million. (This category has disappeared from subsequent budgets, which categories have a habit of doing lately, thus further complicating the task of the would-be budget-fathomer.) Over 30,000 such trips were taken by inmates during the fiscal year, which would bring the average ticket cost to $29. Continental Trailways told me I could get from San Francisco to Salem, Oregon—about 500 miles—for $27.50 (which would leave me $1.50 for a cocktail). This is for their deluxe service and includes hostess, air conditioning, music, magazines, pillows, food and beverage service.

A convict accused of participating in the Folsom work strike describes what it is like to be "movement-processed" as a troublemaker: "First the cold; lying bound, handcuffed, on the ribbed floor of the van, how it bit into the bones! The turning and twisting of half-nude bodies looking for a soft spot on the metal floor. How do four men feel lying trapped and chained in their own sputum, kidneys breaking, backbone trembling?" And he adds: "If you get the chance, find out why the Department of Corrections has such a surplus of men that they can use four of them for a two-day trip with four prisoners. I mean, this would be interesting in light of the department always wanting a budget increase. It cost the taxpayers $400 to transfer four chained men from Folsom to San Luis Obispo . . ."

What of "Administration"? The budget recognizes about 550 positions under this heading, 200 in Sacramento and 350 in the thirteen prisons. The 550 figure, however, represents only the surface if one is interested in how many bodies warm those chairs from the director and his aides—researchers, business managers, clerks, receptionists, etc.—to people who are doing essentially administrative work under other headings like "Treatment," "Inmate Employment," "Housekeeping."

For example, the California Conservation Camp at Susanville has a total staff of 378, with 28 of those positions logged under "Administration." In the remaining program categories, one locates another 38 assorted clerks, typists, administrators, chiefs, and "III"s (a civil service designation of high rank). That brings the total to 66, and a number more lurk behind ambiguous titles of supervisor or manager—persons who may or may not have much direct contact with inmates. Depending, of course, on how one counts, a reasonable approximation for desk jobs at an institution is 25 percent of all positions.

It is, however, to the more obscure corners of the budget rather than to the broad categories that one must look to discover what happens to the convict trapped at the bottom of this pile of money.

Item: From the $28 million dollar "Inmate Support" budget, $9.5 million is allocated for what the department inelegantly calls "Feeding," of which 20 percent is for staff wages, leaving $7,340,000 for food. So the $96 million budget allows 30¢ per meal for each of 21,000 prisoners.

Item: When a man arrives in prison he is issued clothing worth slightly less than $50, which includes jacket, jeans, shirts, shorts, socks, T-shirts, belt, shoes, and bandanas. The overall clothing budget, including initial issue, is $6 per month per person—on paper. However, since the clothing is all made by prisoners in prison industries and bought back by the department, this arbitrarily set figure is, according to a source in the state audit department, "unrealistic and extremely high."

Item: Out of "Inmate Support" the $7,000-a-year man in solitary confinement gets two helpings per day of "Special Isolation Diet." The recipe for this concoction, which smells and tastes like inferior dog food, was purposely devised, says the department in its official regulation on the subject, to be "monotonous and lacking in taste." Cost per serving? The department declined to divulge this information. Judging from the recipe, 5¢ to 10¢ would be about right.

Item: From the same $28 million "Inmate Support" the

indigent prisoner is allowed one stamped envelope a week and one sheet of writing paper for his total correspondence with the outside world.* The indigent's envelopes are colored yellow so all may know his special status.

Item: Another category that has disappeared from the current program budget is "Release Program," last heard of in 1969, when it cost $6 million. This is a multifaceted operation consisting of preparation by counselors of elaborate "Inmate Program Reports" for parole board review, lectures to prisoners by parole officers and other law enforcement men, transfer of records from prison to parole agency.

To the cost of all this paper-shuffling must be added the budget of the Adult Authority—close to $1 million a year. (The San Francisco *Examiner* estimates the cost of each few minutes' interview granted to prisoners by the Adult Authority at $34 and suggests that in view of the way the Adult Authority goes about its work it would be far cheaper and just as effective to hire a man with a dice box to decide who gets paroled.) The goal of the Release Program, says the department, is to assure "a successful but conditional release to the community . . . with reasonable expectations of successful parole." Is it? The department is supposed to allow for $68 "gate money" when a man is released. With deductions from those who have money in their Inmate Trust Account, actual gate money doled out in 1971 to the 9,768 prisoners released that year was $563,-005.20, or an average of $57.65 per person. From this sum was deducted $8.01 for what the department calls "appropriate apparel," leaving $49.64 in cash, from which the prisoner had to pay the cost of transportation from the prison to his home, and survive as best he might.

Prison administrators all over, one gathers, order their budgetary priorities in much the same fashion. Some informa-

---

* Mr. Philip Guthrie of the California Department of Corrections tells me the allowance was recently increased to five envelopes; prisoners say this news has not yet filtered down into the institutions.

CHART I

CALIFORNIA
INMATE POPULATION
AND INSTITUTION EXPENDITURE
1959–73

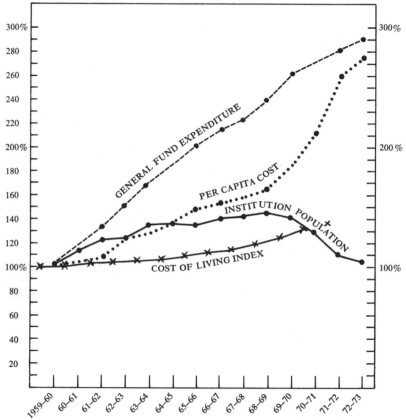

Source of chart: California Department of Industrial Relations,
Labor Statistics and Research Division.

General fund, per capita cost, institution population—See Table I
for source. Cost of Living Index: For Californians, calendar years
1959–71 (latest available).

TABLE I
CALIFORNIA PRISONS
POPULATION AND COST GROWTH
1959–73

Fiscal Year	Average Institution Population[1]	General Fund Expenditure (P&CSD excluded)[2]	Per Capita[3]
1959–60	19,500	$33,164,000	$1701
60–61	21,800	38,551,000	1772
61–62	23,700	43,736,000	1846
62–63	24,200	50,381,000	2085
63–64	26,200	56,887,000	2173
64–65	26,600	61,585,000	2313
65–66	26,300	66,907,000	2539
66–67	27,300	71,674,000	2628
67–68	27,600	73,877,000	2680
68–69[4]	28,500	80,059,000	2811
69–70[4]	27,700	87,359,000	3155
70–71[4]	25,100	90,687,000	3619
71–72[4]	21,400	93,958,000	4384
72–73[4]	20,500	96,364,000	4702

Source of table: *Analysis of the Budget Bill*, 1968–69, with 1972–73 additions; Office of the Legislative Analyst, Sacramento, California.
[1] Includes women and Civil Addicts.
[2] Parole and Community Services Division.
[3] Per capita estimates derived.
[4] Population estimates from 1972–73 *Program Budget*.

tion about how the federal prison system spends its money was furnished by George Pickett, superintendent of Marion maximum-security federal prison, testifying before the House of Representatives Select Committee on Crime in December 1971. Describing Marion as a "model institution," built in 1963 at a cost of over $10 million to hold some 500 "adult male felons who are difficult to manage and control," with an average sentence of thirty-four years, he said the cost per prisoner is $7,600 a year, or more than $20 a day. Pressed by the committee's chief counsel to explain how this money is allocated and how much is spent for food, Mr. Pickett answered that the daily cost of food per prisoner is "roughly 77¢. Total cost per man per day is $1.36. But then everything included, salaries and what-have-you, it comes to approximately $20." After thirty-four years, then, the "salaries and what-have-you" generated by a single prisoner would amount to $241,536, during which time $16,864 would have been allocated for his food and upkeep. As Benjamin Franklin might have said, had he known of this, "One man's time is another man's money."

At the same hearing, Mr. Pickett's boss, Norman A. Carlson, director of the U.S. Bureau of Prisons, offered a ready explanation for any shortcomings in his operation: "As is true in most prison systems in the United States, the federal system has been handicapped by antiquated facilities, insufficient staffs, and limited resources with which to provide adequate programs for offenders," he said. Which moved a subsequent witness, Dr. James A. Bax, commissioner of the Community Services Administration of HEW, to make some salty comments about the boundless rapacity of the prison men. Prisons, he said, "are often incestuous bureaucracies existing unto themselves. Their budgets are stoked by legislators, not on the basis of the numbers of citizens they rehabilitate, but on the numbers of prisoners they keep quietly tucked away out of circulation . . . Institutions are amoral. They are socially irresponsible. They are inherently power-hungry. As every legislator knows, they are always hungry for more public money. In short, institutions are lawless—they themselves must be constantly controlled and rehabilitated. The prison system is no exception. . . ."

Central to the strategies of prison administrations in the era of convict rebellion is construction of new prisons, about which we shall doubtless be hearing a good deal in the coming years. At a 1971 conference on criminal justice sponsored by the

Center for Democratic Studies, James V. Bennett said he estimates that, nationwide, Corrections needs a minimum of $18 billion dollars for new buildings alone. These old bastilles should be replaced, say the prison men; some of them are more than a hundred years old, they are too big, unwieldy, unsanitary, overcrowded. The humanitarian reformer will agree, for he has seen the evidence on his television screen and in magazine picture spreads: the tiny, dark cells, rusty iron bars, overflowing toilets, dank concrete, over all an aura of decay. Incomparably worse than any zoo, he will declare! No wonder riots and disturbances are endemic in these places. As long as we must have prisons, let them at least be decent and fit for human habitation.

Significantly, the occupants of these disgraceful dungeons have in no instance joined the chorus of demands for newer and better-built prisons. Search the manifestoes of convict leaders from the Tombs to San Quentin and you will find no such proposal. On the contrary, prisoner and ex-convict groups throughout the country are urging opposition to new prison building, which they see as leading to a vast expansion of the existing prison empire. The economics are simple: x-million dollars are spent for a new jail. It must be kept reasonably full because if the population goes down jailers are thrown out of jobs—or the per capita cost of operating the jail gets so out of hand that taxpayers may begin to take note. As the authors of *Struggle for Justice* say, "When pressures for reform lead to demands to relieve 'overcrowding' by adding new cell or bed space, the result is inevitable: the coercive net of the justice system will be spread over a larger number of people, entrapping them for longer periods of time."

For example, the anouncement in 1971 by the California Department of Corrections that San Quentin was to be "phased out" was applauded by liberal reformers and editorial writers throughout the state. Soon thereafter the department sought, and obtained, a legislative appropriation of $150,000 for capital outlay to produce plans for a new institution. Those liberal assemblymen who supported the appropriation told me they did so because, having visited the rotting cages of San Quentin, they felt no human beings should be lodged therein and that new, sanitary buildings were an absolute necessity.

The prison administration was remarkably closemouthed about the precise nature of the new facilities and produced no written statement of what was intended, although early in 1972 Raymond Procunier, director of Corrections, told a Senate committee, "The prison to replace San Quentin will be a lot tougher, a lot more stringent." Eventually I was informed by the Legislative Analyst's Office that there are to be two 400-man maximum-security prisons for "problem inmates," small "prisons within prisons." They would be "more secure than Soledad" with double instead of single fencing, and would cost approximately $12 million apiece. Thus the budget request for preliminary planning was the first step toward a more repressive long-term, maximum-security lock-up and segregation for prisoners upon whom the department has bestowed the label "problem inmates."

Lucasville Penitentiary in southern Ohio is worth a detour, as the *Guide Michelin* would say, for anybody who might be curious about the costs, design, and purposes of new prison building. I visited Lucasville, then under construction, in August 1971. From back issues of Ohio newspapers I learned that the new prison was planned following a series of riots in the Ohio Penitentiary and subsequent disclosure of deplorable conditions there; the groundbreaking ceremony, presided over by Governor James A. Rhodes, had taken place in 1968, at which time cost was estimated at $15 million, to be raised through a taxpayers' bond issue. By the time of my visit, construction costs of the "Southern Ohio Correctional Facility" (the designation conferred on the new prison by Governor John J. Gilligan, Governor Rhodes's successor) had risen to $42

million, and according to the superintendent in charge were
expected to reach $60 million.

One's first impression of Lucasville is that of a huge, sur-
realistic barracks rising out of a desolate countryside. It is
90 miles south of Columbus, the nearest town; there is no
public transportation available. The superintendent who
showed me around enthusiastically plied me with facts and
figures: the 80-acre area is surrounded by 2½ miles of two
double-wire, 16-foot-high security fences topped with seven
strands of barbed wire. Twenty feet inside this fence is a concrete wall topped with 14 strands of barbed wire. The 1½-
mile perimeter is guarded by eight gun towers. The prison
proper consists of 22 acres of building under one roof, to
accommodate 1,620 convicts in single cells measuring 6 feet
6 inches by 10 feet 6 inches.

We walked through seeming miles of vast, gleaming ceramic-
tiled corridors to the cell blocks. There workmen were in-
stalling fantastic Rube Goldberg electronic equipment in each
cell door, controlled by a central panel of buttons and levers
that looked something like an airplane dashboard. Television
monitors in three main control rooms allow guards to watch
the prisoners' every move. The cells, with their bars and
catwalks, were indistinguishable from others I had seen—
with one exception: they were variously painted in shades of
powder blue, baby pink, canary yellow.

Of the 1,620 cells, 240 were being especially equipped to
confine the anticipated quota of troublemakers, with unbreakable stainless steel toilets which, said the superintendent, cost
$600 apiece; 550 employees would be recruited from the
surrounding Appalachian foothills at a starting wage for
guards of $2.77 an hour . . . the very poor, guarding the even
poorer.

The eerie sense of observing misery under construction
deepened as we approached the 20-cell Death Row, adjacent

to which was the execution chamber, complete except for the electric chair which had not yet been delivered. (In 1972, after the Supreme Court ruling against the death penalty, the electric chair was countermanded and Lucasville Superintendent W. J. Whealon told the press, "We'll use the room for special treatment facilities for ungovernable disciplinary problems.")

My subsequent efforts to learn something of the background of Lucasville—who stood to gain and how from this vast enterprise—were unsuccessful; my letters to former Governor Rhodes, former Commissioner of Corrections Maury Koblentz and former Assistant Commissioner Beryl Sacks went unanswered. Apparently members of the Ohio Governor's Task Force on Corrections fared no better. One of these, Dr. Harry Allen of Ohio State University, wrote in answer to my inquiry: "I asked a staff assistant to examine the decision-making process by which Lucasville was created and to investigate the implementation procedure, including land purchase, history, and problems of Lucasville . . . In our final report, the task force concluded that the decision-making process could not be reconstructed at this time. In fact, the Lucasville institution is remarkable, in light of our inability to find any documentation in this area."

Two years after my visit, Ysabel Rennie, another member of the task force, told me of some of the uses to which Lucasville, now open for business, is being put. Following a sitdown strike at the London, Ohio, prison over demands for a democratic election of the inmate council, 91 inmates were "busted," she said. The newly elected council was disbanded by the authorities and its chairman was eventually shipped off to Lucasville, "along with every Black Muslim at London." Shortly before Christmas of 1972, the entire population of Chillecothe minimum-security prison conducted a work strike in which the main issues were unfair parole board practices and failure of the authorities to implement the work-furlough law. "They loaded 52 of the strikers into buses and took them off to Lucasville," said Mrs. Rennie.

In their campaign to halt new prison construction, the prisoners may find some unexpected allies. William Nagel, director of the influential American Foundation Institute of Corrections (a privately funded group that is frequently called on by government agencies to furnish research assistance), describes himself as "a prison man at the very core, with a background of eleven years as a disciplinarian, assistant to the superintendent, and deputy in a major institution." At the request of the Law Enforcement Assistance Administration he visited more than 100 new penal institutions in 26 states. He learned that budgets for prison construction, nationwide, in 1973 amount to over $6 billion and are expected to reach twice that amount. He says the prison building boom has become "a huge bonanza for architects, contractors, hardware companies who are cashing in on building all these better mousetraps with the latest in electronic gadgetry."

Mr. Nagel's efforts to discover what the federal Bureau of Prisons is planning in the way of new facilities were at first frustrated, he told me, as the bureau refused to answer any of his inquiries about details and costs of proposed construction. "Finally, I found somebody in the bureau who was willing to talk. I felt a little like Daniel Ellsberg, getting these super-secret plans! My informant says the bureau's budget for new buildings is already over $600 million. He showed me the architectural designs for Butner—Butner frightens me. There are no rooms or cells in the drawings, they are all labeled 'Behavior Modification Units.' "

Once an enthusiast for more cell space to relieve the desperate overcrowding in most jails and prisons, Mr. Nagel says he underwent an "agonizing reappraisal" during his two-year odyssey of new penal institutions, and has concluded that "prisons don't work, period."

He found demands for new prison building coming from every quarter: "The hard-liners are demanding more, not less cell space. The wardens and sheriffs insist their prisons are inadequate and must be replaced. The idealists, sickened by the inhuman conditions in so many of our jails and prisons, are lobbying for bright new replacements for those intolerable places. Civil libertarians argue that since our jails do not provide the basic protections and rights guaranteed by the Constitution, they should be replaced by new jails which do. Architects and contractors are quick to oblige." He advocates a moratorium on all prison building: "The prison is obsolete, cannot be reformed, should not be perpetuated through the false hope of forced treatment, and should be repudiated and abandoned."

In my view, such a moratorium should be a principal demand of all who are concerned with prisoner welfare. For the new prisons, whether the proposed "maxi-maxi" type that New York authorities are planning in response to Attica, the "tougher, more stringent" prisons for "problem inmates" in California, or the Behavior Modification Center in Butner, North Carolina, for "aggressive" federal prisoners, add up to one proposition: the establishment of a form of legal concentration camp to isolate and contain the rebellious and the political militant.

Arbeit macht Frei
—SIGN OVER ENTRANCE
TO NAZI CONCENTRATION CAMPS

11

EMPLOYMENT AND WELFARE

There is across-the-board agreement among prison administrators and reformers alike that "mere warehousing of prisoners" is to be avoided at all costs. This phrase, minted several generations ago by some unknown stylist of the profession, recurs in every treatise, every warden's speech, every popular book on the subject since the turn of the century. "The serious consequences of idleness have often been emphasized," says the American Correctional Association's *Manual of Correctional Standards*. "There is recognition of the great potential work programs have for the building of morale . . . contemporary authorities in the field of correction emphasize that the principal value of work activity is to be found in the opportunity it may afford for the inculcation, or the reactivation, of attitudes, skills, and habit patterns which can be instrumental in the rehabilitation of many offenders."

The description of inmate employment in the text accompanying the California budget is liberally garnished with reference to "meaningful work experience," "constructive employment," "training in work skills," "a means for many inmates to develop financial resources for use after release." In fact, although all prisoners are supposed to work "to the end that each may derive the greatest possible benefit from participation in such a work program," as the Director's Rule Book puts it, 70 percent receive no pay at all. The 30 percent who do get paid are compensated at wages of 2¢ to 16¢ an hour,* $2 to $24 a month. These wages are typical of prison pay throughout the country. (In 1963 the legislature raised the top wage to 35¢ an hour. Unable to find a single prisoner who receives this amount, I made inquiry of the Department of Corrections and was told the maximum can only be granted "with the approval of the director.")

The budget text speaks of an "incentive pay plan" in which the prisoner's "progression through the various pay steps is primarily related to attitudes, interest, performance, and skill level. Thus he is provided an incentive to put forth individual effort . . ." But a departmental directive to the institutions would suggest there are other factors at work in determining pay rates. To circumvent the undesirable situation in which too many inmates would be getting the higher rates of pay, the directive cautions that not more than 15 percent of inmate pay positions should be in the "special skills" category that starts at 8¢ an hour; no more than 40 percent in combined categories starting at 6¢ an hour; no more than 70 percent in the combined categories starting at 4¢ an hour. It is, however,

* From 5¢ to 19¢ as this book goes to press.

possible to rise within the categories, and a chart shows how this can be done. After his first 150 hours, the "special skills" man can get a raise to 10¢ an hour; after 1,500 hours, he may reach the top pay of 16¢. Likewise the laborer, starting at 2¢ an hour or $2 a month, may aspire to the top wage in his classification of 6¢ an hour, or $9 a month, after he has put in 1,500 hours of work.

The largest number of inmate jobs, some 11,000, are not in preparation for industry but for what is called Institution Upkeep, where the "meaningful work experiences" consist mainly of such janitorial tasks as sweeping tiers, bringing hot water to the cells, taking out kitchen garbage. As Raymond Procunier, director of Corrections, told a congressional sub-committee, "Inmates do all the maintenance work. If they didn't, we'd have to quadruple our staff." Two thirds of the 11,000 so employed receive no pay at all; they must perforce be satisfied with the joys of "constructive employment" and the "benefits of participation in such a work program." The majority of the 3,600 paid workers in Institution Upkeep get from $2 to $6 a month.

Since the prison runs almost entirely on convict labor, there are also many highly skilled and responsible jobs filled by prisoners. Whether these are paid or not depends on the whim of the administration. In the culinary department or the barbershop the "lead man" may get $6 to $18 a month, the others nothing; a clerical worker in the food department may get $5 a month; the secretary to the assistant warden, as high as $15.

About 2,000 inmates, 10 percent of the prison population, are employed in prison industries at an average wage of $3.40 a week. Yet a clue to how prison management evaluates the actual worth of convict labor is supplied in the 1968 budget in a "Schedule of Revenue per Inmate" (a table that has dis-appeared from subsequent budgets): estimates range from the woodworker who produces $5,587 worth of goods annually to the dairy worker whose production is valued at $14,279. Thus, assuming the dairy worker is getting the average wage of $3.40 a week, he is worth 86 times his wage.

From Mr. David Moore, chief fiscal officer of California's $13-million-a-year "correctional" industries, I learned that the industries employ 239 civil servants (33 of whom work in the Sacramento headquarters), drawing a payroll of $3,046,000 including fringe benefits, or an average of $12,000 a year, about 70 times as much as the convicts they supervise. Why are not the prisoners entitled to fringe benefits? "No reason I know of," said Mr. Moore. "I guess they're not citizens, so they're not entitled to the same rights."

Nor is there any provision for workmen's compensation and disability insurance for convicts, with the exception of fire-fighters in the conservation camps. Thus the man who is hurt on the job, perhaps permanently maimed, receives nothing in compensation for his injury. (The California legislature has taken pains to underline the hopeless situation of the prisoner injured at work by enacting a specific law which states: "A public entity is not liable for an injury to any prisoner." John Hill, a San Francisco lawyer, is currently challenging this law on behalf of an inmate at Vacaville, a skilled construction worker who was ordered to repair a third-story window despite his protests that the equipment was unsafe. He fell, shattering both legs and ankles, and will never walk again. In his reply brief the attorney general sounds a note of aggrieved indignation that the crippled prisoner should have the gall to sue for damages: "He is reduced to arguing that because he is a skilled worker, and because he was engaging in an alleged 'ultrahazardous activity' when he was injured, he and his injuries should not be treated like other prisoners and their injuries . . . There is no discrimination among prisoners . . . *All* prisoners are given the same rights under the same set of circumstances . . . Were appellant's argument to succeed, public entities would be liable for all injuries sustained by prisoners and the effect would be to hold Government Code section 844.6 wholly unconstitutional.")

Among the products of California prison industries are clothing, furniture, dairy products, canned goods—much of what is needed within the prison is produced by convict-workers. Colleges, mental hospitals, and other state agencies are required by law to purchase their needs in these categories from the prisons, at a price equivalent to the retail market price. The industries' customers, in order of sales volume: state colleges, Department of Corrections, Department of Mental Hygiene, Department of Motor Vehicles, Youth Authority, Highways Department.

As in other states, vehicle license plates are a prison industry monopoly. The license plate factory is a particularly sore spot with prisoners everywhere, since the skills needed to produce the plates are totally worthless on the outside.

Furthermore, prisoners say that when there is a heavy production schedule, key workers in the factory who would normally be eligible for parole find themselves mysteriously denied a release date. (This, they say, is true throughout prison industries—a man with some particular skill, for whom there is no ready replacement, will be out of luck when he comes before the parole board, who will tell him: "You're not ready, come back in a year.") Robert Montilla, for many years assistant administrator in the California Department of Corrections, confirms that the needs of prison industries take precedence over the much-vaunted "programing" and "classification" of prisoners according to their "individual progress." "When I was assistant to Richard McGee I was quite shocked," he told me, "because we could have dropped the population at San Quentin to 2,000 by transferring a number of men with good records to a minimum-security facility. But the conclusion was we *couldn't* reduce the number at San Quentin, there were too many commitments to the correctional industries."

What of the alleged "training in work skills" that the industries are supposed to provide? An appraisal of this aspect is succinctly set forth in a 1969 report by the California legislature's Assembly Office of Research. "California correctional industries consist of a set of relatively small business operations which employ inmates at blue-collar or menial occupations . . . the value of work habits and skills learned cannot be high," says the report. Machinery is "old and obsolete," skills taught are "often antiquated," employment provided is "little better than idleness." The report concludes dryly, "The departmental objective of reducing idleness is obviously achieved by correctional industry, but in a manner that is no more successful than other institutional 'busy-work' programs. The departmental objective of teaching work habits, attitudes, and skills that would be of value after release is not achieved."

However, a cursory look at the literature reveals that in the world of Corrections rehabilitation is in the eye of the corrector. Thus the National Institute for Public Health notes that "working on a chain gang is sometimes justified by the prison administration as helping prisoners to 'work off' hostilities and frustrations and develop 'good work habits.' " And at the 1965 Congress of the American Correctional Association, Mr. Thomas Summers, executive vice-president of a laundry management consulting firm, extols the rehabilitative value of "sorting, folding, and stacking" laundry: "It teaches good work habits, requiring team work."

Since prison industries now exist in every state and in the federal prisons, replacing the old contract labor system of the last century, a word about their development might be in order.

The twin themes of idleness, that well-known Devil's playground, and the reformative effect of hard labor on convicts were much in vogue with the early nineteenth-century penologists, providing as they did an appropriate moral justification for contract labor. Under this system convicts were contracted out to private employers who reimbursed the prison for their labor. The prisons for a while prospered and grew rich; that crime could be made to pay was proved by Auburn Prison, which from 1828 to 1833 netted over $25,000 in profits.

Toward the end of the last century, contract labor came under attack from a number of quarters: the industrial competitors of the contractors, trade unions, humanitarians who deplored the barbarous conditions to which convicts were subjected, and some prison administrators.

From their debates on the subject as reported in the proceedings of early prison congresses, it appears the objections of prison management to contract labor were threefold: the contractors tended to usurp too much authority, sometimes virtually taking over the prison and relegating the warden to a subordinate role. The immense profits from contract labor, much of it siphoned off by the contractor-middlemen, could just as well be garnered in toto by the prison. And, as the chaplain of the Kansas Penitentiary said at the 1870 Prison Congress, "This contract system is ruinous to the moral improvement of the prisoners. There is but little hope of reforming them while they are thus confined to servile labor from early in the morning until late in the evening, without a moment's opportunity to devote to the welfare of their souls."

Opposition to contract labor was formalized in the 1870 Declaration of Principles of the American Prison Association: "While industrial labor in prisons, in whatever aspect viewed, is of the highest importance and utility, we regard the contract system of prison labor as prejudicial alike to discipline, finance, and reformation . . . ultimately it must fall; and the sooner it falls the better." And fall it did, given a strong shove by the emergent labor movement, which regarded this use of convict labor as a threat to trade unionism and a potential strike-breaking weapon.

By the mid-1930's contract labor had disappeared from the scene altogether, supplanted by "prison industries." These have achieved their finest flowering in the federal prison system, initially under the leadership of James V. Bennett, a Herbert Hoover appointee who served for three decades as director of the federal Bureau of Prisons. Something of the missionary zeal that infused the early efforts to establish the prison industries corporation can be inferred from his book, *I Chose Prison*, in which he describes how with the support of FDR and Mrs. Roosevelt he overcame labor opposition to the scheme. Mr. Bennett was called to the White House for a conference with William Green, then president of the AFL. "Roosevelt explained to Green the purpose of the proposed Prison Industries Corporation and the broader importance of rehabilitation, and asked for Green's cooperation." Reluctant at first, Green suddenly caved in and agreed to cooperate—"a political debt Roosevelt doubtless repaid in some other coin," Mr. Bennett surmises.

It is indeed a curious phenomenon that from its inception in 1935 the Federal Prison Industries Corporation has received the active backing of the conservative wing of the labor movement. For years, George Meany has sat on the board of directors with the retired president of the Marshall Field Company, the vice-president of Owens-Corning Fiberglass Corporation, a senior partner of the Universal Vise and Tool Company.

Today, Federal Prison Industries, Inc., is far and away the most profitable line of business in the country. Profits on sales in 1970 were 17 percent (next highest is the mining industry with 11 percent)—the average for all U.S. industries is 4.5 percent. The board of directors' annual report summarizes the success story: over a thirty-five-year period, 1935 to 1970, the industries grossed $896 million, increasing their net worth by $50 million and contributing $82 million in dividends to the U.S. Treasury—thus, like it or not, we are all shareholders in the proceeds of captive labor. Because the Army is a major customer (the industries supply it with everything from military dress shoes to electronic cable), the war years have been especially good to prison industries. A chart in the report depicts successive peak periods under the headings "WW II," "Korea," "Vietnam," the latter responsible for a spectacular rise in sales from $38 million to $60 million over a seven-year-period.

The secret of this immense profitability is not hard to discover; in fact it is laid out for us in the board of directors' report. Pay rates for inmate workers in the federal industries range from 19¢ to 47¢ an hour (as in California the great majority are in the lower pay brackets; the average wage is 26¢ an hour). In 1970, 5,478 inmates earned $3 million for an average wage of $547 a year. In the same year, the report informs us, annual production for each inmate worker was $12,168, and the average profit per worker stood at $2,350.

The report does not mention that in early 1971 a full-fledged strike, supported by over 90 percent of the convicts, broke out in McNeil Island Federal Penitentiary, largely over the inadequacy of job training provided by prison industries and the demand for a 35 percent wage increase. I asked Mr. Norman Carlson, director of the federal Bureau of Prisons, why the bureau refused the demonstrably modest demand for an increase that would have raised the average wage from 26¢ to 35¢ an hour. He answered, as employers are wont to do, "We'd go broke if they got a 35 percent increase." This, in a year when net profits were close to $10 million.

Texas boasts a comparable success with prison industries. "The enemy is inmate idleness, so you put him to work," writes Jack Waugh in the *Christian Science Monitor*. "Working that philosophy, George Beto [director of the Texas Department of Corrections] has built the Texas prison system into a clean, highly disciplined industrial dynasty." Of the 60¢ a day per inmate allotted for food, only 13¢ worth has to be bought. Prison industries in Texas, says Waugh, generated $7,083,077 in sales from September 1970 through August 1971, and he describes the new prisoner's introduction to the clean industrial dynasty: "The first job every inmate gets coming into the Texas system, if he is able-bodied, is six months on the line—hard, back-bending labor in the fields, and recalcitrant, rebellious prisoners are often sent back to the line as punishment. Armed bosses on horseback supervise as the inmates stoop in the fields. A boss called the 'long arm,' with high-powered rifle over his saddlehorn, watches from a distance for any sign of an attempted break."

From the convict's point of view the changeover from contract labor to prison industries is merely a switch in labels, as comments from two widely disparate sources show. In an interview with Mark Lane, published in the *Black Panther,* Huey P. Newton explains why he refused to work while imprisoned in California, choosing instead to suffer the punishment of solitary confinement for more than a year: "'The prison is a capitalistic enterprise. It differs very little from the system where inmates are 'farmed out' to growers. In those instances the growers compensate the state. Most civilized people agree that that system is abhorrent. Yet the California method is to employ the reverse system. The convicts are not farmed out, the work is farmed in. What factors remain the same? The convicts are still exploited by the state; the work still is accomplished; the state is still compensated."

His words were echoed by Milton G. Rector, executive director of the National Council of Crime and Delinquency, addressing an audience of Texan public workers: "Both systems [contract labor and prison industry] have exploited the prisoner literally as a slave worker of the state or federal government. In 1970 over $165 million in goods were produced by convict labor and purchased for government use while the inmates were paid but a few cents per hour or per day. While business and labor have been told prison industry does not compete, government has produced with prison labor what government should otherwise have purchased from private business and industry."

Although contract labor is now specifically prohibited by the California constitution, it still flourishes in certain recesses of the prison. For example, the Director's Rules state that the California Correctional Officers Association, or guards' organization, may "contract with the institutions" for a wide range of personal services for themselves and their families, including shoeshine, barbering, car wash and polishing, laundry, dry-cleaning, tailoring repairs, minor household and furniture repairs, guards' snack bar and store, meals in employees' dining room, clerical work for the association. For many of these jobs the convicts are paid nothing. For others they may rise through the usual pay categories from 2¢ to 16¢ an hour.

The guards, waited on by what amounts to a legion of unpaid servants, come out of it very well indeed. They and their families receive almost every conceivable personal service at a fraction of the normal price: tailoring alterations, household repairs, watch repairs, shoe repairs, all at cost of materials; 12¢ per garment for dry-cleaning, 5¢ for a shoeshine, 60¢ to $1 for a four-course meal cooked and served by prisoners in the employees' dining room. These fees do not revert to the prisoners but are paid into the tax-exempt California Correctional Officers Association.

Clerical work of the organization is performed by convicts for an average wage of $5 a month, for a saving to the guards' organization of $500 to $600 a month per worker at prevailing wages on the outside. Thus the convicts, with an assist from the taxpayers, are in effect financing the lobbying activities of this organization, whose aims include "housing revolutionary inmates in a separate, ultra-maximum security institution where privileges will be held to a minimum"; reinstatement of the death penalty, for which campaign CCOA set aside $50,000 in 1971–72; "investigation and prosecution" of organizations that have assisted convicts such as the National Lawyers Guild, California Rural Legal Assistance, Citizens Committee for Prison and Parole Reform.

The systematic exploitation of the prisoner does not end with his labor. The prisons manage to snatch back for their own use a goodly portion of the convict's meager daily wage, plus money sent to him by his family, through a peculiar piece of extortion variously labeled "Inmate Welfare Fund," "Amusement and Recreation Fund," "Inmate Commissary Fund." These mysterious funds are run in pretty much the same fashion in prisons throughout the country and are a source of intensely bitter resentment among the prisoners, as evidenced by the invariable inclusion of the management of the funds in lists of prisoners' grievances.

In California the Inmate Welfare Fund, established by the legislature in 1945, is clearly an insignificant portion of the total budget (about $3.5 million a year in a budget of $110 million). Yet the administration of this fund perhaps tells us more about the quality of prison life from the convict's viewpoint than any amount of probing into top- and middle-echelon pilfering and mismanagement. We are by now thoroughly inured to misuse of the taxpayer's money by incompetents and grafters at all levels of government—a week's reading of Jack Anderson's column will supply the indignant taxpayer with a year's ammunition on this score. But as Mr. Roy Backman, manager of the Inmate Welfare Fund, told me, "It's not taxpayer's money, it's sort of a stepchild." Rather it is convicts' money, not subject to scrutiny by the Department of Finance or the state legislature, administered and controlled solely by the director of Corrections, who allocates it as he sees fit and is under no obligation to consult the prisoners or anybody else about the use of the money.

Resources of the fund include interest on convict trust accounts held in the state treasury, profits from prison canteens and handicraft sales, "forfeiture of inmates' earnings prescribed by law," a 10 percent charge to outside organizations and research projects that avail themselves of convict labor, occasional gifts from philanthropists who contribute to the fund in the fond belief that they are providing some extra treats for the prisoners.

The inmate's first introduction to his Welfare Fund comes when he enters prison and is required to sign a power of attorney which contains three provisions: (1) He authorizes "deposit in the Welfare Fund of all interest on monies held in trust" for him—*but* he is not informed that he will never see this interest again, that he is donating it to the fund, that he will have no say at all as to how it will be spent. (2) He appoints the director of Corrections as his "true and lawful attorney-in-fact" with authority to collect checks, drafts, warrants, "or other securities that become due to me from any source whatsoever" for deposit in his Inmate Trust Account, thus relinquishing all rights to handle his personal transactions. (3) He consents to having his mail opened and examined. Should he balk at signing this three-pronged agreement he forfeits all rights to correspond with the outside world, for the Director's Rules specify that "you shall not be permitted to send or receive a package or communication of any nature until you have signed the required form consenting to the opening of same and examination of its contents." He will also be barred from buying in the canteen.

Neither is he permitted to send his money to an outside savings account where interest could be accumulated for him against his release date, except in increments of $100, and only then if he maintains a balance of $200 in his Inmate Trust Account—and less than 5 percent of all California prisoners have $200 or more. He may not send any of his money to family or friends except in "special circumstances" with the approval of the director. (Until 1972 money could only be sent out in increments of $500. The new rule, like some other recent innovations, was enacted at the insistence of a group of legislators who make it their business to intervene from time to time against some of the more flagrant injustices of prison.) Thus if a man serves, say, a ten-year sentence and maintains an average balance of $100 in his trust account, he will have forfeited to the state approximately $55 at current interest rates by the time he gets out.

Money scraped together by the prisoner's family cannot be sent directly to him, for the Director's Rules state that: "funds may be sent to you only by money orders or certified checks made payable to the Department of Corrections." Gifts of cash from outside and the convict's earnings in prison, if any, are deposited in his trust account, held in the state treasury, and invested in U.S. securities. About $50,000 a year is realized for the Inmate Welfare Fund from interest on these trust accounts.

The principal source of revenue for the Inmate Welfare Fund is profits from the canteens, about $500,000 a year. The prison canteen is a paradigm of the infamous company store that once flourished in remote mining towns, textile centers, southern plantations. As a condition of their employment, workers were compelled to buy in the company store at extortionist prices set by the employer; in many instances workers were paid in scrip to assure against their trading elsewhere.

In prison, cash money is likewise contraband. The prisoner is allowed to draw up to $40 a month in scrip from his Inmate Trust Fund (although very few have sufficient funds to draw this amount). All purchases must be made through the canteens, which, in the incomparable language of the Director's Rules, "contribute to good morale among the inmates, permit the enjoyment of harmless luxuries which the state cannot in good conscience supply, and promote the self-respect of inmates by providing a legitimate means for them to obtain items which they might otherwise attempt to secure through irregular channels." The harmless luxuries consist of ice cream, canned goods, cheese, soft drinks, stationery, cigarettes, soap, toothpaste—the kind of merchandise stocked in a rural Mom and Pop store, or an Army PX. Prices are fixed by the individual canteen manager (there is no central pricing policy), pegged anywhere from 10 to 50 percent higher than those in the supermarket; the canteens realize an average gross profit of over 22 percent and a net of 13 percent, compared with a prevailing 1 percent net that is claimed in the outside market. (Nor do they ever put merchandise on special sale. In response to a written question about this from the Assembly Office of Research, the department replied with unaccustomed candor: "Since the canteen sales are made only to the 'captive population,' the potential revenue is limited. Therefore, the fund cannot run specials on loss-leader items to encourage more sales. This may indicate that inmates are paying premium prices if the normal prices are compared to sale items in local communities.") Some canteens even levy a surcharge on postage. A price list from Men's Colony East shows "postcards, 2 for 15¢." Why? Because, I was told, the canteens only deal in multiples of a nickel. Air mail letters run 3¢ higher for the same reason. Thus the 2¢-an-hour man must work for 1½ hours just to pay the overcharge on his postcards or air letters.

Should the prisoner want to order something not in stock, the transaction must go through the canteen, which levies a 10 percent surcharge on a sum compounded of the cost of the merchandise, sales tax, and postage. As one wrote, "When the inmate orders an item (say, a footlocker from Sears for $11.97), he has to pay the initial cost of the item, then add California state sales tax, then add the cost of postage from the vendor to the institution, then—and only then—add an additional 10 percent of the entire sum of the above, which purportedly goes to the Inmate Welfare Fund. And the end result of an $11.97 order is in the neighborhood of $15 or $16." What if the prisoner's family wants to make him a present of the footlocker? They are barred from sending it to him, instead must send enough cash, computed as above, through the regular channels.

The inmate handicraft worker, who produces leather goods,

ceramics, and the like for sale in the prison gift shop, is penalized at both ends of the transaction. He buys his own tools and materials from the prison (again, he is not permitted to have them sent from outside) and is charged 10 percent above the retail cost for these. If he makes a sale, 10 percent is deducted from the price received. Prison artists fare even worse; they must forfeit 25 percent of the price realized from their paintings. (Until recently, prison writers were docked 25 percent of fees paid them by publishers, a "rule" struck down as unconstitutional by the California Supreme Court in 1971.)

What of expenditures from the fund? These are carefully concealed from the convict population in the financial summaries that are posted from time to time in the prison libraries and canteens, which merely list assets and liabilities.

The Penal Code provides that the fund shall be used for "inmate benefits," defined as "an item or service for the exclusive use of inmates for entertainment, recreation, and other leisure-time activities." As interpreted by the prison administration, these include:

1. Salaries and fringe benefits for some 50 civil service employees, including several guards: about $450,000 a year, or an average wage of $175 a week.

2. Wages (but no fringe benefits) for 500 convict employees of the fund: $16,000, or an average of 60¢ a week.

3. Printing presses, duplicating machines, and operating expenses for the so-called inmate newspaper, a vehicle for staff communication with the prison population; as set forth in the *Administrative Manual*, its purpose is "the dissemination to the inmates of information from the administration." Content of the newspaper is controlled by the warden, and convict writers are prohibited by the Director's Rules from criticizing the prison in its columns; the publication "may not be used to attack any law, rule, or policy to which inmates may object," nor may it "take an editorial position on matters pend-

ing before the legislature." Although the printing equipment is theoretically owned by the Inmate Welfare Fund, it is used by the prison administration and the California Correctional Officers Association for printing announcements, official documents, directives to staff, and the like—without reimbursement to the fund. There is no inventory of any of the equipment allegedly "owned" by the inmates.

4. Pro-rata charges, amounting to some $40,000 a year, levied against the fund by other government departments. Example: the Inmate Welfare Fund reimburses the General Fund to the tune of $18,000 a year for "legislative services," a designation that merely means a payment toward the general cost of the legislature. "The Inmate Welfare Fund bears a hell of a disproportionate burden of the pro-rata costs of central government," said my source in the State Audit Department. "Basically, it's a charge for administrative costs." Until 1972 the fund was assessed around $1,600 for the Finance Audits Department. But in 1971 Assemblywoman Yvonne Brathwaite Burke, at the request of prisoners, introduced a bill requiring a biennial audit of the fund, copies to be posted in the prison canteens and libraries. Of a number of prison reform bills passed that year this was the only one that was unopposed by the Department of Corrections and that survived Governor Reagan's veto. The reason becomes clear when one learns that under the new law the Inmate Welfare Fund will be charged $15,000 a year for the same kind of audit it has been getting—formerly, for the pro-rata charge of $1,600 to the Finance Department.

5. Television sets, movies, "fiction books" for the libraries, athletic supplies—all considered by prison administrators to be indispensable to the smooth running of the prison. "Television might have been considered a luxury when it was first introduced in the fifties," said Mr. Montilla. "Today it's a necessity, an adjunct to custody essential to the maintenance of order and discipline."

As summed up by my source in the audit division, the Inmate Welfare Fund is in fact merely an accounting fiction, a convenient source of petty cash to be dipped into at will by the administration. "It doesn't belong to the inmates, it belongs to the state," he said. "It's not a trust fund, any more than the general state fund is. In effect they run the joints out of money from the Inmate Welfare Fund—it's an extortion racket, an illegal use of prisoners' money. It's just another fund for accounting purposes, a euphemism called 'inmate welfare' to make it sound good."

So good does it sound that in 1969 Johnny Cash and Columbia Records were moved to make a contribution of $10,000 apiece to the Inmate Welfare Funds of Folsom and San Quentin as an expression of gratitude to the convicts for their participation in making the hit records "Johnny Cash in Folsom Prison" and "Johnny Cash in San Quentin." Johnny Cash received assurance from Mr. Philip D. Guthrie, information officer of the Department of Corrections, that the money would be used "only for the purchase of recreational and entertainment items for inmates . . . money in the Inmate Welfare Fund cannot be diverted to other purposes, but is reserved exclusively for inmate benefit expenditures. The life of men in prison is at best very difficult and lonely. The money will be put to good use in behalf of all the men in Folsom and San Quentin." Cash had asked that the gift be given no publicity, but said he would like the inmates to be informed of it. To this, Mr. Guthrie responded that it would be unwise to tell the inmates because "most of the major columnists have sources of information inside the prisons. It is likely they eventually would pick up news of the gift if it became generally known to the inmate body."

In spite of administration efforts to keep the contribution secret, rumors of it spread through the prison grapevine, but the convicts were unable to discover what had happened to it. My inquiry to the business managers of Folsom and San

Quentin, three years after the donation had been received, elicited this information as to how Johnny Cash's generous gift was being used to cheer the "difficult and lonely" lives of prisoners: the largest single expenditure from the fund was for a jitney train at San Quentin for visitors to ride in (never seen by the prisoners, as visitors are permitted only outside the prison proper). Other expenditures were for folding chairs, furniture, two television sets. None of Folsom's share had been spent. An unspent balance of $10,000 remains in Folsom's treasury and $4,772 in San Quentin's, drawing interest for the nonexistent Inmate Welfare Fund.

Reports from around the country would indicate that prison administrations learn from each other in regard to the handling of inmate funds. In the spring of 1972, striking prisoners in the Arizona State Prison charged in their ten-point "Curriculum for Reform" that "the current monies existing within the Athletic and Recreation Fund are being misused and misappropriated by the present administration. We demand all monies spent from the A. and R. Fund have the approval of a convict committee and that the general population be kept abreast of the amount of money in the existing fund."

One of the 28 demands in Attica was "Investigate the alleged expropriation of inmate funds." A year earlier, strikers at Folsom demanded "annual accounting of the Inmate Welfare Fund and formation of an inmate committee to give inmates a voice as to how such funds are used."

A letter from Indiana State Prison describes how the fund works in that institution: "There's a neat little scheme called the 'Inmate Commissary Fund' which at times has had balances in excess of $80,000. Cons are ripped off at the commissary with exorbitant prices on almost every single item. Supposedly the profits from commissary go into this fund to purchase recreation equipment, but that's a laugh. In addition, all commissary personnel wages are paid from this fund, although most of the workers are hired in as guards and are funded through regular legislative budget allowances. Recently Michigan City residents donated a mobile trailer to the prison so that inmates might display and sell handicraft items, but the state has placed a 10 percent claimer on all items sold from the trailer, supposedly to pay the civilian clerk."

Lastly, work furlough, a new star in the correctional firmament. Modeled after systems long in use in socialist regimes and Scandinavian countries, the program permits the prisoner to work on an outside job while returning to prison at night, the idea being that he should support himself and family while being simultaneously punished for his misdeeds and prepared for reentry into society. Since the late fifties, work furlough has found increasingly wide acceptance in American prison administration circles; as James V. Bennett put it, "The work release program is basically sound in concept and a surpassingly useful and practical method of promoting the rehabilitation of the offender and prevention of recidivism."

It is also a surpassingly useful and practical method of supplementing county jail and state prison budgets, providing sinecures for an inordinate number of guards and other "correctional" employees, and supplying cheap labor to nonunion employers.

In California, work furlough was initiated on an experimental basis for county jail inmates in 1957 and expanded to include state prisoners in 1966. By the early seventies the program had grown to accommodate some 700 county and 200 state prisoners at any given time. Some are housed in county jails, others in centers established for the purpose, still others commute to work from San Quentin.

A Department of Corrections handout, titled "Work Furlough: A Success Story," depicts several happy-looking, smartly dressed men and women, some striding purposefully to work with attaché case in hand through a door marked "Administration," others on the job as salesman, office worker, carpenter, executive, woman doctor, with these captions: "This man is a prisoner. While in jail, he is able to continue earning a living and supporting a family—because of work furlough." "This woman is a prisoner. Because of work furlough, she can continue her professional career." "This man is a prisoner. He is the sole support of his mother, brother, and sisters. Because of work furlough, they need not go on relief." The work furlough program, says the leaflet, "saves people, preserves man's dignity and respect, aids in rehabilitation."

A more accurate portrayal would show convicts engaged in "stoop labor" in the fields of California's giant farming industry, washing dishes in skid-row cafeterias, sweeping out warehouses and garages. Far from the pleasant white-collar occupations depicted in the handout, work furlough jobs are overwhelmingly of the unskilled, nonunion, minimum wage, dead-end variety for which the take-home pay is in the neighborhood of $10 to $16 a day—most of which, it develops, the prisoner never sees.

On entering the program the prisoner signs an agreement under which, in addition to promising never to be late getting back from work ("willful failure" to return promptly is "punishable as an escape"), he assigns "ALL MONEY to become due me" (caps in the original) to the program administrator. The latter parcels out the pay check as follows: off the top comes a per diem charge, which ranges from $3 to $7 a day, depending on where the prisoner is housed. If the prisoner's family is on welfare (ascertained in advance by his keepers), a portion goes to reimburse the Welfare Department. He may also be required to pay off outstanding fines and debts. An amount determined by the administrator is returned to the prisoner for his personal expenses.

For jail and prison administrators, the per diem collected from men and women on work furlough represents something of a windfall. Tim Fitzharris, a criminologist who spent some time studying work release in a number of states, concluded that the dollar return is the "selling punch" which convinces local officials to experiment with the program. Thus the sheriff of San Joaquin County, which maintains a work furlough population of 350, was able to report to his board of supervisors in 1967 that "new dollar income" for the county from work furlough was "well over half a million dollars."

The California Department of Corrections in its 1970–71 budget report says that over a four-year period 1,071 state prisoners on work furlough earned a total of $840,000, of which almost half was appropriated by the state: $200,000 to the counties for "cost of care," $100,000 to the Department of Corrections for "administration and supervision," $100,000 in withholding and income tax. There are additional hidden financial benefits to the prison. The work furlough man buys his own clothing. He is not entitled to receive the $68 "gate money" on his release; thus, in four years the prison chalked up a saving of $72,828 in gate money alone on these 1,071 prisoners.

Employers, Fitzharris found, are enthusiastic about work furlough, referred to jocularly by some as "rent-a-con." In response to his questionnaire 75 percent of the agricultural employers said they have come to rely heavily on convict labor to see them through the peak periods of cultivation and harvesting. One farm labor contractor said, "It's been good for me. Since I got into it, it would be hard to do without it"; if work furlough inmates were removed from the market, he added, he would probably have to cut his fleet of ten buses in half. And an aircraft parts foreman: "I'll tell you, if it hadn't been for county inmates we would have had trouble keeping the plant operating at times."

A particularly attractive feature of the program from the employers' viewpoint is the fact the men are still prisoners, subject to the iron discipline of jail and thus unlikely to be late for work, show up with a hangover, be absentee—or join a union. "Less of a problem than the regular employee," "Sober and clean," "In better condition than some men I get off the street," were typical employer verdicts. In fact, a Los Angeles probation officer told Fitzharris that many employers had hopefully inquired whether it would be possible to keep the men on the furlough program past their release date: " 'They never worked so well,' say the employers."

To qualify for work furlough the state prisoner must be within five months of parole. From those who remain in San Quentin, the prison exacts $36.75 a week, or $159.25 a month, for what they are told is "room and board." (In contrast, guards who live on the grounds of San Quentin pay $35 to $75 a month rent for pleasant two- or three-bedroom family homes.)

A prisoner writes: "This 'work furlough' swindle I'm into has me uptight but good. It has turned out to be nothing but another arm of the extortionary canteen, another 'inmate welfare' scam. They charge us $36.75 per week rent and feed us the same garbage the men on the mainline eat. We are compelled to furnish our own transportation and come and go on a schedule they make up on pain of getting 'rolled up' and losing our parole dates. Everybody here is hot-hot-hot about it. They do nothing to help us but do everything to exploit and keep us all angry. If your per diem is not paid up to the moment (including paying $5.25 for the day of your release), they will not give you your 60-day time cut as per Adult Authority resolution. Moreover, they stall the paperwork on say four out of six men from one to two weeks so that they may suck more of our blood in the form of rent. This swindle is shocking to the conscience, believe me . . ."

Since the prisoner's room is already there, and his board, according to the budget, amounts to less than $7 a week, why this high charge? I asked Mr. Philip Guthrie, chief of Community Relations and Information for the Department of Corrections, how the figure was arrived at. It turns out the per diem is not for room and board at all. He told me, "This rate is computed on the basis of reimbursing the state for the salary costs for one parole agent, one sergeant, and four officers."

At first glance this seems odd of Mr. Guthrie, whose job it is to cast the department and all its works in the most favorable light possible. For while it might seem reasonable to require the prisoner with an outside job to pay the actual cost of his upkeep, it does not seem right that he should be compelled to pay the wages of his guards. It develops, however, that the department may offer this explanation of the fees charged to avoid legal culpability, for in 1971 the California Supreme Court raised some questions about the constitutionality of charging prisoners for room and board.

The court's opinion in this case, *Pitts v. Reagan*, contains some revealing facts about the uses to which the state puts work furlough. In 1967, Governor Reagan announced he had "authorized the use of prison labor in Merced County to assist in the harvest of figs and prevent a disastrous crop loss." He instructed the Department of Corrections to set up an Emergency Harvesting Program, under which several hundred prisoners were bused to work each day at the expense of the growers, who also paid the salaries of their guards. Wages were paid on a piecework basis. "These wages, however, were delivered to the state, which retained a portion to cover 'expenses incurred,'" said the court. "Among the 'expenses incurred' by the state was a charge of $5 per day against each man for room and board." At one prison, the total wages paid to the inmates by the growers were $43,585—of which the state pocketed $20,122. Observing that picking figs "does not resemble a rehabilitation program," the court concluded that the Emergency Harvesting Program was in violation of the California constitutional prohibition against letting out convict labor. It added: "Although unnecessary to our resolution of the appeal, it is noted that the evidence would support a finding that part of the convicts' wages was in fact retained by the state and not credited to the convicts' accounts . . . Since the men were prisoners confined, even during the harvesting, in state prisons, the state was under an obligation to maintain them . . ."

In San Francisco, some 70 state and county prisoners on work furlough are housed in a disused warehouse in the heart of the industrial district. "It's a horrendous place, a foul barracks," I was told, yet no description could have prepared me for the scene: a parody of desolate bleakness, a contrived stage-set for an avant-garde play about the despair of the human condition. One enters through a "day room" guard station and offices to the right, to the left rows of straight wooden benches for the residents. Beyond that is a vast, barnlike dormitory crammed with steel bunk-beds and metal lockers, a broken television set in one corner; men sleep two-tiered, there are no partitions, no chairs, the only lighting some naked overhead bulbs.

There are no cooking facilities, so the residents are obliged to pay restaurant prices for their meals. The charge for occupying one of those bunk-beds: $21 a week for those on furlough from the county jail, $28.70 for men from San Quentin—the extra $7.70 being for "state administrative costs of the program."

From Mr. T. Wallace Takiguchi, administrator of this bizarre place, I learned some work furlough facts and figures. There is a staff of 13 to watch over the 70 residents: 4 from the probation department, a state coordinator and his aide for the state prisoners, 7 guards. "We have custody here twenty-four hours a day. The guards work on round-the-clock shifts, two in the daytime hours and one on the midnight shift." What, I wondered, could keep this large staff busy all day? "The guards' duties are strictly custody. They check the inmates in and out for work and meals." The inmates are allowed one hour for eating, said Mr. Takiguchi. If a man is late checking in, he risks arrest for escape. No visitors are allowed except on Sundays, between 10 A.M. and 3 P.M. Has he ever considered trying to make some improvements in the place? "I asked for $200 a year for television repair, but that was refused. I also put in a request for bars on the back windows, to prevent escapes, but I was turned down on that too." What would be the point of having bars—if they are out on the job all day, couldn't they just walk away? "Oh, they're like children—it's more fun to escape out of the window." The median age of these fun-loving kids is thirty-eight.

Since the work-furloughee is ineligible for the $68 "gate money" normally furnished to released prisoners, yet is compelled to pay over most of his earnings to the state, he frequently ends up worse off than the man released to the streets. Tim Findley, writing in the San Francisco *Chronicle*, relates a typical work furlough experience in the San Francisco establishment. "Tony," inmate of San Quentin, had a couple of good-sounding job offers, both requiring personal interviews. He was put on work furlough to allow him to make those interviews. The interviews fell through, through no fault of his own, so after a week the authorities got him a job driving a truck at $1.90 an hour. By the time Tony got his first paycheck he was two weeks behind in rent alone. Including money loaned to him for meals, he owed the state $88, and his paycheck was $89. "He would pay his rent from his paycheck, but that would leave him with almost nothing to live on the rest of the week and no place to sleep once he was off work furlough," writes Findley. Tony, now broke and homeless, told Findley: "It's like I did all this time for taking money, and now here I was again. It was almost like I was being forced to do wrong."

Thus throughout his term in prison, and for as long thereafter as he remains in custody of the Department of Corrections, the prisoner's wretchedly meager resources are methodically tapped by the prison establishment for its own uses, to provide sinecures for guards and other civil service personnel. In those three minuscule areas of the budget where one might suppose there was some opportunity for the prisoner to improve his lot by his own efforts and to exercise a degree of independent decision-making—prison employment, the Inmate Welfare Fund, and the work furlough program—he encounters systematized exploitation and officially sanctioned thievery, much of it in direct violation of the law and the California constitution, all carried out in the name of "rehabilitation" and "inmate benefits."

In the course of my reading—by no means confined
to law—I have reviewed many of the world's religions.
The tenets of many faiths hold the deity to be a trinity.
Seemingly, the parole boards, by whatever names
designated in the various states, have in too
many instances sought to enlarge this to include
themselves as members.
— JUSTICE HUGO BLACK
U.S. Supreme Court

12

PAROLE

" 'Parole granted'—the most breathlessly anticipated phrase
in the English language for more than 200,000 individuals
now serving time in this nation's prisons. 'Parole denied'—
the most terribly feared phrase ever uttered to any of the
same 200,000 individuals." So writes one of the authors of
An Eye for an Eye, a book by four convicts in the Indiana
State Penitentiary.

Nationwide, for some 60 percent of the inmates of state
and federal prisons, parole is the prescribed path to eventual
freedom. Another 38 percent are discharged at the expiration

of their sentence; the remaining 2 percent achieve release by escaping, or dying in prison. Within these figures there are wide variations by state: in eight states, including California, more than 90 percent of prisoners are paroled, in four others, less than 20 percent.

What happens then? Of those released on parole, large numbers are soon returned to prison. Not only does the newly paroled convict face staggering difficulties in such rudimentary matters as finding a job, a place to live, adjusting to an unfamiliar world after long years in prison, but he also lives under the shadow of arbitrary re-imprisonment at the decision of his parole agent.

"They've set up the whole system to make you fail," said one parolee. "I guess they have a business going in this state and once they get you hooked into the system they don't want to let you go. They want you to come back. They let you out of here on a yo-yo. You're out there a little while, then they pull the string, zap, you're back. They got a good thing going here, man, can't you see it. They don't want to lose you."

The desperate situation in which the newly released parolee finds himself was described to me by Mark Dowie, executive director of a San Francisco convict-help organization called Transitions to Freedom. "He arrives without a job in an urban area, after years in prison, with perhaps $20 or $30 in his pocket. Surviving is a trick, even if he's a frugal person, not inclined to blow his few dollars on drinks and women. The parole agents—with some remarkable exceptions—don't give a damn. He's deposited in the very middle of the city, where all he can find is a fleabag hotel in the Tenderloin. He has an aching determination to make it on the outside, but there are hustlers all over him; gambling con games, dollar poker."

If he is black and under thirty, he joins the largest group of unemployed in the country with the added handicap of his ex-convict status. Some of his problems are more subtle: he has literally forgotten what the outside world is like, is disoriented, unable to cope with the simplest aspects of everyday living—ordering something at a hot-dog stand, producing the right change for a bus ride, even crossing a busy street. In *The Felon*, John Irwin quotes a newly released convict: "The first time I started across the street, I remember, I was watching a car coming and I couldn't judge his speed very good. I couldn't tell if he was going to hit me or not. It was weird."

The twin objectives of parole are protection of the public through surveillance of the ex-convict, and his rehabilitation through the guidance and help of the parole agent. As defined in the President's Crime Commission Report: "Supervision consists basically of a combination of surveillance and counseling, drawing partly upon the methods identified with social casework, but distinguished by the need to enforce authoritative limits and standards of behavior." And as described by former U.S. Senator Charles E. Goodell and Andrew von Hirsch of the Committee for the Study of Incarceration, testifying before the House Judiciary Committee: "Parole involves placing the offender under supervision by an official who is supposed to combine the function of maintaining surveillance over him with that of providing him with supportive services. These dual roles—of policeman and helper—tend to conflict."

The parolee has been described as a "walking suspension of the constitution." Deemed to have lost all rights, he is in a state of "civil death." His legal status (if one may call it that) rests on a mishmash of common-sense-defying legal fictions that have grown up over the last century derived from case law, legislation, administrative fiat of the parole board, and ancient tradition. To summarize its main aspects:

The theory of grace: The granting of parole is an act of grace, comparable to the pardoning power that was once the prerogative of the monarchy. As such, it is infected from the outset with the arbitrariness and unpredictability that is characteristic of penal institutions and other autocracies. The prisoner theoretically has no right to any reduction of his sentence from the maximum imposed by the judge, or prescribed by law under the indeterminate sentence. But in fact in the more "advanced" prison systems, parole is eventually granted to virtually all prisoners; far from being an occasional act of clemency, it has evolved into an integral and essential part of the penal system.

The constructive custody theory: Although the prisoner is walking the streets, he is still in the custody of the parole board, subject to many of the same controls as when he was in prison. He is not really at liberty, but continues to serve his sentence outside prison walls.

The contract theory: In return for his liberty, the parolee signs a contract with the parole board in which he agrees to abide by numerous arbitrarily imposed conditions—a curious sort of "contract," in which one side has all the bargaining powers and in which the contracting parolee, if accused of breaking it, has no redress in the courts. (The courts in their wisdom have ruled that the prisoner cannot be forced to sign the contract; but if he refuses, he will, of course, stay in prison.)

The contract, which reads like a parody of the white middle-class notion of appropriate behavior for the lower-class "deviant," is designed to circumscribe every conceivable aspect of the parolee's existence, from his means of livelihood to his sex life. Among the standard clauses: he may not leave the county, change his residence, change his job, drive or buy a car, sign contracts, or even get married, without permission of his parole agent. In four states he must get permission before suing for divorce. He is prohibited from associating with other ex-convicts or "individuals of bad reputation." He must obey all laws, conduct himself as a "good citizen," and "maintain gainful employment." In 44 states he may not "consume any alcoholic beverage or liquors"; in two others he may not "drink to excess." A catch-all clause states he must "cooperate with his parole agent at all times." In Nebraska, regular church attendance is compulsory for all parolees. In California the Adult Authority imposes an unwritten condition: the parolee may not live with a member of the opposite sex without benefit of marriage. If the parole board thinks these clauses insufficiently restrictive, it has discretionary authority to add "special conditions."

Responsibility for enforcement of the contract lies with the parole agent, in whom is vested the right to enter and search the parolee's house at any time without warning or warrant, to arrest and jail him without possibility of bail on mere suspicion of breaking one of the rules, and to suspend parole pending a hearing by the parole board. It is the agent, lowest ranking employee in the parole department, who reports violations or suspected infractions to the parole board, which almost always follows his recommendations as to disposition of the case.

In practice, the exercise of these extraordinary powers varies greatly from agent to agent. Christopher Nuttall, an English sociologist who spent months studying the California parole system, found the agents he met "a fascinating mixture," their differences of approach "amazing." Individual qualifications and backgrounds range from master's degrees in social work to experience as ex-prison guards and policemen. Some are tolerant, compassionate men whose prime concern is to help the parolee in the arduous task of "making it" in the outside world; others, authoritarian in outlook, regard themselves as street jailers and act accordingly. One of these displays a picture of the San Quentin gas chamber on his wall and a twelve-foot whip on his shelf. Thus "success" or "failure" of the ex-convict hangs largely on the individual characteristics of his parole agent and the manner in which the latter chooses to interpret and enforce the all-encompassing terms of the "contract."

Some indication of how this game of chance may affect

the parolee, whose stake in it is years of his liberty, is afforded by a study conducted by James O. Robison and Paul Takagi in which they sought to discover how the decision-making process works out in practice. Subjects of the study were the entire staff of a state parole agency, including regional administrators, district supervisors, caseload-carrying agents, and the chief of the agency, all governed by the same rules and regulations and all responsible to the same parole board. They were given ten actual case histories involving suspected violations of parole, and asked to make a judgment in each case: should the alleged parole violator be continued on parole? Or should he be returned to prison?

Judgments of the 316 agency staff members varied wildly. Among them were five who recommended ten returns to prison, and one who recommended only one return. About half the staff members would have returned either six or seven of the parolees—however, even those who would have returned the same *number* of cases were not in agreement about *which* cases they would return. Agents who came from a background of prison work would have returned many more alleged violators to prison than those who came from some outside social work position. Higher-ups in the organization, supervisory and administrative staff, recommended return to prison in fewer cases than parole agents. There was also variation by geographic region: in "District X" the supervisor recommended sending nine back to prison, whereas the supervisor of "District Y" would have returned only four. A further study was made by Professor Michael Hakeem of the University of Wisconsin, in which he requested ten trained parole officers and ten laymen with no correctional experience to make a series of predictions on parole survival on the basis of case summaries of 200 parolees, half of whom had been recommitted for parole violations and half of whom had not. He found that the laymen were substantially *more* accurate predictors than the parole officers. Moreover, both groups combined made fewer correct identifications of the nonviolators than would have been made by random selection.

If the parolee is "violated" by his agent (this curious solecism is used, without any sense of irony, by everyone in Corrections, from the parole board to the convict), he is back to Square One. An agent's report of "deterioration of behavior and attitude" is enough to send a parolee back behind bars—a handy method of effecting preventive detention.

In California, the re-imprisoned parolee is eventually brought before representatives of the Adult Authority, ordered to enter a plea of guilty or not guilty to the charges, and asked if he has anything to say. The hearing typically lasts from five to ten minutes. He is not afforded the right to have counsel present at the hearing.

If found guilty, his parole is canceled, and the Adult Authority automatically resets his sentence at the maximum. (The power to do this, never granted by the legislature, was arrogated to the Authority by its own resolution in 1951, a particularly sore spot with convicts.) The cycle of annual hearings before the Adult Authority for sentence setting and paroling now starts all over again. The parolee may end up serving more time for breaking an administrative rule than for the criminal offense for which he was originally convicted.

The parolee sees the contract as a delicately triggered trap. Since it is obviously impossible for the parolee to abide literally by all the conditions, the agent who wants to keep his charge on the street must, and does, shut his eyes to many violations of which he is aware. But he records them nevertheless (convicts call this "banking violations") against the day when he may decide to slam the trap shut. Some agents will give *oral* but not *written* permission for the parolee to leave the county, or drive a car, and then "bank" these as technical violations.

As for the amount of recidivism, there are statistics to suit every taste. Morris and Hawkins say there is a "legend that two thirds return to prison," but that studies which have attempted to follow up on what happens to those released "suggest on the contrary that about two thirds do *not* return." In *Crime in America,* Ramsey Clark says that "80 percent of all felonies are committed by repeaters" and that "better than one half of all the people who leave prison return convicted of a serious crime." The President's Task Force on Corrections estimates that among adult offenders 35 to 45 percent of those released on parole are subsequently returned to prison. Thus the impression is fostered that released prisoners are a dangerous lot; few employers will hire them, few landlords will knowingly rent to them, they are generally shunned by respectable folks.

David Greenberg, staff member of the Committee for the Study of Incarceration, having observed that released prisoners he met did not seem particularly dangerous, analyzed data made available in 1972 by the National Council on Crime and Delinquency on the success or failure of 50,000-odd male parolees released in 1969.

"At first glance," he writes, "the numbers seem to confirm the popular belief; at the end of the first year, 20 percent of the men were back in prison. If the follow-up had been extended for a second and third year, this number would undoubtedly have increased." However, a closer examination revealed that of the 20 percent sent back to prison only 5 percent of the total re-imprisoned were sent back with a new major conviction; the other 15 percent were returned as technical violators. What were the new, major offenses committed by the 5 percent? The bulk of the returns, says Greenberg, "are for various forms of theft, and violation of alcohol and narcotics laws." Only 0.79 percent were returned because of a new commission or allegation of a violent offense, and another 1.1 percent for "potentially violent" offenses. Greenberg estimates that had these more than 50,000 men been confined for an additional year instead of being released, the rates for homicide, rape, burglary, assault, and auto theft would have declined *at most* by less than 1 percent: "To prevent this very small amount of crime by keeping these men in prison would have been quite costly to taxpayers, but most of all to the prisoners themselves, 98 or 99 percent of whom would *not* have committed one of those violent offenses so alarming to the public."

In approximately two thirds of California parole revocations the official reason given is violation of rules in the "contract." The other third result from new criminal convictions. But behind most of the rule-violation cases lie what convicts call "silent beefs," criminal charges for which the parolee has been tried in court and acquitted, or suspected crimes with which he has never been charged because the police lacked sufficient evidence. In the former case the parole agent has the awesome right to set his own judgment above that of the jury and nullify its verdict. In the latter, the parolee is deprived entirely of trial and his fate is decided by administrative fiat. Mr. Joseph Spangler, administrative officer of the California Adult Authority, told me that in such a case its decision would be based on "a comprehensive report, including the facts of the new felony," as written by the parole agent. What if the accused denies his guilt? "He's not charged with, say, *robbery*; that would be a legal determination. He's charged with *behavior* in violation of his parole, and if he's found guilty of that we can reinstitute his maximum sentence." The procedure by which years of a man's liberty can be forfeited for "behavior," without benefit of trial for his alleged crime, is justified by the claim that trials would be too costly, would clog the courts, and are not required under the present law.

A violation report from the California Parole and Community Services Division illustrates the despotic power of the parole agent who, should he choose to blow the whistle on a parolee for technical infractions of the rules, can in effect impose a long prison sentence for acts that are in no sense criminal. The report concerns one JRW, imprisoned in February 1959 for burglary second degree, a crime that carries a sentence of one to fifteen years. Ten years later, in 1969, JRW was paroled from Folsom. The following year his parole agent, reporting to the Adult Authority, wrote: "1. JRW violated Condition 5B of the Conditions of Parole by consuming beer as evidenced by his own admission on 2-6-70. 2. JRW violated Condition 10 of the Conditions of Parole by display of sexual material, and behavior as observed by this agent during a home call on 2-6-70." (Condition 10 states, "You are to cooperate with the Parole and Community Services Division and your parole agent at all times.")

For drinking beer, displaying "sexual material" in the privacy of his home, for unspecified "behavior" and failure to "cooperate," JRW is subject to re-imprisonment for five more years, his sentence now reset at the maximum of fifteen years.

Summarizing parole as it has developed in practice, Goodell and von Hirsch told the House Judiciary Committee: "Parole has meant the creation of a system of discretionary drumhead justice for those under supervised release. While the rest of us can be subjected to the state's sanctions only if we violate the criminal law and only after a fair trial, parolees face instant discipline without trial at the hands of parole boards and parole agents if they are believed to have violated the law, to have committed technical infractions of parole, or to have led a lifestyle or been seen with associates displeasing to the authorities. One of the prisoners who died at Attica was a paroled check-forger who was returned to prison for driving without a license."

The day may not be far off when the agent's surprise visit to his charge's home, there to catch him drinking beer or ogling the *Playboy* foldout, will have been rendered unnecessary. Donald J. Newman, professor of criminology at New York State University, speaking at the 1970 Congress of the American Correctional Association, noted that: "there are some recent developments in electronic tracking of probationers and parolees by means of which the almost total surveillance and control system of the prison can be carried into the street." In a monograph published by the Public Health Service, Dr. Ralph K. Schwitzgebel, a pioneer in this use of electronics, describes "the development, in prototype form, of small, personally worn transmitters that permit the continual monitoring of the geographical location of parolees. This system . . . is known as an electronic rehabilitation system." Nor will the parolee be able to shed his transmitter, for "special security equipment has been designed and is being further developed to prevent the removal or compromise of personally worn equipment by parolees." All the components of the system "have been developed in a design or protoype stage in various laboratories," says Dr. Schwitzgebel.

The tracking device, which transmits signals giving the parolee's location to a base station, is being further perfected to supply other information: "In addition to monitoring the location of a person, other characteristics might also be monitored," including blood pressure, physiological activity, and penile erection. The electronic rehabilitation system need not be a one-way proposition: "A complete communication system could also permit the transmission of signals to the offender within the community." The alcoholic or narcotics addict could be required to wear "a small, portable shock apparatus with electrodes attached to the wrist," to be activated when he succumbs to the temptation of drink or drug.

Unlike the best things in life, the device would not be free. Another enthusiast of electronic tracking for the millions, Joseph Meyer, computer specialist with the National Security Agency, and originator of the Crime Deterrent Transponder System, feels the taxpayer should be spared the cost of financing the program. He writes in *Transactions on Aero-*

space and Electronic Systems: "The obvious way to pay for the transponders is to lease them to the subscribers at a low cost, say $5 per week, and make the subscribers responsible for damages." More recently, in the fall of 1972, Dr. Barton Ingraham and Dr. Gerald W. Smith advocated the permanent implantation of radio receiver-transmitters in the brains of parolees. They envision the automatic monitoring of parolees by a computer, which, if it detected a *probability* of misbehavior by the parolee, would cause him to desist by delivering an electrical "zap" to his brain and/or by calling the police to his radio-monitored location.

Musing over the constitutionality of all this, Dr. Schwitzgebel observes that: "The use of antinarcotic testing to determine the frequency of illegal behavior and reduce it, hints at the possible acceptability of other methods of recording and preventing behaviors in the community. Electronic monitoring and tracking devices would not seem to be directly prohibited by the cruel and unusual clause within a broad view of the issue . . ." Is there also a broad hint for the rest of us concealed in here somewhere? For if "behaviors in the community" can be electronically spotted and corrected for parolees, why not for the entire population?

It used to be up to about 4 or 5 years ago that there was a real balance of people in prison. There were some violent people, some revolutionary type of people, but there were also some real sensible people who really didn't belong in prison. We don't have so many of those sensible types any more.

—RAYMOND PROCUNIER,
California director of Correc-
tions, in testimony before
Subcommittee No. 3 of the
House Judiciary Committee,
October 1971

13

PRISON PROTEST

In the past few years, something resembling a state of war between keepers and kept has existed in many prisons across the country and is fast developing in others. The war is waged on a variety of fronts: within the prison fortresses themselves, in the courts, the press, the state and federal legislatures. In character and extent, the prison upheavals of the 1970's are unlike anything seen heretofore. But they are not without antecedent. Ever since the first U.S. prison was established in Philadelphia in 1790 there have been prison riots, uprisings, escapes. These incredibly daring acts of protest, cries for help

against intolerable conditions, occurred sporadically throughout the last century; in this century, three successive waves of
rebellion preceded the current uprisings, in the years just before the First World War, in the early thirties, and again in
the fifties.

In his book *Violence Behind Bars,* Vernon Fox lists some
400 known prison uprisings between 1855 and 1955. These
may be just the tip of the iceberg, for he observes that most
riots are never reported to the newspapers, since "it is not to
the advantage of a prison administration to let it be known
that a riot has occurred." Once the news does get out, the
administration will make the best of it by ascribing the disturbance to insufficient funds and calling upon the legislature
to increase the budget.

A number of the uprisings recorded by Fox seem to have
been acts of solidarity among convicts. In 1857 an inmate of
Auburn Prison, New York, was ordered into solitary confinement for refusing to work; two days later, 60 inmates armed
with hammers demanded and obtained his release back into
the prison population. In 1914, 700 prisoners at Blackwell's
Island, New York, rioted for the release from solitary of 40
others. In 1952, 50 inmates of Trenton State Prison conducted
a four-hour protest over the failure of a prison orderly to
provide medical attention to a prisoner.

Demands in these early rebellions centered around brutality
of guards, bad food, inadequate medical care, conservative
parole board practices; more recently, a major demand was
publication of prisoners' grievances in the press. In 1926,
mutineers in Kansas State Penitentiary's mine requested their
demands be published and "copies of the newspapers thrown
down the shaft so they could not be double-crossed by officials. The demands were refused and they were starved out."
In 1944 inmates at Atlanta Federal Penitentiary seized
hostages and refused to surrender until a special edition of
the Atlanta *Journal* printed their story.

The wave of disturbances that engulfed the prisons during the early fifties was described by Richard McGee, pioneer reformer and then director of the California Department of Corrections, at the 1953 Congress of the American Correctional Association: "During the past 2½ years we have had a series of riots and mutinies in our prisons unequalled in history . . . We stand at the cross roads . . . the threat is real and present. The disorders in our prisons, so prevalent during the past two years, must be stopped—initially by gas and gunfire if need be, but ultimately by a complete reexamination of the place, function and purpose of prison."

There is a dearth of information from the convicts' point of view about these uprisings, for as in the slave revolts, which they resemble, the voice of the rebels was until recently effectively smothered by their overseers. As Dr. Clarence Schrag of the University of Washington told the American Correctional Association at the 1960 congress, in what must have been the understatement of that year: "Clearly, the perceptions of riot causes are disposed to vary according to the social positions of the persons making the judgments." But the administrators had their say, contained in innumerable official reports, testimony before legislative committees, speeches at meetings of prison people. In general, they placed the blame on a few disgruntled, hardened ringleaders, on "mass contagion" caused by newspaper and radio reports that reach into the prison to stir up unrest, and on those perennial scapegoats for all society's ills, the outside agitators.

Thus, in 1913, Ralph E. Smith, president of the Wisconsin Association of Governing Boards, told his colleagues in the American Prison Association, "In spite of the fact that great advancement has been made in methods of reform, it is also undoubtedly true that in no corresponding length of time have there been more serious outbreaks and revolts in prison." The cause, he believed, was "the agitation of so-called social workers. Their misrepresentations of the conditions of prisons and prison life have led prisoners living under admirable prison conditions to believe that they are treated worse than the worst, and that their condition is nothing more nor less than that of abject slavery. They are today not only causing unrest within prisons but are contributing a great deal to the development of lawlessness without."

More than half a century later, at the 1969 American Correctional Association Congress, Warden R. W. Meier of McNeil Island Federal Penitentiary expanded on the same point: "We can without question blame some of our problems on outside influences. I think you know what I mean . . . there is the problem of well-organized disturbances brought on by the resisters, draft dodgers, professional agitators, Communists, hippies and revolutionaries . . . Former prisoners, militants, far-out liberals, subversives, and even a few clergymen, educators, and social workers on the outside seem to delight in fomenting unrest in prisons."

Again, in 1971 in response to a question by Congressman Charles B. Rangel about the causes of the peaceful demonstration of convicts at Raiford, Florida, in which scores were injured by guards' gunfire, Director of Corrections Louie Wainright said he thought Jack Anderson "contributed to the disturbance" by his columns about conditions in that prison. Which caused Congressman Rangel to declare, "The last warden we had testify said it was a Communist conspiracy. Now we have another warden saying that Jack Anderson has created a major part of the problem. How can you have faith in a system like that?"

Protest behind the walls, when heeded and acted on by outside agitators, has historically been the only significant factor in calling public attention to the prisoner's plight and in wresting from the prison authorities any sort of amelioration of conditions. Largely due to the activities of convicts themselves, the prison has in recent years become Topic A in the media. Formerly, prisons and jails were considered fair enough copy for the occasional exposé, the random sob story. Now, they are the subject of featured news accounts in the metropolitan papers, television specials, long analyses by columnists.

As manifestations of rising militancy in the black population—from southern sit-ins to northern ghetto riots—focused public attention on black demands in the sixties, so the current wave of prison disturbances (itself a spillover of black militancy on the outside) is forcing the public, the legislatures, and the judiciary to turn unwilling eyes in the direction of that long-neglected, secret world. In the early sixties Black Muslims in the prisons forced an opening wedge. Regarded as prime troublemakers by the authorities, subjected to brutal punishments and long stretches in solitary, they nevertheless won important court decisions affirming their right to practice their religion behind bars. Today prison administrators look back to those days with a certain nostalgia; the associate warden of San Quentin told me he now considers the Muslims to be quite a constructive influence, especially compared with the Panther and La Raza groups that are now forming in all the institutions.

Radical and revolutionary ideologies are seeping into the prisons. Whereas formerly convicts tended to regard themselves as unfortunates whose accident of birth at the bottom of the heap was largely responsible for their plight, today many are questioning the validity of the heap. Increasing numbers of prisoners are beginning to look upon the whole criminal justice system, with the penitentiary at the end of it, as an instrument of class and race oppression. In spite of administrative vigilance, inmates manage to come by copies of the underground press, the works of Che Guevara, Frantz Fanon, Mao Tse-tung. Books like *Soledad Brother, The Autobiography of Malcolm X, Soul on Ice,* the holy writ of latter-day prison rebels, are passed from cell to cell until they fall apart, then surreptitiously duplicated page by page on prison Ditto equipment.

A new and more sophisticated type of prisoner is entering the system: the civil disobedient, the collegiate narcotics user, the black and brown militant. These maintain links with radical organizations in their respective communities via smuggled letters, the good offices of sympathetic "free-world" prison employees (teachers, chaplains, etc.), illicit radical publications.

Racial antagonisms, traditionally fostered by guards as a convenient method of divide and rule, are beginning to break down. California State Senator Mervyn Dymally, who made a personal investigation of Soledad, reported that prison guards, greatly outnumbered by inmates, "divert hostility from themselves by encouraging the racist tendencies of the white and Chicano inmates and playing them off against the blacks." In the early sixties, efforts by a small group of militant blacks to integrate the dining room in Folsom Prison were met with violence from both white prisoners and guards. But by 1968 *The Outlaw,* underground newspaper in San Quentin, was issuing repeated calls for unity against a common oppressor: "Some of us cons don't seem to know which side we're on. We're obsessed with nearsighted disputes based on race, ideology, group identity, and so on. We expend our energies despising and distrusting each other. Don't be so critical of the other races. All of this is helping the California Department of Corrections. We permit them to keep us at each others' throats. But a handful of us are calling for unity. This is for a purpose. We want to crush this empire that has been built upon our suffering." In late 1970, prison rebels in San Quentin, Soledad, and Folsom for the first time united across color lines, establishing black/white/brown committees to press their demands. Even some of the self-styled "Nazis," white prisoners who flaunt swastikas burned or tattooed into their flesh, began to make common cause with Chicanos and blacks.

Thanks to "mass contagion" spread by media accounts of these occurrences, the new spirit of interracial unity leaped from prison to prison. In 1971, the Attica manifesto began: "We the imprisoned men of Attica Prison want an end to the injustice suffered by all prisoners, regardless of race, creed, or color. The preparation and content of this document has been constructed under the unified efforts of all races and social segments of the prison . . ." In 1972, a "curriculum for reform" issued by striking inmates of Florence State Prison in Arizona declared, "This is a unified movement of all convicts for reform of present conditions. There has been a unified decision reached by the majority of all convicts to elect a convict counsel. As such, there are committees now representing all of the Black Brothers, White Brothers, Brown Brothers, and Red Brothers."

To what extent the new militants speak for their fellow-convicts can only be a matter of conjecture. Prison administrators will tell you, as their predecessors did, that the rebels are a handful of hard-core troublemakers spurred on by outside agitators and by the unaccustomed attention they are getting from the media, that the vast majority of convicts would prefer to "do their own time" undisturbed by sit-downs, riots, and uprisings. However there is some evidence that the revolutionary philosophy of the new breed of prison rebel is spreading like a brush fire, no longer confined to prisons, like those of New York and California, which house convicts drawn from predominantly black, politically explosive urban areas. A white correspondent writes from the Indiana State Penitentiary (in which three quarters of the inmates are white), "Here in Hoosierland we're awash with the 'new militancy.' The most abysmally ignorant now can articulate all the political and sociological grievances. Men who two or three years ago might have experienced difficulty phrasing even the most simple thought now quote lengthy passages from Fanon and Cleaver, and identify righteously with Angela, the Soledad Brothers, Berrigan, et al. I believe the new militancy is widespread in the prison system. I've had occasion to speak with men coming here from other states, men who have been in other prisons, and it's apparent that moods and attitudes have been, and are, changing. Only this morning the radio had news of a night-long riot in Walpole, Massachusetts . . ."

Convicts and their keepers alike agree that traditional prisoners' grievances have undergone fundamental change. As characterized by a black ex-convict at a meeting called shortly before Attica by the San Francisco Prisoners' Union, the demands of prisoners today are essentially the same as those of the Watts and Detroit rioters in the sixties: survival and the elementary necessities of life, to be sure, adequate and decent food, medical care, educational and trade training opportunities, worthwhile jobs at prevailing union wages. "But beyond that," he said, "they are fighting for human dignity, for empowerment, for self-determination, for political rights —which many believe will lead to the eventual overthrow of the system that enslaves them."

Manifestoes, convicts' bills of rights, strike demands issuing from prisons everywhere would seem to bear this out. The Tombs demands of August 1970, while protesting food "not fit for human consumption," centered on "injustices we suffer in the courtrooms of the Criminal Court and the Supreme Court of Manhattan County." In Arizona State Prison, striking convicts demanded the state minimum wage, workmen's compensation, the right to due process in disciplinary procedures, a law library, an end to mail censorship, "human and constitutional rights to freedom of expression." The first Attica manifesto, presented to Commissioner Oswald in May 1971, demanded such simple improvements as a new prison doctor, a baseball diamond, better food. By July, a new manifesto was issued containing this language: "We, the inmates of

Attica Prison, say to you, the sincere people of society, the prison system of which your courts have rendered unto you is without question the authoritative fangs of a coward in power. Respectfully submitted to the people as a protest to the vile and vicious slavemasters."

"A Convict Report on Major Grievances," prepared in secret by prisoners at San Quentin in 1968–69 over a thirteen-month period of intense study and discussion for presentation to the State Assembly Criminal Procedures Committee, consists principally of an analysis of the unconstitutionality of paroling procedures. It proposes abolition of the indeterminate sentence law, removal of sentence-setting power from the Adult Authority, and introduction of due process in parole violation proceedings.

In a memorandum entitled "Power to the People!" addressed to prison and law enforcement administrators, James W. L. Park examines "some characteristics of the new rebellion" as evidenced in two 1968 disturbances at San Quentin. Mr. Park is a veteran of the California prison system; he got his start in the early fifties as clinical psychologist in Chino Prison, worked in the Sacramento headquarters of the Department of Corrections, and spent some years in Soledad before becoming associate warden of San Quentin.

Observing that this institution is situated close to "major centers of social ferment" like Berkeley, the Haight-Ashbury District, four ghettos, "and thirty or more enclaves of the disillusioned, the drop-out, the dissident, or the revolutionary," Mr. Park writes: "These two experiments were successful from the viewpoint of the instigators because they demonstrated, perhaps for the first time in American penal history, that outsiders could conspire with prisoners to cripple the normal operation of a prison. The age-old dissatisfactions of the convict were translated into a well-planned and sophisticated attack on state laws and policies, the operations of the paroling agency, the limitations on legal rights of parolees, the indeterminate sentence, and other issues far removed from the usual minor food grievances." He notes that "the intake of young inmates in the next few years will include many who have been exposed to the concepts of social revolution," and he counsels administrators to read books on revolutionary techniques, as these "have been studied by many inmates and may be useful in understanding the thinking of inmate leaders."

A danger to which prison administrators should be alert, says Mr. Park, is "environmentalistic idealism: a belief that man is inherently good and acts in an antisocial manner because the dominant political and economic structure forces him to. A corollary position discounts the reality of ingrained sociopathic traits . . . This belief is reinforced by limited contact with prisoners. Students, volunteer workers, and new employees who observe prisoners functioning in an effective manner in confinement often assume that they could do the same in free society if given the proper opportunities and hence conclude that incarceration is unjust and unnecessary."

Under the heading "Social Movements Impinging Upon Prison Management," Mr. Park cites "racial and ethnic consciousness: under rallying cries of 'Black Power' or 'Viva la Raza,' Black and Mexican Americans seek dignity, self-respect, a fair share of the economy and political power . . . practically all participants are more aggressive and less patient than in the old Civil Rights Movement." He concludes: "Administrators of penal units near urban and academic centers should review their disturbance control plans with the participation of outside demonstrators in mind. Advance planning with local law enforcement agencies regarding crowd control and the closing of access roads would be prudent."

Professor Anthony Platt of the School of Criminology at Berkeley, who has closely watched these developments, believes there is a converse to Mr. Park's theory that prisoners are influenced by outside revolutionaries; in his view, militant prisoners have in turn had a powerful effect on the radical movement as a whole. "While there is a danger of romanticizing prisoners—something that irks *them,* too—contemporary prison rebels have provided some of the best insights into American society," he told me. "In terms of the struggle against oppression, they furnish a strong example to people outside. Men like Malcolm X and George Jackson are a product of the prison, much as men and women like Frederick Douglass and Harriet Tubman were products of slavery."

Where outsiders are concerned, wardens tend to be an uncommunicative lot; they do not welcome inquiries about their operations from the press, nor are visitors permitted to intrude upon their association meetings. Among themselves, in the privacy of their own organization, it is another matter. Their voices come through loud and clear in the columns of *The Grapevine,* semisecret house organ of the American Association of Wardens and Superintendents, to which only members are permitted to subscribe. Leafing through a year's back issues of this modest publication, a three-page multilith pastiche of newspaper stories, down-home jokes, letters from wardens to the editor and to each other, I detected a grim determination to hold the fort against the enemy within and without: convicts, courts, lawyers, legislators, a hostile public—the conspiracy to undermine the prisons seems to be spreading its tentacles everywhere, even into the White House.

As Warden Wayne K. Patterson of Colorado said in his letter to Warden Louis Nelson in California, reprinted in the February 1972 *Grapevine,* "I think our position of attempting to maintain control of a large institution will eventually become impossible when radicals from within and without, aided and abetted by a multitude of liberals, leftists, crusading attorneys, and misguided humanists, are daily undermining all constituted authority. In addition, I read in the newspaper that the President of the United States calls for prison reform and labels all prisons as 'colleges of crime.' The United States

Attorney General quotes extensive statistics and calls on the people to 'reform the prisons.' Then I receive a newsletter from a newly formed coalition for prisoner rights . . . As a result of all this, you and I will become brutal sadists and political sheep to be slaughtered indiscriminately as the great reforms take shape."

The Grapevine gives the good news: "South Bend, Indiana: Unless exceptional circumstances are present, state prison officials may continue using chemical irritant sprays on unruly inmates. U.S. District Court Judge Robert A. Grant denied a motion for a temporary restraining order which would have prohibited the use of such sprays at the Indiana State Prison . . ." And the bad news: "Madison, Wisconsin: A federal judge here believes prison authorities do not have the right to limit personal freedoms of convicts dealing with length of hair, visiting, and mail privileges. U.S. District Judge James E. Doyle said inmates should be treated the same as people who are not imprisoned . . ."

Exhorting each other to close ranks against all critics, the wardens urge courage: "It is absolutely amazing how soft our courts have become," writes editor G. Norton Jameson. "Not only the courts but the entire public has become infiltrated with a sloppy sentimental attitude." Paraphrasing François Villon, he laments, "What has become of the 'guts' of yester-year?" And Reverend James P. Collins, president of the New York prison chaplains: "A strong courage of convictions is especially needed in light of the recent criticism of the Corrections profession by the media. We in Corrections today need a king-sized dose of courage and old-fashioned guts." (To which the editor rejoins: "Amen! Father Collins is my kind of chaplain.") Again, the editor: "We need this know-how more now than ever—keep speaking out—the nin-com-poops and revolutionaries will eventually die from eating their own offcum." Deploring a Harris poll that showed "23 percent of the public say the authorities are too easy on the inmates, while

58 percent say the authorities don't understand inmate needs,"
the editor declares, "We must redouble our efforts to get before
the public the true picture, otherwise prisons are headed for
that deep dark bottom of inmate rule." However, Don R. Erick-
son, president of the association, feels things are beginning to
look up somewhat. Proposing to make 1972 "the Year of the
Warden," he notes that "the pendulum is coming back toward
the middle and we as wardens should grasp the opportunities
and not lose control of our institutions. Remember, let's get
off the defensive and on the offensive in 1972."

The response of wardens to these calls to action is reported
in a column spryly captioned "Here and There": "Raymond J.
Gaffney, warden of Kansas Penitentiary: 'If necessary we will
use force. We will not negotiate with prisoners or an outside
mob.' " "Warden Patterson reports, 'The strike was concluded
with no concessions whatsoever by me, regardless of their possible merit.' " "Michigan City, Indiana: 'We've been locking
up the strike organizers since Monday,' Warden Russell E.
Lash said. 'They are still determined, but they're locked up.'
Among the demands made by the militant tagshop workers,
he said, was an increase in wages from about 70¢ a day to
the federal minimum of $1.65 an hour." "Warden Frank A.
Eyman of Arizona State Prison revealed that he had refused
three black legislators admittance beyond his office to meet
with black prisoners last year. They stormed out of his office
in a rage, he said. As the prison's more than 1,200 strikebound
male inmates would probably testify, Eyman is nobody to bet
against . . . 'I'll make Attica look like a picnic,' the warden
said today."

Most of these items are culled from metropolitan newspapers, but once in a while *The Grapevine* runs its own in-depth
exclusive account of some particularly praiseworthy feat of
prisoner management, as in Warden Bill Bannon's letter in the
January 1972 issue on his handling of a sit-down by 62 women
prisoners in the yard of the Detroit House of Corrections. "You

should have seen the requests!" writes Warden Bannon. "Shorter skirts, more money, lower prices in the commissary, better programs, and many other demands that we all have wrestled with over the years. My matron and the guard force wanted to go in and drag them out but I knew if we hit the worst one out there, she would become more important than the Queen of England, so we surrounded them and let them sit; I prayed for rain but no answer. They sat for four days and four nights, then came in . . . after they gave up, we kept them locked for a few days and then put them back in the general group and to work. I thought our trouble was all over, but two bleeding hearts on the City Council called me before their august body. This is when the stew hit the fan . . ."

Worse was to come, says Warden Bannon, in the shape of a matrons' strike in which 32 of the 52 matrons walked out. This was followed by a "flare-up" of women prisoners in one of the eight cottages: "We had two cars with four state policemen come in, we locked the cottage up tight with 46 women in it. We were just too busy to feed them all the next day. The second day, they were unlocked and we had no more trouble. The union took us to Labor Relations and we didn't give an inch; we told them we were running as good—if not better—without the matrons. So all the matrons gained was the loss of five days' wages." In a forthright display of the guts of yesteryear the warden concludes: "You will remember, I told you in Florida that I was getting out . . . I will be damned if I will quit now. I have never been fired, but I will stay until I do get fired as I will not give in to the bleeding hearts."

In the past, prison administrators were wont to blame many of their troubles on public and official apathy to their field of endeavor. One senses that today they would welcome a return to this traditional public indifference to the plight of those in captivity. As Ed Cass, member of the New York Commission of Corrections, wrote to the editor of *The Grapevine*:

"As you well know, the courts and certain types within the institutions have taken over and it is amazing to me how much outside sympathy they manage to get not only from the press but people generally . . . the emphasis seems to be in the area of the constitutional rights of prisoners . . ."

The dimensions and dynamics of what has come to be called the "Prison Movement" are indeed amazing, a new phenomenon on the American scene. It comprises legislators, newspaper men and women, lawyers, academicians, students, citizens from all walks of life and of a variety of political persuasions. The overwhelming majority of those caught up in it are people who until a few years ago had no interest whatsoever in what went on behind those walls, who have in fact been stirred to action by "certain types within the institution" whose muffled protests are at last being heard outside, and by the proliferating ex-convict organizations which serve as a liaison between their fellows behind bars and the community.

The wardens notwithstanding, the Prison Movement is by no means confined to ex-convicts and political activists of radical bent, although these undoubtedly spearheaded it in the first place. It is fast acquiring astonishing breadth, much as the antislavery movement did before it. In my travels around the country I have come across the most unlikely people who, having become obsessed with the evil of prison, are now full-time outside agitators. Some bring to mind those stalwart abolitionists of antebellum days. To cite two examples:

David Rothenburg got his start in the theater world in 1959, when he was twenty-six years old, working for a theatrical press agency. Within five years he had established his own immensely successful agency, representing such Broadway productions as *Hair, Beyond the Fringe,* and Richard Burton's *Hamlet.* In 1966, a colleague gave him a copy of *Fortune and Men's Eyes,* John Herbert's grim play about the gang-rape of a teen-aged prisoner. "I read it at a sitting," he told me. "I knew it was absolutely the truth. Against the advice of my friends, who thought it too downbeat for the public taste, I did a workshop production of it and eventually it opened off-Broadway, to very mixed reviews—people either loathed it or loved it."

About four months after the play opened, Rothenburg initiated nightly discussions in which the audience was invited to stay on following each performance and exchange views with the many ex-convicts who came to see it. "One thing led to another. A group of us, theater people and ex-convicts, decided to form an organization—the Fortune Society. Our aim was to inform the public about prisons and to furnish what help we could to men and women just released." What started as a spare-time hobby, says Rothenburg, became a vocation; by 1968 he had forsaken the theater agency business and turned his office into a headquarters for the Fortune Society, of which he is full-time executive director.

In some respects, the Fortune Society is a prototypical reform group. Staffed almost entirely by ex-convicts, it seeks to instill "motivation" into those newly released from prison, and to change their "attitude," to the end that they might more easily adjust to society. It works with employers, unions, and vocational training agencies to open up job opportunities for ex-convicts, it conducts a public education and information program aimed at building support for prison reform. But it also maintains strong ties with the militants; David Rothenburg and two colleagues were among those named by the Attica rebels at the height of the uprising to serve on the observers' committee. Its publication, *Fortune News*, which by 1972 had reached a circulation of 20,000 including 3,000 prisoners, reports prisoner demands and prison disturbances around the country, and furnishes a forum for prisoners and ex-convicts. Its legal department, originally established to handle the individual legal problems of inmates and ex-convicts, is now involved in a series of test cases challenging prison rules and administrative practices.

Mrs. Ysabel Rennie of Columbus, Ohio, now in her middle fifties, served during World War II as intelligence analyst for the Office of Strategic Services and later as an officer with the State Department. Educated at Stanford and Radcliffe, she has written several books including a history of Argentina, is married to an insurance company executive, and is an active member of the Episcopalian Church. She hardly strikes one as likely material for insurgent activity aimed at a stronghold of American political power.

"For seventeen years I had been driving past the Ohio Penitentiary," she said, "asking myself what life could possibly be like behind those gray stone walls, and a question nagged at my mind. Supposing it turned out that dreadful things went on inside: would I be any different than all those 'good Germans' who passed Dachau and Buchenwald and never asked questions? Yet, I am ashamed to confess, it took two riots and at least five deaths to confirm me in the resolve which had been slowly, and so reluctantly, growing within me—to find out what goes on after we have condemned a man to the spiritual wastebasket we call the penitentiary."

Following the 1968 riots, Mrs. Rennie happened to see a notice of a federal court hearing involving two prisoners who had brought suit for an injunction against cruel and unusual punishment. What she learned in that hearing (at which the injunction was denied), and subsequently at eight riot trials, drove her to make a firsthand inquiry into conditions in the penitentiary. In the autumn of 1968 Mrs. Rennie took a proposal to the Christian Social Responsibility Commission of her church for a study of the entire penal system. There followed "two years of continuous investigation, interviews, and conversations with former prisoners, with families of men inside, guards, Corrections officials, and countless weeks spent in Federal and Common Pleas Court listening to testimony of inmates, guards, and prison officials."

Early in 1970 she related her findings in testimony before Senator Thomas J. Dodd's committee, a lengthy and horrifying recitation of officially sanctioned Macings, beatings, sexual assaults, killings of prisoners by guards. "We have yet to find one institution in Ohio, either the best or the worst of them, which does not, to some degree, degrade, corrupt, pervert, and dehumanize the men committed to its charge," she told the committee. "You will be told of wonderful programs of rehabilitation, education, vocational training—all the right words and phrases. If Ohio prisons could walk to heaven on a bridge of press releases, we should long since have been saved. The truth, I regret to say, is something else again . . .

"Men can stand only so much abuse, and in June 1968, the Ohio Penitentiary exploded. Utensils were hurled about the dining room, windows were smashed, fires set. When asked the reason for this behavior, our commissioner of Correction, Maury Koblentz, told the papers that 'outside influences stir things up,' a statement for which he was awarded the Flying Fickle Finger of Fate award by Rowan and Martin's *Laugh-In*."

Among the atrocities to which Mrs. Rennie testified was an incident in which some guards collected several pet cats the prisoners had befriended at Chillecothe Correctional Institute, including six four-day-old kittens, and dashed their brains out in sight of the whole prison population. "*This* is what captured the imagination of the press and public, not the murders and beatings of prisoners!" she said indignantly. "Judging by the letters to the editor, irate cat-lovers all over the country must have taken pen to paper to protest against the cat massacre. Several even sent death threats to the warden!"

Due to the persistent efforts of Mrs. Rennie and the movement she has built in Ohio, some changes have come about. In the aftermath of the cat massacre, Mr. Koblentz resigned as commissioner, and a more liberal commission now administers the Ohio prisons. In 1971, Governor John J. Gilligan appointed a Citizens Task Force on Corrections, of which Mrs. Rennie is a member. "We spent all that year investigating the seven Ohio prisons, and we produced more than a hundred recommendations," she told me. "In the summer of 1971 the governor lifted censorship of first-class mail, an unprecedented step for any prison system, since followed in a couple of other states. But it took sit-down strikes at six of the prisons before any of the other recommendations were adopted, several months later. The striking inmates won an immediate doubling of their wages from 5 to 10¢ an hour, and the $300 limit on going-home pay was lifted—before this, any inmate's savings over $300 were kept by the state." In July of 1972, the new commissioner issued a number of detailed administrative orders based on the task force recommendations, placing severe restrictions on punishment of inmates and granting extensive rights to those called before the Rules Infraction Board: the right to call witnesses, to cross-examine accusers, to appeal the decision. "Unfortunately, nobody is checking up to see whether any of these orders are being carried out," said Mrs. Rennie. "At Chillecothe, where a number of 'troublemakers' from the Ohio Penitentiary are in administrative segregation, men are being put in strip cells and Maced without the slightest attention to these rules." How does she now assess the results of her years of effort? "Changes have occurred in the Ohio system since my 1970 testimony before the Dodd Committee, but I should certainly hesitate to take credit for them; and I am not at all sure, from the standpoint of the average inmate, that the environment has visibly improved. The record is decidedly mixed. I keep on nagging, but truthfully, there's very little I can claim credit for except keeping a basilisk eye on the prison scene."

No advocate of reforms intended to shore up the prison system, Mrs. Rennie thinks prisons should be abolished. As she told the Dodd Committee, "You want to appropriate money for better prisons. I say, don't do it. Giving money to the states to build better prisons is like giving money to Himmler to build better concentration camps: it is wrong in principle."

I would like to say one thing this committee should consider: That one of the astounding facts about prisons is this, that they are probably the most lawless place in our society . . . this is a dominating factor every place, that they are lawless.

—HON. RICHARD KELLY
Judge, Sixth Judicial Circuit Court,
State of Florida, testifying before
Select Committee on Crime, House of
Representatives, December 1971

14

THE LAWLESSNESS OF CORRECTIONS

As seen by the prison people, the most worrisome threat to their absolute dominion over the lives of the convict population is the gradual entry in some areas of the rule of law into the world of prison.

Until very recently judges traditionally adopted a "hands-off" policy in matters of prison administration, thus placing prison, alone of administrative agencies, outside the reach of judicial intervention. The Thirteenth Amendment to the U.S. Constitution states, "Neither slavery nor involuntary servitude, except as a punishment for crime whereof the party shall have been duly convicted shall exist within the United States." Interpreting this, courts took the position that the prisoner because of his criminality has forfeited all individual rights, is in a state of "civil death." According to an 1871 case, "He has, as a consequence of his crime, not only forfeited his liberty, but all his personal rights except those which the law in its humanity accords to him. He is for the time being the slave of the state." A corollary of this doctrine holds that judicial interference with the conduct of prison administrators "would be prejudicial to the proper administration of discipline." Since the prisons are run for the benevolent purpose of rehabilitation and are staffed with experts in that art, the courts have reasoned, procedural restraints would be inappropriate. As expressed in a 1954 opinion, "Courts are without power to supervise prison administration or to interfere with the ordinary prison rules or regulations." And again in 1962: ". . . supervision of inmates of . . . institutions rests with the proper administrative authorities and . . . courts have no power to supervise the management of disciplinary rules of such institutions." In effect, the courts were delegating the final word on acceptable prison practices to the guard on duty, and were saying to the prisoner, "Once the jailhouse door has clanged behind you, there *is* no further law. You have no legal redress."

Via the "hands-off" policy, the courts had invested prison officialdom with all functions of government within the walls: administrative (it is the prison authorities who regulate all aspects of the prisoner's daily life and who make all decisions affecting his standard of living, the work he shall perform, the wages, if any, he shall receive), legislative (it is they who are empowered to make all rules governing the prisoner's conduct), and judicial. Furthermore, it is the prison authorities who determine what is "administrative" and what "judicial"—

that is, when and in what circumstances an inmate may be subjected to the internal judicial process of trial and punishment.

To get some notion of how the prison autocracy carries out its mandate to perform the judicial function, I explored the disciplinary procedures of the California Department of Corrections. These, incidentally, are in full compliance with procedures outlined in the American Correctional Association's *Manual of Correctional Standards* (Valhalla edition) and are typical of practices in prisons throughout the country.

As stated in the Director's Rules, department policy regarding inmate discipline is "to develop in the inmate self-reliance, self-control, self-respect, self-discipline," and "the ability and desire to conform to accepted standards for individual and community life in a free society." To this end, rules (some of which sound as though they had been lifted from a deportment manual for Victorian young ladies) have been established which "every inmate is expected to obey." Among them:

"Always conduct yourself in an orderly manner . . . Do not agitate, unduly complain, magnify grievances . . ."

"Promptly and politely obey all orders or instructions given by employees."

"Do not use profane or obscene language. Do not boo, whistle, shout, or make other loud and disturbing noises."

"Do not participate in any sexual or immoral act. Do not place yourself in a position which might lead to such an act."

"Be attentive and respectful toward state employees and officials. Address any such person as 'Mr.,' 'Mrs.,' or 'Miss," followed by his or her last name or by their proper title followed by the last name. Examples: 'Mr. Jones,' 'Lieutenant Smith,' etc."

"Be properly clothed at all times and keep your clothing as neat and clean as conditions permit."

"Keep your shoes clean and as well polished as circumstances permit."

"Bathe frequently; keep your teeth clean; keep your hair properly cut and neatly combed; be clean-shaven and wash your hands when needed, particularly before meals and after using the toilet."

"Have only the standard type of haircut, pictures of which are posted at each inmate barbershop . . . Do not wear a moustache or beard unless approved by the institutional head. Female inmates shall dress their hair in a feminine style, in accordance with institutional regulations."

Are these rules really taken seriously by the "line-men" whose job it is to oversee the convicts in their day-to-day comings and goings? To what extent are they enforced? This is entirely within the discretion of the individual guard. Some intimation of the despotic power invested in the "line-man" can be glimpsed in an article written by a San Quentin guard for *Correctional Review*, a Department of Corrections house organ. He describes his mandate to make or break at whim convicts in his custody:

"Recently, as an officer, I had to make a decision that was part of a routine day. A young inmate, twenty years of age or so, a first-termer new to prison life, had failed to report to his school assignment. When I brought him in and explained that he must stay on his assignment until changed by proper authority, he referred to me in terms unpleasant and unprintable. I knew this would be his first 'beef' at San Quentin. I knew that under California's indeterminate sentence a prisoner can shorten or lengthen his sentence by his behavior pattern. Should I send him to disciplinary court with all the details written down? Or should I merely cite him for nonattendance at school? Perhaps I held an extra year of this inmate's life in my hands at the moment." (The writer does not divulge which of these alternatives he chose.) Thus the first rule of prison justice is that the guard can decide, out in front, whether or not there will be any at all.

"When rules are broken, discipline shall be administered," says the rule book, "in such a way as to conserve human values and dignity and to bring about desirable changes in attitude." Attainment of these goals is the task of a three-member hearing committee consisting of the associate warden or his delegate and two other officers, before whom the prisoner accused of breaking the rules is brought. The hearing will typically last from two to ten minutes. The prisoner is not permitted to confront or cross-examine his accuser, or to call witnesses in his defense, nor may his lawyer be present.* If found guilty (and any other outcome would seem inconceivable, in view of the nature of the proceedings), he may at the pleasure of the hearing committee be given punishments ranging from loss of mail and visiting privileges to days, months, or years in solitary confinement. Or the committee may prescribe what the prisoners call "bus therapy." As one ex-convict explained it: "You may be in Chino minimum-security prison, and be accused of some minor infraction—you'll find yourself on the 8 A.M. bus for Folsom. Bus therapy has rewards as well as punishments. If you're in Folsom, and you snitch to a guard on another prisoner who has a knife, you can be in Chino by morning. There are hundreds of men on the move on any given day in this curious game of chess. Custody status is the authorities' biggest weapon. Top is AAA—can drive a car outside prison. End of the road is F, meaning Folsom, and Final." The punishment does not end with these privations. His record

---

* In the months following the decision of Judge Zirpoli in *Clutchette v. Procunier*—as this book goes to press, still on appeal in the U.S. Court of Appeals for the Ninth Circuit—inmates were permitted to cross-examine adverse witnesses at the pleasure of the investigating officer. No counsel was permitted.

blotted, the prisoner who falls afoul of the disciplinary committee will be moved out of the category of "normal," and so
may serve more than the term normally imposed for his crime.

Jurisdiction of the prison disciplinary committee extends
not only to infractions of the prison rules but to major felonies
up to and including murder. While these are as a matter of
policy reported to the district attorney, he seldom prosecutes
—why should he, the reasoning goes? The accused is already
serving a long sentence. Under the indeterminate sentence law
he can be locked up almost indefinitely by the simple expedient
of referring the case to the Adult Authority, which will readily
accommodate and leave his sentence at the maximum. In
1968, for example, San Quentin authorities recorded a total
of 126 "major infractions" ranging from fatal assaults to
possession of weapons and narcotics. Of these, but 16 were the
subject of prosecution by the district attorney. The balance,
including four "fatal assaults" and twenty "assaults on inmates," were handled by the prison disciplinary committee.

What if the prisoner accused of a felony maintains he is
innocent and demands a court trial with all of the procedural
safeguards—right to counsel, right to cross-examine his accusers and to call witnesses in his defense? I pursued this
question with Mr. James Park, associate warden at San
Quentin, and Mr. Raymond Procunier, director of the California Department of Corrections.

"He hasn't a right to a trial," said Mr. Park. "We find him
guilty or not-guilty administratively."

"But—how can you be sure he is guilty if no witnesses
are called and no evidence given?"

"That's simple, we *know* who did it from other prisoners,"
explained Mr. Park with the weary patience of one who has
suffered through these questions before. "If several reliable
prisoners point to this guy, or refuse to clear him, we know
he's guilty. We don't have the type of case we could take to
court, it would be too dangerous for our inmate-informers to

have to testify. You middle-class due-processers don't understand, it's an administrative matter, not judicial."

And Mr. Procunier: "We have to deal with communities within communities. We must decide where the inmate is to be housed. He stabs somebody—we can't prove it, but we know he did it. We don't have the arresting officer at the hearing because we don't want to get involved in an adversary sort of argument."

The views of Messrs. Park and Procunier are shared by Clinton Duffy, a pioneer of California prison reform, of whom one of his erstwhile charges said, "He represents the 'kind' school. But the way he sees it, the kindnesses are given as collateral for the loss of all civil and constitutional rights. Types like Duffy manage to fritter away the rights of prisoners with their kindness."

Mr. Duffy, now retired, was warden of San Quentin from 1940 to 1951. Before his regime, he told me, mere possession of any newspaper or magazine was a disciplinary infraction. He abolished this rule and for the first time inmates were allowed to subscribe to the newspaper of their choice—"as long as it wasn't communistically inclined, of course." (Asked what publications he considers communistically inclined, Mr. Duffy cited the California *Eagle*, a now defunct Los Angeles black-owned weekly.) To men locked up in solitary confinement, whose reading was traditionally limited to the Bible, he would often send a favorite of his own: *How to Win Friends and Influence People*, by Dale Carnegie.

To accord a trial to the prisoner accused of a felony would, he said, cost millions in taxpayers' money: "Why refer him to the district attorney when the man already has a fifty-year or life maximum? Why would we need a new charge? We refer the whole incident to the Adult Authority. We've had hundreds and hundreds come before the Adult Authority and protest their innocence. The A.A. is supposed to weigh all the facts. True, he hasn't had his day in court, but he's had it before the

Adult Authority. He *could* be wrongfully accused and wrongfully convicted, but there's only a small handful of those." (Not for prison administrator Sir William Blackstone's ancient maxim, "It is better that ten guilty persons escape than one innocent suffer.")

Is it true, as the prisoners charge, that they only get a two- to ten-minute hearing by the disciplinary committee? Mr. Duffy thought that would be about right, but he recalled one case that took almost half a day. "An inmate was charged with plotting to kill another. He had served twelve years of a twenty-year maximum sentence, his parole date was set, he was due to be released in seven days. He was a screwball type, like many people in your neighborhood or mine. We took his credits—or rather, the parole board did—which meant that he had to serve the full twenty years. When the twenty years were up, we took him before the Superior Court, which adjudged him insane and committed him to Atascadero Hospital for the criminally insane. As far as I know, he's still there."

"Why didn't you take him to court in the first place, when he was first accused?"

"Because he hadn't committed any crime, he had only been *plotting* a crime. So we didn't have the kind of evidence against him that would be needed to convict in a law court."

The legal assault on the unfettered discretion of prison authorities began with the prisoners themselves who, heartened by the limited courtroom successes of Black Muslims in the early sixties, began to bombard the courts with writs.

Mr. Park told me that the number of writs prepared by "jailhouse lawyers," prisoners who write their own, rose in San Quentin alone from a scant 50 or so in 1960 to more than 5,000 in 1970. (In the heads-I-win-tails-you-lose prison setting this even presents certain advantages to the administration: writ-writing and the study it involves can serve as a tran-

quilizer for the convict who undertakes it; it also enables
the authorities to identify him as a malcontent and deal with
him accordingly.) Few prisoner writs are successful. Yet their
very volume exerts some pressure on the courts.

A more promising route to legal redress for the convict may
be at hand. The ranks of lawyers willing to undertake the
difficult and unremunerative task of representing convicts are
being fast augmented by a mutation of the genus lawyer emerging from the law schools. Tops in his or her class or editor of
the law review, the new breed of lawyer turns a deaf ear to the
siren call of Wall Street law firms with their $15,000 starting
salary and promise of future millions. Instead these young
lawyers batter at the doors of the impecunious civil liberties
firms, or work in a neighborhood OEO office, or happily join
in the relative poverty of a legal services commune. Their
work brings them into daily contact with delinquents, "deviants," lawbreakers. Having successfully challenged arbitrary
administrative power in the vast public welfare domain, where
because of recent court decisions the clichés of "grant" and
"privilege" are giving way to new legal concepts of "entitle-
ment," they are ready to champion the rights of prisoners,
which they see as inextricably linked with the rights of students, draftees, the mentally ill—all subject to the arbitrary
rule of administrative despotism.

"We must mount a careful, concerted legal attack on the unconstitutionality of prisons," one of these, Steve Elias, told
me. "The total discretion of prison authorities is the real issue.
The composition of the parole board isn't important—even if
it *wasn't* loaded with cops, the prisoners wouldn't be better off.
What's needed is a tool, a mechanism, a vehicle to review the
deprivation of prisoners' rights within the closed prison world.
Until we get that, even legislation won't help. If a bill were
passed tomorrow granting all conceivable rights, as long as the
courts say they won't go into the prison, the prisoner in reality
has no rights, no way of enforcing the law."

The brief and spectacular growth of prison litigation was traced for me by Fay Stender of the Prison Law Project in Oakland, California. Whereas in the mid-sixties there were perhaps half a dozen lawyers who engaged sporadically in this work, she estimates that today at least 50 lawyers throughout the country are spending full time on it, plus 300 to 500 more who have taken on some prison cases. "There is tremendous interest among law students," she said. "When I was in law school in the middle fifties, I never heard the word 'prison' mentioned. Most major law schools now offer a course in prison law. Many have established legal assistance programs in which students actually go into the prisons and help prisoners with their legal problems." The new interest is reflected in a spate of law review articles and case notes on prisoners' rights, several distinguished law reviews having devoted whole issues to symposiums on the subject.

In the three years of its existence, the Prison Law Project, staffed by approximately five lawyers and five legal workers, has initiated class action suits challenging almost every aspect of the California prison operation: censorship of literature, punishment for political activity, denial of medical care, disciplinary and parole procedures, punitive transfers, conditions in the Adjustment Center. In an average week, the project receives over 150 letters from prisoners. "We answer every one," said Mrs. Stender, "and we almost never tell the writer that nothing can be done. We suggest a lawyer, or if the prisoner is preparing his own case we try to direct him to the legal materials he'll need."

The project has recruited some 35 established lawyers to take on individual prisoners' cases and class action litigation. These do not confine their efforts to the larger issues of due process, censorship, or cruel and unusual punishment but also go after some of the day-to-day injustices and harassments suffered by prisoners. For example, Leigh Athearn, a prominent corporation lawyer recruited by the project, has donated many hours of his expensive time and has made several trips to Sacramento chasing down one problem: the loss of inmates' property that frequently accompanies transfer from one prison to another. "The inmate has a watch, maybe worth $5, photographs of his family which are of course irreplaceable, legal papers he has accumulated. He's transferred from Chino to Folsom and finds all his stuff missing. He complains, and is told he never had a watch in the first place." Accustomed as he is to the well-regulated world of high finance and corporations, in which property rights are supreme, Mr. Athearn has clearly sustained many a severe shock in his dealings with the prison authorities and their allies in the Board of Control, to which he first applied for redress. "I went in expecting a fair hearing," he said indignantly. "The hearing turned out to be a total disaster. Chairman Laurence Robinson, Jr. took the position that, in essence, since the prisoner/claimant had himself committed a crime it was all right to let prison personnel rip him off at will. My suggestion that this was not a very good method of rehabilitation simply bounced off him." In a class action suit against the Department of Corrections, Mr. Athearn intends to press for cash damages for the missing objects. He was appalled to discover that there is a "barbaric state law" which denies a prisoner the right to sue for negligence or to make a claim against the state for loss of his property. "Assumpsit bring, and God-like waive the tort!" he said in his lawyerly fashion, meaning that by dipping into ancient common law he had found a way to circumvent this statute, and sue as though the department had made a contract to pay for the missing property at its reasonable value.

Several law groups organized to fight the battles of welfare recipients, tenants, victims of police repression have sprung up in various parts of the country and many of these are deeply involved in prison litigation.

The old, established civil liberties groups are now devoting much of their time and resources to prison work. William B.

Turner of the San Francisco office of the NAACP Legal Defense Fund, the organization that initiated southern school integration and right-to-vote cases in the fifties and sixties, told me that ten years ago the fund had no prison cases. "Since 1970, there's been an explosion of prison litigation," he said. "Stan Bass in our New York office and I in San Francisco spend almost full time on it. We're involved in at least forty cases."

Philip Hirschkop of the American Civil Liberties Union in Alexandria, Virginia, was first propelled into prison work in 1968 when he received a call from an inmate of the Virginia Penitentiary asking him to represent prisoners in their demand for improvement in the penal system. "That call precipitated intensive litigation on my part on behalf of prisoners," he said. "Since that time, I have made dozens of visits to prisoners in the penitentiary, in the state farm, in road camps and county jails. I have taken statements from hundreds of prisoners and received from five to twenty letters each working day from prisoners. Many reveal horrors that defy twentieth-century perception."

Hirschkop's operation, largely staffed by volunteers, consisted at first of methodically building a voluminous record against the Virginia Division of Corrections based on prisoner interviews and letters.

Following Hirschkop's assault on the Virginia prisons and his disclosures of bestial conditions in the state's penal institutions, ACLU affiliates in Virginia and New York started independent prisoners' rights projects. In 1970, the ACLU national office designated prisoners' rights as an area of major concentration, and assigned Hirschkop, together with Herman Schwartz, law professor at New York State University in Buffalo, to serve as coordinators for the National Committee for Prisoners' Rights. Of the 50 ACLU state affiliates, Hirschkop estimates that at least 30 are now actively engaged in prison litigation.

By the early seventies, these intensive organizational efforts were beginning to bear fruit in the shape of some landmark decisions signifying a new willingness on the part of some courts to intervene on behalf of prisoners. In a few cases, judges went so far as to set forth detailed regulations covering all phases of prison management, from living conditions to disciplinary procedures, to which the authorities were ordered to adhere. Some examples:

In a class action case brought by a number of Arkansas inmates, an Arkansas District Court found in 1970 that "confinement itself within a given institution" where conditions are "so bad as to be shocking to the conscience of reasonably civilized people" may amount to cruel and unusual punishment. The court declared that the Arkansas penitentiary system as it exists today is unconstitutional, and ordered prison administrators to "make a prompt and reasonable start toward eliminating the conditions that have caused the court to condemn the system . . . The lives, safety, and health of human beings, to say nothing of their dignity, are at stake . . . The start must be prompt and the prosecution must be vigorous." The court appended a lengthy memorandum outlining specific standards that officials had to meet.

In New York (whose prison system has been rated by some experts as second only to California's for its humane, enlightened policies), a U.S. District Court in 1970 reached some conclusions which call into question existing disciplinary procedures in every penal system in the country: "The prisoner carries with him to prison his right to procedural due process which applies to charges for which he may receive punitive segregation or any other punishment for which earned good time credit may be revoked . . . prisoners do not lose all of their rights under the Constitution when sentenced to prison." Finding that the inmate plaintiff was subjected to punitive segregation without due process for more than one year under "conditions which violate present standards of decency," the court awarded punitive damages against the prison authorities of $13,020, to be paid over to the inmate. Although the Second Circuit Court of Appeals reversed substantial portions of this ruling, including the punitive damages award and some of the due process requirements, the district judge's opinion nevertheless represents a significant break with traditional judicial attitudes to prison cases.

In October 1971, a U.S. District Court judge, ruling for the prisoners represented by Philip Hirschkop, wrote a searing denunciation of Virginia prison authorities, observing that the atrocities revealed in ten days of testimony at the trial were "not isolated deviations from normal practice but rather indicated traditional procedures in the state penal system." Among the traditional procedures cited by the judge: punishments including a bread-and-water diet of 700 calories which he termed "a technique designed to break a man's spirit . . . inconsistent with current minimum standards of respect for human dignity," and the use of chains, handcuffs, tear gas, beatings administered for such offenses as talking to civilians on the highway, writing letters to the press, filing petitions with courts. One prisoner, the court found, was "placed in a meditation cell by reason of the fact that he was mentally disturbed and his behavior sometimes uncontrollable . . . he screamed day and night apparently seeking help . . . until he died."

Ordering an end to these atrocities, the judge went further to require a drastic overhauling of prison disciplinary procedures. "Good time has been taken in amounts at least as large as one year on the basis of the briefest of guard's reports," he wrote. Henceforth the authorities "will cause to be put into full force and effect" due process standards in disciplinary hearings, including notice in writing of the charge, the right to cross-examine witnesses, a decision based on evidence in the record, and "in instances where proceedings may result in the loss of a substantial right" such as transfer to maximum security or loss of good time, the right to counsel.

As a result of the ruling, says Hirschkop, there have been vast changes. "Several hundred prisoners were released immediately on the good-time issue," he told me. "All inmates get hearings now before they can be disciplined. There's a tiny fraction of the number formerly locked up in solitary confinement. Beatings and the bread-and-water diet are things of the past."

There is, however, plenty of evidence that this degree of compliance with a court's orders is the exception rather than the rule, that by and large the Corrections crowd still turn a blind eye to the law and Constitution in the day-to-day job of confining and controlling their prisoners. When courts and legislatures make sporadic forays into the Corrections stronghold, occasionally securing limited rights for inmates and eliminating some of the more flagrant abuses, too often prison authorities arrogantly ignore their directives. As Professor Fred Cohen wrote in the *Buffalo Law Review*: "No one who is familiar with correctional administrators believes that a courtroom victory for an inmate is followed by a staff meeting on how best to implement the letter and spirit of the decision. Indeed, it is far more likely that the meeting will involve the problem of how to avoid the ruling or achieve minimal compliance . . . The prison community is viewed, and rightly so, as a lawless enterprise lacking in substantive and procedural safeguards . . ."

A case in point is the 1971 ruling of U.S. District Judge Alphonzo J. Zirpoli in the case of *Clutchette v. Procunier,* requiring San Quentin authorities to provide rudimentary procedural due process safeguards in any disciplinary hearing where serious punishments may result, such as indefinite confinement in segregation or extension of an inmate's prison term. Judge Zirpoli ordered that the prisoner be given notice of the right to cross-examine adverse witnesses and call witnesses in his own behalf, access to legal counsel or a counsel-substitute, a decision by an impartial tribunal based on the evidence. During the negotiations over implementation of Judge Zirpoli's decision, Director of Corrections Procunier declared in the presence of State Senator Dymally that rather than submit to due process requirements they would simply change the nomenclature and put men into solitary confinement labeled "administrative segregation" rather than "punitive segregation."

Subsequently, Professor Cohen attended some disciplinary hearings at San Quentin and observed how authorities were complying with the judge's order. "A guard is appointed to represent the inmate as counsel-substitute," he told me. "In one case, a guy was accused of murdering another inmate. The guard 'counsel' came in to the hearing before the accused appeared and told the disciplinary committee, 'He's guilty, we know he did it. We can't disclose the name of the inmate who witnessed the killing, it would put him in jeopardy.' Then the accused inmate came in, and his 'counsel' repeated, 'We know he's guilty.' The lieutenant who was conducting the hearing said, 'What have you got to say for yourself?' The inmate said he was innocent. The lieutenant said, 'We find you guilty.' There was no kind of proof. The whole procedure, from accusation to conviction, took seven minutes. Ironically, the district attorney had refused to prosecute the case for lack of evidence."

Examples of this lawlessness could, as any lawyer involved in prison cases will affirm, be multiplied indefinitely. To cite a few:

In 1968 the state legislature amended the California penal code to permit prisoners the right to subscribe to any magazines and newspapers "accepted for distribution by the United States Post Office" with the exception of obscene publications or material inciting to murder and violence. The warden of San Quentin, construing this in his own fashion, allows inmates to subscribe to *Playboy,* but disallows a number of other publications, including *Ramparts.* Why *Playboy* and not *Ram-*

parts? I asked the director of Corrections. Does not the new law state that unless courts have ruled that a publication is "obscene" or "incites to violence," it cannot be arbitrarily banned by the authorities? His reply, a succinct statement of prison officialdom's cavalier disregard of the law: "I guess the warden doesn't like *Ramparts*."

The new statute also requires that prisoners be permitted confidential correspondence with their lawyers and public officials. But lawyers' letters are still routinely opened and scrutinized at San Quentin. Why? "You can't trust lawyers, their letters are opened for inspection of contraband," explained Associate Warden James Park. How about letters to public officials? "We couldn't care less if they correspond confidentially with the governor," said Mr. Park with a sardonic grin.

Again, in 1966 a U.S. District Court, noting that this was the first inquiry of its kind into the procedures and practices of a state penal institution, made a firsthand investigation of maximum-security cells (described in Corrections handouts as "special units for problem inmates") in California's Soledad Prison. The court declared that prison authorities had "abandoned elemental concepts of decency by permitting conditions to prevail of a shocking and debased nature," and ordered them to restore "the primal rules of a civilized community." Yet four years later, in 1970, a committee of black legislators investigated charges that black inmates of the self-same "special units" under jurisdiction of the self-same warden were targets of unbridled racism and brutality on the part of guards. The legislators concluded, "If even a small fraction of the reports received are accurate, the inmates' charges amount to a strong indictment of the prison's employees on all levels as cruel, vindictive, dangerous men."

Leading Edge of the Law (house organ of Bancroft Whitney, legal publishers) for January 1972 reports, "The Arkansas prison system, which was recently declared unconstitutional by a federal court as involving cruel and unusual punishment, continues to have its troubles. Despite Supreme Court rulings that indigents may not be compelled to work out their fines, the practice continues in Arkansas where such prisoners are used to work profitable county farms. In a recent incident, a fifteen-year-old prisoner was drowned while working in a swollen stream at bridge-building. He was buried without a death certificate being filed and exhumed only after an attorney for his mother obtained a court order."

Within hours after the Attica massacre a group of lawyers including Herman Schwartz of the ACLU, fearful that horrible reprisals would be visited on the prisoners by the authorities unless outside observers were present, rushed to the home of Federal Judge John T. Curtin and obtained a court order requiring the prison to admit 33 lawyers and doctors "upon demand." Arriving at the prison in the early hours of the following day, the lawyers and doctors were denied entry. As described in the official report of the New York State Special Commission on Attica, "A 'hot-line' conversation at midnight between Commissioner William Baker, acting as the duty officer at Attica, and Commissioner van Eekeren in Albany concluded no one was to be allowed into the prison. Van Eekeren, a lawyer, stated later he had understood when he issued them that his instructions violated the court order. But he had felt strongly that prison officials should have the prior opportunity to assess the prison's condition . . ."

Two and a half months later, the Second Circuit Court of Appeals described how prison officials made use of this prior opportunity. On December 1, 1971, the court, issuing an injunction to stop further reprisals and physical abuse, found that "beginning immediately after the state's recapture of Attica on the morning of September 13, and continuing until at least September 16, guards, state troopers, and correctional personnel had engaged in cruel and inhuman abuse of numerous inmates. Injured prisoners, some on stretchers, were struck, prodded, or beaten. Others were forced to strip and run naked through gauntlets of guards armed with clubs . . . spat upon or burned with matches . . . poked in the genitals or arms with sticks. According to the testimony of inmates, bloody or wounded inmates were not spared in this orgy of brutality."

What, then, are the prospects for accomplishing any significant results via the judicial process? Lawyers involved in prison litigation are generally agreed that their single most important contribution has been to pry ajar the massive door to that closed world and, as in the civil rights litigation of the fifties and sixties, to supply ammunition and momentum to the popular movement for change. Moreover, in the courtroom and in the proliferating legislative hearings on Corrections, prison officials are increasingly being called on to justify not only their practices but their very existence. As Philip Hirschkop observed, "Once you put a prison administrator on the stand and you make him answer 'Why,' you've made a step forward. It may be the first time he's ever had to explain an action he's taken."

Prison litigators point to substantial victories won over the past few years in at least four areas. A number of courts have acted to proscribe cruel and unusual punishment, generally arising out of conditions in solitary confinement. The prisoner's right of access to the courts, counsel, and legal materials is now well established. "The earlier legal status of a prisoner was scarcely recognizable as the equivalent of human status," writes Professor Cohen; indeed, he had fewer rights than those fought for and won by humane societies for domestic animals, such as the right to minimal care and protection from brutal treatment. This transformation from "nonperson" to a "jural entity," says Cohen, is not lost on the prisoner, who has acquired a new sense of his own identity and new legal weapons to fight for that identity. Nor is it lost on prison officials, who are "nervously beginning to detect that their absolute power over the lives of inmates is threatened."

The successful litigation of the sixties establishing freedom of religion for prisoners is being followed up in several jurisdictions with an effort to extend First Amendment rights: an end to mail censorship, the right to communicate with the outside world and with the media, the right to receive and read political literature disapproved by the prison. Many of these cases have been won, and some have moved judges to strong language: "Censorship is utterly foreign to our way of life; it smacks of dictatorship," said a federal court, ruling against a ban on the Fortune Society newsletter by the New York State prisons. "Correctional and prison authorities, no less than the courts, are not above criticism, and certainly possess no power of censorship simply because they have the power of prison discipline."

More and more courts are dealing with the all-important matter of due process in prison disciplinary proceedings. And some measure of relief through the courts may be at hand for the parolee. In 1972, the United States Supreme Court decided the case of *Morrissey v. Brewer*, in which the issue, as stated by the chief justice, was "whether the Due Process Clause of the Fourteenth Amendment requires that a state afford an individual some opportunity to be heard prior to revoking his parole." The court decided it does, and ordered that in parole revocation cases the parolee be accorded two hearings: a preliminary fact-finding inquiry to determine whether there is probable cause to believe the parolee had violated the conditions of parole, and (if the hearing officer decides there is probable cause) a subsequent hearing to evaluate contested facts and determine if there is a basis for revocation. The parolee, said the court, has the right to written notice of the claimed violations and disclosure of evidence against him, to present witnesses and to cross-examine adverse witnesses, to a "neutral and detached" hearing body such as a traditional parole board (members of which need not be judicial officers or lawyers), and to a written statement by the fact-finders as to the evidence relied on and reasons for revoking parole.

Analyzing *Morrissey*, Professor Fred Cohen points out that nothing in the opinion requires that the parolee be fully informed of his rights, and that conspicuous by its absence from the due process rights is the right to counsel. In New York, he says, where an alleged violator does have a right to counsel, the experience is that "the mere presence of counsel leads to dismissals, favorable dispositions . . . where parole officials have been arbitrary and abusive in the past, their behavior improves considerably when faced with legal counsel." The Supreme Court's action in *Morrissey*, Cohen believes, is not likely to cause more than minor adjustments in parole revocation practices, but it does furnish lawyers with a "foundation for raising other compelling issues," such as right to counsel and challenges to the content of parole conditions.

Assessing the achievements, limitations, and future outlook of the current surge of prison litigation, Professor Fred Cohen reflects the views of many thoughtful prison lawyers. Among his observations:

"However one may ultimately assess the actual gains of prison litigation, one point is abundantly clear: an educational process has occurred.

"It remains to be seen whether the ostensible gains achieved through litigation serve to advance or retard the effort to deal with prisons as the most flagrant example of the race-class bias which pervades the entire criminal justice system."

He concludes, "This article has approached the matter of prison reform with both a profound distrust for prison administration and a sense of *déjà vu* about current reform efforts. The litigation efforts to date deserve credit for forcing a small opening in a system sorely in need of ventilation . . . The task now, as I see it, is to avoid the exaggeration of what is possible through litigation, to inventory and consolidate gains and to link up with other reform efforts—ranging from high-level study efforts to action-oriented groups—and move in the direction of achieving overriding objectives. Bringing decency and regularity to the prison should be viewed as a transitional step on the road to the elimination of the fortress prison . . . The burden of demonstrating the viability of our prisons is on those who manage them and it is a burden they cannot meet."

If any person is addressing himself to the perusal of this dreadful subject in the spirit of a philanthropist bent on reforming a necessary and beneficent public institution, I beg him to put it down and go about some other business. It is just such reformers who have in the past made the neglect, oppression, corruption and physical torture of the old common gaol the pretext for transforming it into the diabolical den of torment, mischief and damnation, the modern model prison.

— GEORGE BERNARD SHAW,
The Crime of Imprisonment

15

REFORM OR ABOLITION?

That "prisons are a failure" is a cliché dating from the origin of prison, repeated by top people throughout the last century and by at least the last four Presidents of the United States. The failure has given rise to demands for reform. The authors of *Struggle for Justice,* a report prepared by a Working Party of the American Friends Service Committee (several of whom are ex-convicts), summarize the "reformist prescription" which, they say, after more than a century of persistent failure, is bankrupt: "More judges and more 'experts' for the courts, improved educational and therapeutic programs in penal institutions, more and better trained personnel at higher salaries, preventive surveillance of predelinquent children, greater use of probation, careful classification of inmates, preventive detention through indeterminate sentences, small 'cottage' institutions, halfway houses, removal of broad classes of criminals (such as juveniles) from criminal to 'nonpunitive' processes, the use of lay personnel in treatment—all this paraphernalia of the 'new' criminology appears over and over in nineteenth-century reformist literature."

Anyone with the fortitude to read that forbidding literature will recognize the formula. Witness the Declaration of Principles adopted by the first Congress of the American Prison Association in 1870, which in addition to urging classification, indeterminate sentences, treatment of the offender, opted for "preventive institutions for the reception and treatment of children not yet criminal but in danger of becoming so," education as a "vital force in the reformation of fallen men and women," and prisons of "a moderate size," preferably designed to house no more than 300 inmates.

Or the 1931 report of the Wickersham Commission, appointed by President Hoover in 1929: "We conclude that the present prison system is antiquated and inefficient. It does not reform the criminal. It fails to protect society. There is reason to believe that it contributes to the increase of crime by hardening the prisoner. We are convinced that a new type of penal institution must be developed, one that is new in spirit, in method, in objective. The commission recommends . . . individual treatment . . . indeterminate sentences . . . education in the broadest sense . . . skillful and sympathetic supervision of the prisoner on parole . . ."

Skip now to *The Challenge of Crime in a Free Society,* the 1967 report of the President's Crime Commission, which calls for more intensive parole supervision, establishment of "model, small-unit correctional institutions," the strengthening of screening and diagnostic resources "at every point of significant decision," the upgrading of educational and vocational training programs.

These calls for reform invariably follow in the wake of riots and strikes by prisoners protesting intolerable conditions. Thus the pattern over the past century tends to be circular: an outbreak of prison disturbances—followed by brutal suppression of the insurgents—followed by newspaper clamor for investigation—followed by broad agreement that prisons are horrible, destructive places fulfilling none of their supposed objectives —followed by a restatement of the penological nostrums of preceding decades.

There have always been those who looked beyond palliative reform proposals to the essential character of prison, found it intrinsically evil and not susceptible to reform, hence have advocated abolishing prisons altogether. To cite four examples, spanning just over a century:

According to the minutes of the 1870 Congress of the American Prison Association, "Judge Carter, of Ohio, avowed himself a radical on prison discipline. He favored the abolishment of prisons, and the use of greater efforts for the prevention of crime. He believed they would come to that point yet . . . Any system of imprisonment or punishment was degradation, and could not reform a man. He would abolish all prison walls, and release all confined within them . . ." (The next speaker, we are told, "dissented in toto" from these remarks.) Speaking to the inmates of the Cook County Jail in Chicago, in the year 1902, Clarence Darrow said: "The only way in the world to abolish crime and criminals is to abolish the big ones and the little ones together. Make fair conditions of life. Give men a chance to live. Abolish the right of private ownership of land, abolish monopoly, make the world partners in production, partners in the good things of life. . . . There should be no jails. They do not accomplish what they pretend to accomplish. If you would wipe them out there would be no more criminals than now. They are a blot upon any civilization, and a jail is an evidence of the lack of charity of the people on the outside who make the jails and fill them with the victims of their greed." Dr. Frank Tannenbaum, a pioneer student of prison, wrote in 1922: "We must destroy the prison, root and branch. When I speak of the prison, I mean the mechanical structure, the instrument, the technique, the method which the prison involves." In 1972 Federal District Judge James Doyle of the Western District of Wisconsin, ruling on a prison mail censorship case (*Morales v. Schmidt*), wrote: "I am persuaded that the institution of prison probably must end. In many respects it is as intolerable within the United States as was the institution of slavery, equally brutalizing to all involved, equally toxic to the social system, equally subversive of the brotherhood of man, even more costly by some standards, and probably less rational."

I share this conviction. But I also agree with the authors of *Struggle for Justice,* one of the most thoughtful and important texts to come out of the current prison turmoil, when they note "the impossibility of achieving more than a superficial reformation of our criminal justice system without a radical change in our values and a drastic restructuring of our social and economic institutions . . ."

They caution against proposals for prison abolition that are really exercises in label switching: "Call them 'community treatment centers' or what you will, if human beings are involuntarily confined in them, they are prisons." They suggest an easy way to test the real intent of the proponents of abolition: Is the proposed alternative program voluntary? Can a person enter at will and leave at will? If the answer is No, "then the wolf is still under the sheepskin."

In the wake of Attica many scandalized liberals joined with the radicals in embracing the slogan "Tear Down the Walls." The test proposed in *Struggle for Justice* may usefully be applied to this rhetoric. A case in point is a headline in the San Francisco *Chronicle* (November 22, 1971): "Ramsey Clark's

Solution: Abandon Prisons Entirely." According to the story, which is somewhat murky, Mr. Clark had told the press that "anti-social offenders" should be "treated as one human being at a time rather than as columns of dehumanized statistics," and that "the ideal spot for their containment" might be "a section of an apartment house or the wing of a Y." On closer examination, his position as set forth in his book *Crime in America* reveals that he is in reality advocating larger doses of the same old reformist prescription. He asserts that "Corrections is by far the best chance we have to significantly and permanently reduce crime in America," and he bestows his unqualified blessing on the indeterminate sentence which, he says, "gives the best of both worlds—long protection for the public yet a fully flexible opportunity for the convict's rehabilitation . . . the prisoner would have the chance, however remote [!] of release at any time. The correctional system would have its opportunity to rehabilitate." Mr. Clark's brand of "abolition" adds up to more money for Corrections, more supervision of the offender at every stage of his progression from probation to parole, a vast extension of discretionary power of captor over captive.

Again, in 1971, Arthur Waskow, resident fellow at the Institute for Policy Studies in Washington, circulated a proposal for a "five-year campaign around the demand that by July 4, 1976, all the prisoners in all U.S. jails must be released and the jails closed." The following year he wrote in a guest editorial in *Saturday Review*, "Forget about reform; it's time to talk about abolishing jails and prisons in American society." He proposes these alternatives: for those convicted of violent crimes, "a fenced-off town (or farm) where the gates are closed in one direction only, closed to exit by the initial residents . . . but open to entrance by *all* visitors or joiners invited by those residents." For burglars, embezzlers, shoplifters, vandals, tax-evaders—"even corporation executives who have given orders that resulted in poisoning the air and water with cancer-producing agents"—he would have a self-governing kibbutz-like community where all share work and income equally.

Mr. Waskow seems to have overlooked a few practical difficulties: would he not have to erect gun towers and guard houses around the fenced-off town and the self-governing kibbutz to prevent the "residents" from walking out with the "visitors or joiners"? But aside from that, he apparently accepts prevailing notions of what constitutes "serious crime," for he would segregate the "violent" criminals in the fenced-off city but admit the carcinogenic corporation executive to the less punitive kibbutz. Absent a transformation of the American criminal justice system and the society it serves, his alternative prisons would still be repositories for the same mix of poor-white/black/brown offenders that fill the traditional prisons, for who else gets convicted of the crimes he has enumerated: violent crimes, burglary, vandalism, shoplifting? Given the realities of cops, robbers, and courts in America today, the embezzlers, tax-evaders, and miscreant corporation executives are not likely to find themselves confined in that kibbutz.

The objectives of prison, as traditionally set forth by penologists, are threefold: protection of the public by locking up the lawbreaker, deterrence, and rehabilitation. (A fourth one, punishment, has virtually been dropped from the lexicon of the modern prison man, although this is the only objective that prison actually achieves.) Today, few would seriously argue that prison rehabilitates. The proponent of abolition will, however, meet with deeply felt objections on the other counts: "My God, if you let all those killers, rapists, thugs, burglars on the streets, it wouldn't be safe to venture out!" And, "If we had no prisons, the crime rate would soar."

Protection of the public is no doubt uppermost in the minds of both the hard-line law-and-order advocate and the liberal who, while he would like to see prisoners better treated, would fear the consequences should the prison gates be swung open. Does not the law-abiding citizen feel a twinge of self-satisfaction in these days of mounting terror of crime and criminals as he drives by the fastness of San Quentin or Sing Sing to think that behind these walls are locked away those ruffians who would rape his daughter, steal his television set, mug him on the street?

His belief that the prison protects him is, it turns out, illusory. Only a minuscule fraction of lawbreakers are in prison, the vast majority are all around us in the community.

The President's Commission on Causes and Prevention of Violence says that for an estimated nine million crimes committed in the United States in a recent year, only 1½ percent of the perpetrators were imprisoned. Carl Rauh, advisor to the deputy attorney general of Washington, D.C., describes the process: "Of 100 major crimes [felonies], 50 are reported to the police. For 50 incidents reported, 12 people are arrested. Of the 12 arrested, 6 are convicted of anything—not necessarily of the offense reported. Of the 6 who are convicted, 1.5 go to prison or jail."

What of the categories of crime that send the public temperature soaring the highest—murder, sex offenses, street muggings? Does not imprisonment of the perpetrators protect the public from their depredations?

In recent years the nationwide annual figure for "willful homicide" has run about 15,000. Thus the gruesome fact must be faced that within the next twelve months approximately that number of people will meet violent death at the hands of a killer. But it is also self-evident that the murderer of tomorrow's headlines is at large in the community tonight. Of those who have been caught, prosecuted, and imprisoned, the number who murder again when eventually released (as most of them are) is so negligible that it is not even recorded on the "recidivism" tables so beloved of criminologists: for example, a study by the Philadelphia Bar Association of 215 persons pardoned after serving terms for murder shows that only seven were later arrested, and of these only one, or .05 percent, was for murder. Murderers, prison and parole officials will tell you, frequently make model prisoners and are the best "risk" of all; most of them could be let out tomorrow without endangering the public safety. They have generally acted out some desperate personal frustration against a member of their family, are most likely to repent, least likely to repeat—unless, of course, they are psychotic, in which case they don't belong in prison at all.

Of those convicted of sex offenses (and thereafter forever stigmatized in police records as "sex-offenders"), only an estimated 5 percent have committed crimes of violence. The other 95 percent are in either for activities which, while they may be annoying, do not physically harm anybody, such as voyeurism and indecent exposure, or for types of sexual behavior arbitrarily labeled "criminal" like statutory rape, homosexuality, and the mysterious "unspeakable crime against nature" which turns out to be what lots of respectable married couples do. Contrary to popular myth, the nonviolent sex-offender almost never escalates into a dangerous rapist or sex-fiend type. Nor are the violent sex-offenders usually repeaters: actually, of all serious crimes, only homicide shows a lower record of recidivism.

As for street muggers, few are ever caught, since it is in the nature of their crime to strike at night or in unfrequented places. New York, dubbed "Fear City" by its inhabitants, is today in the grip of an almost palpable terror of street attacks, muggings, beatings. A white middle-class New Yorker told me: "People are afraid of three main types of criminal: underprivileged blacks and Puerto Ricans, drug addicts, and aberrant psychotics. That's what crime means to people." His views would no doubt be shared by many a ghetto-dweller, on whom the burden of such crime falls most heavily. Is prison the solution to any of the problems he enumerated—poverty, drug addiction, insanity? If so, to protect New Yorkers from all who suffer from these disabilities it would be necessary to turn half the city into a prison. At that, it might be wise never to let any of the prisoners out again, since it is popularly believed that people emerge from prison "worse" than when they went in.

This is in fact exactly what Governor Rockefeller has proposed as a solution for New York's drug problem. He would take all persons convicted as peddlers of heroin, LSD, amphetamines, barbiturates, and hashish, and lock them up for the rest of their lives without possibility of parole. He would do the same to all persons convicted of crimes of violence while under the influence of these drugs. Charles Howe of the San Francisco *Chronicle* analyzed what this would mean if applied to California, where there are an estimated 60,000 heroin addicts, at least half of whom are selling drugs to support their habit. In 1971, 56,700 Californians were arrested for possessing or selling heroin and other illegal drugs. If 20,000 of these were convicted of peddling and incarcerated for life, says Howe, 50 new prisons costing about $10 million apiece would have to be built. He estimates the cost of keeping the 20,000 locked away for life at more than $4 billion.* Meanwhile those who were not caught would, presumably, continue to ply their trade and their numbers would continue to multiply. In New York City there are an estimated 150,000 addicts. Extrapolating from Howe's figures, the Rockefeller proposal would require 125 new prisons at a cost of $1.25 billion, and the lifetime imprisonment of 50,000 New Yorkers, which would amount to $9 billion.

The net effect of Rockefeller's proposal would be to send the crime rate soaring. Aryeh Neier, executive director of the American Civil Liberties Union, says "every new get-tough law enforcement approach to narcotics only has the effect of

* His figure is low; projecting from the Department of Corrections' 1972–73 budget, the cost would be over $5 billion.

driving the price of heroin higher and forcing addicts to commit additional crimes to satisfy their habits."

The prevailing estimate is that narcotics addicts are responsible for about 50 percent of the property crime in New York. In the early part of this century there were more narcotics addicts per capita in the United States than there are today (the typical addict in those days was a white, affluent woman over 40; only 7 percent of addicts were "lower class"), but because narcotics were cheaply and legally available they were not a crime problem. The ACLU advocates adoption of the English drug maintenance system, under which heroin and other drugs are legally prescribed for addicts by doctors, a system that Consumers Union recommends as "magnificent," thus eliminating the demand for black market heroin.

What of crimes committed by psychotics? A conversation with a New York friend comes to mind. One of his co-workers, a young woman in her early twenties, had gone into a Manhattan church during her lunch hour and knelt down to pray. An unknown assailant attacked her, beat her brutally and cut up her face with a razor, stole her purse, then disappeared into the noonday crowd. This is, of course, a perfectly hideous story and one that unfortunately can be matched in varying degrees whenever two or three New Yorkers are gathered together. I deliberately chose this one from dozens I have heard because of its sensational overtones: the innocent young victim praying, the bizarre, incredibly savage nature of the attack on her . . . but what is the moral? The threat of prison evidently did not deter the assailant. Nor, had he been caught, convicted, and imprisoned, would he have been "rehabilitated."

The friend who related this episode did so as an argument against abolishing prisons: "What do you *do* with people like that?" But in the event the person who did this nasty piece of work was never caught, should one then punish the rest of the prison population (the great majority of whom have done nothing of the sort) for his crime? Such crimes as his, which arouse the greatest horror and revulsion, are psychotic and aberrant—indeed it is their psychotic and aberrant nature that evokes such passionate reaction. The question then is whether prison is an acceptable means to cope with such behavior, and whether it is worth maintaining the monstrous prison bureaucracy with all its cruelty and irrationality to preserve the illusion that it protects us from such random, senseless acts of violence.

To what extent is fear of prison successful as a deterrent to crime? Obviously those who have been caught and convicted were not deterred, and from the large numbers of repeaters one must infer that the prison experience did not turn them into the paths of righteousness. Criminologists scratch their heads over the deterrent effect of fear of prison on the general populace; most have concluded that respectable people are kept that way mostly from fear of the shame of *any* brush with the law, and that the principal deterrent for such folks is fear of arrest. Most of us can attest to this from our own experience. We are deterred from speeding by the fearful whine of the Highway Patrol siren; but are we deterred from carving up our friends and relations only by fear of execution or life imprisonment?

In 1968 the California Assembly Committee on Criminal Procedure published a report on the deterrent effect of criminal sanctions in a period when the legislature was drastically increasing penalties for a number of crimes. The committee analyzed the effects of these increased penalties on the rate of criminal violations, using as examples a crime of violence and a victimless crime: assault on policemen, and possession of marijuana.

Before 1961, a person who assaulted *anyone* with a deadly weapon *could* receive up to one year in jail, or up to ten years in a state prison. By 1966 the sentence for attacking a policeman with a deadly weapon had been set by the legislature at five years to life in a state prison. During the same

period, 1961–66, the rate of attacks on Los Angeles policemen rose from 8.4 per 100 officers per year to 15.8, an
increase of 90 percent. Thus after five years of increased
penalties, a Los Angeles policeman was almost twice as likely
to be attacked as he was before the increases.

In 1961 the legislature removed the sentence of one to
twelve months in the county jail as an *optional* penalty for
the possession of marijuana and *required* that possessors serve
one to ten years in a state prison. In 1961 less than 3,500
persons were arrested for marijuana offenses. But in 1966
marijuana arrests had risen to over 18,000, an increase of
over 500 percent, despite the widely publicized stiffer sentences
decreed by the legislature.

As proof that long prison terms do not deter but have the
opposite effect, the committee cited a number of studies, one
of the most striking of which arose out of a 1963 U.S.
Supreme Court decision, *Gideon v. Wainwright,* in which the
court affirmed the right of indigent felony defendants to
counsel. As a consequence of the decision the State of Florida
was obliged to discharge long before the normal release date
1,252 indigent prisoners who had been tried and convicted
of felonies without counsel. The Florida Department of Corrections conducted a study of these early releases, comparing
their recidivism rate with an equal number of full-term releases.
Result: twenty-eight months after discharge, 25 percent of
the full-term release group had returned to criminal activity
compared with only 13.6 percent of the early release group.
Commenting on this study, the American Bar Association
observed, "Baldly stated . . . if we, today, turned loose all
of the inmates of our prisons without regard to the length of
their sentences and, with some exceptions, without regard to
their previous offenses we might *reduce* the recidivism rate
over what it would be if we kept each prisoner incarcerated
until his sentence expired . . ."

From these findings the assembly committee concluded that

"the amount of time served has no measurable effect upon crime among released convicts," and that "time served can be reduced without increasing recidivism." It made the further comment that "what is often neglected in official statements is not that prisons fail to rehabilitate but the *active* nature of the destruction that occurs in prison." But it did not explore the next question that logically arises from these conclusions: if prisons were abolished and thus "time served" reduced to zero, would *this* have any measurable effect on crime?

An experiment currently underway in Massachusetts, first of its kind anywhere in the country, may point to some answers. During the sixties the Massachusetts juvenile prisons (the official designation for which was "state training schools"), housing offenders and abandoned children aged seven to seventeen, were notorious for their horrible living conditions, overcrowding, and brutality. In October 1969, the governor appointed a new commissioner of the Department of Youth Services, Dr. Jerome Miller, whose avowed intention was to abolish all juvenile institutions in the state.

The cost of jailing a juvenile for one year was $10,000, he said, "enough to send him to Harvard University* with a $100 a week allowance and a summer vacation in Europe." He told the press, "We made a basic decision that it would do no good to pump more money and more programs into the existing system because the system can chew up reforms faster than you can dream up new ones. It's a sick system that destroys the best efforts of everyone in it, and we decided to look for alternatives."

In Dr. Miller's first two years in office the population of the juvenile prisons was cut in half, from 1,200–1,500 to 650–750. By the autumn of 1972, the institutional population had been reduced to 80–100, about 6 percent of the numbers imprisoned when Dr. Miller took office three years earlier.

* A yardstick I have heard used by prison critics from coast to coast.

The erstwhile prisoners have been released to their own homes, or placed in foster homes, prep schools that generally cater to upper- and middle-class youngsters, residential centers where they are free to come and go. "We don't allow locks or handcuffs," said Dr. Miller. A youth placed in one of these programs is not re-imprisoned if he commits another crime but is shifted to another program. Some of the older boys and girls are encouraged to find their own place to live and may be given a regular stipend, ranging from $5 weekly pocket money to $90 a week for a short period to help them get started in their new life. Only those considered "seriously assaultive," about 40 to 50, are housed in the one remaining "secure facility," and these are placed in the custody of a private ex-convict group. Another 50 to 60 youths are in a special psychiatric facility for those deemed "disturbed." (Despite the closing of the institutions, the anticipated budgetary saving did not quite come up to expectations. Although the department was able to return $2 million of its $10 million budget to the state treasury, as of mid-1972 it was unable to find substitute jobs for most of the former guards. They proved unsuitable by temperament and inclination to serve as foster home parents, so they remain on the department's payroll, guarding the now empty prisons.)

Miller has virtually no interest in "general deterrence," which he says is a middle-class concept that does not apply to most of the youngsters committed to his department. He assumes that imprisonment and the threat of imprisonment have no measurable effect on the rate of crime. As of January 1973, his views on this would seem to be empirically borne out: preliminary reports showed there was no discernible increase in overall juvenile crime rates as a result of shutting down the prisons—if anything, there had been a slight drop in arrest rates. Moreover, since the closing of the prisons there has been a "dramatic drop in the amount of violence among those committed to the department," says Miller. "The institutions generate violence. Taking the kids out has resulted in de-escalating the violence."

The new programs are not limited to those committed for minor offenses but include offenders in every category, Dr. Miller told me. There are four or five who were committed for murder, numerous armed robbers and youths convicted of aggravated assault housed in open settings: "Institutions are not the answer to those problems, either, unless you're going to keep them in until they're middle-aged. The large majority don't need residential treatment, they need to be in their own homes with additional help which we supply through college students who act as 'big brothers.' " The 80 to 100 kept in secure institutions are youngsters who had committed "really weird, crazy crimes," and even in these cases the goal is to re-locate them in the community as soon as possible.

Evaluating the Massachusetts experiment, an unpublished working paper of the Committee for the Study of Incarceration concludes that it represents an important departure from traditional methods of selection for release on probation or parole in which there is merely a culling process: only those regarded as the "best risks" are not incarcerated, while the less good risks are still imprisoned. In Massachusetts, "for the first time there is a genuine attempt at de-institutionalization, not merely a continuation of the culling process," for young offenders who seem quite likely to (or do) commit further crimes are not re-imprisoned. However, the process of de-imprisonment is not complete, "as certain types of special risks —viz. 'dangerous' offenders and 'psychiatric' cases—are still retained in secure institutions."

There is much that is debatable in the content of Dr. Miller's alternative to prison. As the Committee for the Study of Incarceration points out, it is conceived very much within the tradition of the "individualized treatment model" to which so many injustices suffered by prisoners for more than half a century can be laid. The staff has wide discretion; there are few standards or rules to determine whether the offender shall be placed in one of the rather regimented residential units or sent home with minimum supervision. This may present the "familiar problems of inequality of treatment, bias and lack of predictability" that have beset well-intentioned reform programs of the past. All depends on the attitude of the staff; should the present idealistic, child-oriented staff be replaced by more cautious or punitive types, the entire tenor of the program could change overnight.

I cite the experiment not to enter this debate, but as the only extant example of virtually complete de-imprisonment and its consequences in terms of the crime rate and "deterrence." What inferences does Dr. Miller draw for adult prisons from its apparent success in this regard? "At the risk of sounding naïve and simplistic, I believe the same approach could be implemented for offenders of all ages. Out of every 1,000 in prison there are probably no more than 20 who couldn't be safely out on the streets."

The notion that 75 percent, or 80 percent, or 90 percent of the prison population could be freed tomorrow without danger to the community or increase in the rate of crime finds amazingly wide acceptance in prison administration circles. Even the toughest wardens of the roughest prisons will quote some such figure off the record. Somewhere between 10 percent and 25 percent of "hard-core" criminals are "too dangerous" to be loosed on society, according to this dictum. Ronald Goldfarb and Linda Singer report in their exhaustive study *After Conviction*: "We have asked every experienced, practicing prison official we know how many of the inmates currently held in confinement really need to be incarcerated in order to protect the public from personal injury. All agree that only a small minority of all the present inmates in American prisons—most estimated between 10 and 15 percent—could be considered to be so dangerous."

Benjamin Dreyfus, a San Francisco lawyer with wide experience in criminal law, tells me that in the early sixties he heard the then deputy director of the California prison system speak at an ACLU meeting: "One of the things he said in his speech was that 80 percent of the prison population did not belong there. I had a later opportunity to quote that figure to Carl G. Hocker, then captain in charge of custody at San Quentin. He is now warden of the Nevada State Prison, known throughout the system as a stern disciplinarian and a tight custody man. I expected him to denounce the idea that anybody who was in prison did not belong there, and probably to advocate a healthy increase in prison populations. To my surprise, Warden Hocker told me that he thought the figure was too low, and that in his opinion 90 percent of the people in prison do not belong there."

Should the wardens be taken at their word, and 90 percent of their captives freed, this would be a giant step in the direction of abolishing prison. Yet the very concept of the "dangerous" 10 percent, and the prison as an appropriate place to confine them, is fraught with peril. Those so designated can, under the indeterminate sentence, be held sometimes forever in what amounts to lifelong preventive detention.

Somebody has to decide who is dangerous. The decision rests first of all with the sentencing judge, and there is no consensus among judges as to who is "dangerous." A criminologist told me of a sentencing institute for federal judges in which each judge was given an identical fictional pre-sentence report on a fictional offender. "The variety of sentences proposed was unbelievable," he said. "For the same offense one judge would have given probation; another, twenty years in the penitentiary."

Once a person is committed to prison, the decision as to his dangerousness rests with his keepers. An exchange on this subject took place at a forum arranged by the American Friends Service Committee in February 1973 at which Mr. Philip Guthrie was representing the California Department of Corrections. A woman in the audience asked, "What is a dangerous person? Traditionally all levels of prison—state, federal, local—say that a person who protests or resists the inhumanities of prison, for example in a food strike or a work strike, has now become a dangerous element. So isn't it true that dangerous can also mean, according to the people who run the system, one who protests, one who resists that authority? So it really is a catch question what that dangerous person is." To which Mr. Guthrie replied, "I agree. I suppose if you asked what a dangerous person is, everyone in this room would have a different definition. In Sacramento, in the Department of Corrections, or in the institutions which undertake the responsibility we don't have the answer either."

Be that as it may, the label "dangerous" is increasingly used by the authorities to immure protesters and political militants in the dungeon recesses of prison. The case of George Jackson, who spent eleven years of his short life in prison—most of them in solitary—for the original offense of stealing $70, is now known the world over. His book *Soledad Brother* was hailed by distinguished critics here and abroad as "the voice of a free black man in white America," "letters that chart the spiritual and political growth of an extraordinary man," "a work reflecting the love, the strength, the revolutionary fervor characteristic of any soldier of the people." In contrast are the views of L. H. Fudge, associate superintendent of a California prison camp, who wrote in a confidential memorandum to his colleagues: "This book provides remarkable insight into the personality makeup of a highly dangerous sociopath . . . This type individual is not uncommon in several of our institutions. Because of his potential and the growing numbers, it is imperative that we in Corrections know as much as we can about his personality makeup and are able to correctly identify his kind . . . This is one of the most self-revealing and insightful books I have ever read concerning a criminal personality."

Yet another function of prison, generally omitted from the penological catalogue, is coercion. The distinction between deterrence and coercion is real. It is one thing to say you must not do this and that; it is something else again to say that you must do such and such. A case in point was the Selective Service Law: thou shalt register, thou shalt accept induction, thou shalt kill when ordered to do so by a superior officer. Failure to do so will result in imprisonment. Here the law and prison become coercive instruments of political policy. In the 1960's the prison as an instrument of political coercion became conspicuous, not only with respect to the draft and the Vietnam war generally, but also with respect to commandments as to where people might eat, sit in a bus, drink water, or pass it out as urine. The number of persons imprisoned as an exercise in such political coercion soared into the thousands. The term "political prisoner" gained common currency.

This term has been adopted by prisoners convicted of offenses that, in common usage, are not considered political. They argue that they are the victims of class and/or ethnic oppression, that imprisonment is employed to coerce their acquiescence to a status quo of deprivation, indignity, injustice. Huey Newton perceives two kinds of political prisoners: "First there are the great majority of prisoners who are illegitimate capitalists. These are the unemployables, the blacks, browns, and poor whites who have no choice, no real method of partaking of the good things in life except by ripping off the system. They may have no political consciousness, but their attack upon the property system, motivated as it is by the institutionalization of unemployment and underemployment under capitalism, is in a sense *political*.

"Then there are the truly political prisoners, those who, like the Panthers, do not accept the legitimacy of the social order . . . they understand why they are in prison; they recognize that to be a legitimate capitalist is to exploit the oppressed and that to be an illegitimate capitalist will only perpetuate a social order where the privileges of some are based on the poverty and powerlessness of others. The truly political prisoners are growing in numbers and influence; they pose a real threat to the prison system today."

Is Newton's definition of the political prisoner valid? Envision, if you can, a prison system populated primarily by the white and well-to-do, convicted of crimes that are peculiar to the affluent: price-fixing, purchase and sale of political influence, product adulteration, industrial pollution, criminal neglect of industrial safety standards, fraudulent stock manipulation, manufacture of unsafe, death-dealing cars, violation of the minimum-wage law . . . That this notion seems like the wildest flight of fancy is already a commentary on the class character of the prison system. After all, no one would expect that those who command political power and control the criminal justice system would use these in such a manner as to make them the likeliest candidates for imprisonment. It is axiomatic that as long as privileges of class and skin color prevail in the society this state of affairs will be reflected in its prisons, and will determine who coerces whom. As the authors of *Struggle for Justice* observe, "Criminal justice is inextricably interwoven with, and largely derivative from, a broader social justice. The construction of a just system of criminal justice in an unjust society is a contradiction in terms."

Newton's analysis is underscored by Samuel Jordan, inmate in the Pennsylvania state penal system, writing in the *Criminal Law Bulletin*: "Of the 1.2 million criminal offenders handled each day by some part of the United States correctional system, 80 percent are members of the lowest 12 percent income group—or black and poor," he writes. "These facts testify to the systematic use of prison as a weapon. It is used against the poor, particularly poor people of color."

Jordan discerns three general categories of prison reformer. There are those who would redefine crime and criminals, decriminalize a range of victimless crimes: "It is not accidental that this concern happens to include most of the young white people from middle-class and upper-class families who are now in jail for marijuana and other 'excusable' offenses." In this connection it is interesting to note that in listing drugs whose sale he would punish by life imprisonment, Governor Rockefeller omitted marijuana. Could this be because he does not want to see his pot-smoking young relatives behind bars? Conversely, might not Samuel Jordan support a proposal, like that of the ACLU, to decriminalize heroin offenses, the punishment of which now falls most heavily on young blacks and browns?

A second category of reformer, says Jordan, is the "bourgeois humanist" with the "case-worker-counselor approach, three decent meals a day, work-release programs, honor blocks, movies." This approach results in "harsh social stratification . . . inmates are induced to add competition for honor merits to existing in-group tensions. Perhaps this competition for status is what the bourgeois humanist considers adequate preparation for successful reentry into his society." The third type of reformer, the "bourgeois realist" who interprets all things in terms of dollar value and sound business practice, simply says prisons are too costly and are not doing their job: "Fortunately, the reforming realist presently is convinced that prison is a bad investment, tying up monies more profitably invested elsewhere."

In the course of current prison upheavals, says Jordan, the prison system "has been revealed as incapable of the control and conditioning for which it is intended . . . prisons have become unwieldy and burdensome." Thus the task of the reformer is to "make prison a viable institution in American life," his objective to "make prisons work."

Discussing the current emphasis by all stripes of reformers on reducing prison populations and substituting small, manageable prisons for the huge fortresses now in use, Jordan points out that "even the reformers who recognize racism do not seek to alter the racial or economic composition of the inmate population. If this population were cut in half tomorrow but remained composed of the same percentages of black, brown, and poor people, the use of prison as a class weapon would remain unchanged." He concludes, "The prison reformer—wittingly or unwittingly—is an agent of capitalism, a used-car salesman. His mission is to repaint, adjust, or gloss over the flaws in one of society's potent control mechanisms."

Nor are prisoners the only ones to discern that reforms may strengthen the system in the long run by refurbishing the façade of prison and thus assuaging the public conscience. A tactical question that nags at many political activists engaged in the struggle to improve prison conditions and advance prisoners' rights is that their very achievements may tend to confer legitimacy on the prisons and thus help to perpetuate the system. As posed by Professor Cohen: "Do you retard the reduction of prison populations, or even the eventual demise of prison, by winning such items as the right to read *Playboy,* to exercise more frequently, to be notified in writing of a disciplinary charge, or to receive and send uncensored mail?" The rejoinder of one lawyer was that "I am not the one to tell a prospective inmate client that he should remain in solitary until the Revolution." Which is much the same answer as one I received from a convict of whom I had asked, Should prisons be abolished? Should they be reformed? Do you see reform and abolition as antithetical goals? He wrote back: "Sure, prisons should be abolished. But don't let up on reform. If I've got cancer, don't wait for the definitive cure to be discovered before treating me."

Thus it becomes imperative to distinguish between two types of reform proposals: those which will result in strengthening the prison bureaucracy, designed to perpetuate and reinforce the system, and those which to one degree or another challenge the whole premise of prison and move in the direction of its eventual abolition.

In the first category are reforms that call for more money for Corrections, more prison employees at higher salaries, more researchers, more experts, more utilization of the latest scientific know-how in "treatment" of prisoners, building new correctional therapeutic communities to replace the old fortress prisons. These are projected by Corrections as essential for prisoner rehabilitatior and for prevention of further disturbances. They sound attractive to the well-intentioned reformer, who believes they will make life more tolerable for the prisoner.

As the prison crisis deepens, we shall doubtless hear earnest appeals for such measures, not only from the prison bureaucracy itself but from the ever-proliferating ancillary interests that stand to gain from the widespread demand for prison reform. New tentacles of the prison octopus are growing, nourished by immense sums made available through government agencies, universities, private foundations. There's gold in them thar therapeutic correctional communities, model small-unit institutions, youth training schools. For example, in 1971, Attorney General John N. Mitchell announced that the Law Enforcement Assistance Administration had earmarked $178 million for "correctional aid to the states and localities" and would double that amount in the following year, bringing the total LEAA contribution to Corrections to well over a quarter of a billion dollars. A National Clearinghouse for Criminal Justice Architecture had been established, he said, "to provide technical assistance for improving existing facilities and for designing new buildings."

A spot-check of government prison research funding for 1971–73 reveals these allocations: LEAA, $8½ million; Manpower Administration, $5½ million; National Institute of Mental Health, $2¼ million. Among the research projects underway: "Misconduct at Kennedy Youth Center," "Investigation of the Effects of Anxiety on Behavior in a Correctional Setting," "Youthful Offender's Aggressive and Automatic Reactions to Predictable and Unpredictable Events," "Sickline Abuse in a Correctional Setting as Related to Self-Image."

There is little wonder that architects, researchers, professionals in half a dozen lines of endeavor are standing in line with their hands out. There are fortunes to be made, and professional prestige to be gained, on the correctional trail. As we have seen, to the extent these worthies have succeeded in entering the lucrative prison field, the result has almost invariably been further degradation of the prisoner, and more specifically the punishing repression of those prisoners who dare to assert their constitutional rights or challenge institutional policies.

Reform proposals in the second category, most frequently originating with the prisoners themselves, are aimed at reducing the discretionary power of authorities all down the line, at reducing prison populations, and at restoring to prisoners those constitutional rights that will enable them to organize and fight injustice within the system. As defined by the authors of *Struggle for Justice*, they are "actions that shift power relationships, that place power in the hands of the heretofore powerless, and have the potential for creating basic change . . . the movement for prisoners' rights runs directly counter to the growth of unfettered discretionary powers; it calls for shifting power from administrators toward those who are on the receiving end." More than this, they are actions that would restore human dignity to the convict and remove him from the status of "nonperson" to which he has traditionally been relegated.

If the starting point is that prisons are intrinsically evil and should be abolished, then the first principle of reform should be to have as few people as possible confined, and for as short a time as possible. Thus a broad range of offenses should be made noncriminal: prostitution, gambling, vagrancy, adult-consenting sexual acts, all drug use. Cash bail should be abolished, and those now jailed awaiting trial released.

Sentences, which for most crimes are longer in the U.S. than in any other Western country, should be.vastly reduced in length. While there should be a great many educational, medical, psychiatric, vocational, and other services available to prisoners, these should be independent of the prison system with no coercion attached: the prisoner should be free to take them or leave them, his decision in no way affecting length of time served. Parole, beloved of reformers as a "helping service" and loathed by convicts as just an extension of prison servitude, should be abolished and replaced by unsupervised release—again, with a vast range of "helping" services available on a voluntary basis to the man or woman coming out of prison.

The untrammeled discretion now invested in the authorities via indeterminate sentences should be eliminated. In practice, these set up a penal system within a penal system, the first ostensibly governed by due process, the second totally uninhibited by the vaunted principles of Anglo-Saxon jurisprudence. In fact, it is a system of double jeopardy, in which the accused is sentenced twice, once in a court of law and the second time by the parole board.

Influential voices are now being raised in support of many of these proposals. In 1972, the Annual Chief Justice Earl Warren Conference, sponsored by the Roscoe Pound-American Trial Lawyers Foundation, devoted its entire agenda to prisons. Participants included judges, nationally known trial lawyers, professors of law, criminology, and philosophy, prosecutors, even a few enlightened prison administrators and commissioners of Corrections.

The conference overwhelmingly rejected the idea that prisons can be reformed. Only two of the participants refused to go along with the proposition that "there is no convincing evidence of the effectiveness of rehabilitative programs in prison." According to the foreword to the final report, "The conferees clearly felt that the time for minor, piecemeal 're-forms' is long past. Rather, the report challenges the funda-mental value of today's prison as an institution. In effect, as we read the findings and as we heard them formulated, their plain-spoken direction is toward the elimination of prisons, now too often just a way to cage society's castoffs. A similar con-clusion is reached on our bail system." Among the conference recommendations: "The ultimate goal should be no indetermi-nancy whatsoever in sentences." "Bail as a prevailing system should go. An end to it would, of course, also serve to further reduce prison and jail populations." "The state has a duty to provide economic, social, educational, and medical services in prisons, as well as in the communities, but . . . their accept-ance by prisoners should be voluntary . . . they should have no bearing whatsoever on the length of a prisoner's incarcera-tion." ". . . prisoners should be permitted to organize, without fear of reprisal, for the purpose of effective expression and negotiation of grievances."

The emergent organization of prisoners into something akin to a trade union within the penitentiaries is an entirely new phenomenon, an outgrowth of the prison rebellion of the past decade. For the first time prisoners are attempting to unite and demand a voice in their own destiny. The Prisoners Union, a national organization with headquarters in San Francisco, controlled and staffed by ex-convicts, is coordinat-ing these efforts in prisons throughout the country. The union's three-point objective: "Abolishment of the indeterminate sen-tence and all its ramifications; establishment of workers' rights for the prisoner, including the right to collectively organize and bargain; the restoration of civil and human rights for the prisoner." To implement these, the union would "organize convicts into a body which can keep public pressure on the

Department of Corrections, work toward the abolition of hand-picked inmate advisory committees and replace them with a democratically elected, unionized body of convicts, demand unrestricted access to the judicial system and the press." In spite of the almost insurmountable difficulties attendant on organizing within the prisons, by March 1973 the Prisoners Union had recruited 3,000 members in 68 state and federal penitentiaries. Its publication, *The Outlaw*, named after the underground news sheet of the 1968 strike in San Quentin, reaches some 5,000 prisoners, despite the efforts of authorities in many prisons to exclude it.

To the correctional bureaucracy a union of prisoners is a contradiction of penal terms, for it is an affirmation of community and of rights, two attributes a prisoner is supposed to shed along with civilian clothes in the induction process. Since a prison regime is absolutist, and hence peculiarly susceptible to the absolute corruptions of power, a ruthless attempt to crush the incipient prison movement is a clear and present danger. Only informed, insistent, massive public support of the prisoners can counter this threat.

The union movement is no modest reform proposal, no effort to gild the cage. By striving to establish the rights of the prisoner as citizen and worker, it seeks to diminish the distinctions between him and those on the other side of the walls. In a profound sense the ultimate logic of such a movement is abolition, for to the degree that those distinctions are obliterated, to the same degree the prison is stripped of its vital functions.

Unhappily, the distinctions can be diminished not only by the acquisition of citizenship rights on the inside, but also by erosion of those rights on the outside. Do prison experiments in behavioral manipulation and ubiquitous surveillance foreshadow a Clockwork Orange society to come? Society created the prison in its own image; will history, with its penchant for paradox, reverse those roles? The questions are chilling because empirical data, as well as the prophecies of artistic perception, suggest such a direction.

When people come upon the celebrated statement of Eugene V. Debs—"While there is a soul in prison, I am not free"— they are prone to regard it as an affirmation of extraordinary human compassion. This it is. But it also may be viewed as a profound social insight. And not only because the prison system, inherently unjust and inhumane, is the ultimate expression of injustice and inhumanity in the society at large. Those of us on the outside do not like to think of wardens and guards as our surrogates. Yet they are, and they are intimately locked in a deadly embrace with their human captives behind the prison walls. By extension so are we.

A terrible double meaning is thus imparted to the original question of human ethics: Am I my brother's keeper?

APPENDIX

Two California convicts write in the National Lawyers Guild *Practitioner*: "We wonder, have some of you become bored with this fad—this movement? Has the exercising of your limited freedoms exhausted you? Has the rule of order, maintained by the threat of force, frightened you? Or— maybe, your awareness of our fight has faded with the dimmed public concern. Our days pass in the shadow of gun-towers; our nights are disturbed with these unanswered questions. A prisoner's life is an endless reaching out, for the hand that is never there."

For readers who would like to extend that hand—and for prisoners who need assistance—I suggest getting in touch with one of the many organizations engaged in various aspects of the fight for prisoners' rights. In the following list, compiled with the help of the Prison Law Project, the American Civil Liberties Union (ACLU), and the National Prison Project, I have attempted to give a sample of publications, and of organizations in each state that welcome and solicit members, volunteer workers, or both.

PUBLICATIONS

Civil Liberties Review
22 East 40th Street
New York, N.Y. 10016

Committee for Prison Humanity &
*   Justice Newsletter*
1029 4th Street
San Rafael, California 94901

Fortune News
29 E. 22nd Street
New York, N.Y. 10010

The Freeworld Times
314 Social Science Tower
University of Minnesota
Minneapolis, Minnesota 55455

Midnight Special
23 Cornelia Street
New York, N.Y. 10014

Prisoners' Digest International
P.O. Box 89
Iowa City, Iowa

Prison Law Reporter
(a project of the Young Lawyers
    section and Commission on
    Correctional Facilities and
    services of the American
    Bar Association)
15th Floor Hoge Bldg.
Seattle, Washington 98104

Southern Patriot
c/o SCEF
3210 W. Broadway
Louisville, Kentucky 40211

The Outlaw
1345 7th Avenue
San Francisco, California 94122

ORGANIZATIONS

ALABAMA

Alabama CLU
P.O. Box 1972
University, Alabama 35401

CLU
Box 6144
University, Alabama 35401

ALASKA

Alaska CLU
Box 80625
College, Alaska 99701

Civil Liberties Union
820 East 8th Avenue
Anchorage, Alaska 99501

ARIZONA

Arizona Civil Liberties Union
822 A Mill Avenue
Tempe, Arizona 85281

Civil Liberties Union
Arizona State University
Law School at Tempe
Tempe, Arizona 85281

ARKANSAS

Arkansas CLU
P.O. Box 61
Fayetteville, Arkansas 72701

CALIFORNIA

Berkeley

Black Law Journal Prisoners
    Program
Boalt Hall School of Law
University of California
94720

Los Angeles

American Civil Liberties Union of
    Southern California
323 West 5th Street, Room 202
90013

Coalition Against Repression
8162 Melrose Avenue
90046

Committee United for Political
    Prisoners
701 West 34th Street
90007

Elizabeth Fry Center
3429 West Olympic Boulevard
90019

Pasadena

American Friends Service Committee
980 North Fair Oaks Avenue
91103

Project J.O.V.E. II
814 North Fair Oaks Avenue
91103

Sacramento

Friends' Committee on Legislation
    Organizations
1107 9th Street, Room 1030
95814

Friends Outside
P.O. Box 15865
95813

San Jose

Friends Outside
State Office
712 Elm Street
95126

San Francisco

American Civil Liberties Union of
    Northern California
593 Market Street
94105

American Friends Service Committee
2160 Lake Street
94121

Austin MacCormick Center
American Friends Service Committee
1251 Second Avenue
94122

Connections
3189 16th Street
94103

Contact
Center for Peace and Social Justice
109 Golden Gate Avenue
94102

Sam Melville Memorial Books
    for Prisoners' Program
143 Highland Avenue
94110

NAACP Legal Defense Fund, Inc.
12 Geary Street, 8th Floor
94108

Organizations at 558 Capp Street
94110
    National Lawyers Guild
    People's Law School
    Prison Law Collective
    San Francisco Medical Committee
        for Human Rights
    Women's Jail Project

Prisoners Union
1345 Seventh Avenue
94122

Transitions to Freedom, Inc.
1251 Second Avenue
94122

San Rafael

Committee for Prison Humanity and
    Justice
1029 Fourth Street
94901

San Diego

Project J.O.V.E.
722 Broadway
92101

COLORADO

ACLU of Colorado
1711 Pennsylvania Street
Denver, Colorado 80203

American Friends Service Committee
346 Acoma Street
Denver, Colorado 80223

Colorado National Lawyers Guild
1450 Pennsylvania, Room 27
Denver, Colorado 80203

CONNECTICUT

Connecticut CLU
57 Pratt Street, Room 713
Hartford, Connecticut 06103

Connecticut Prison Association
340 Capital Avenue, Room 343
Hartford, Connecticut 06115

DELAWARE

ACLU of Delaware
2409 West 17th Street
Wilmington, Delaware 19806

Community Legal Aid Society
204 West 7th Street
Wilmington, Delaware 19801

Delaware Council on Crime and
    Justice, Inc.
701 Shipley Street
Wilmington, Delaware 19801

WASHINGTON, D.C.

American Friends Service Committee
Pre-Trial Justice Program
1800 Connecticut Avenue, N.W.
20009

Bureau of Rehabilitation
412 5th Street, N.W.
20001

Board of Church and Society
United Methodist Church
Department of Law, Justice &
    Community Relations
100 Maryland Avenue, N.E.
20002

Committee for the Study of
    Incarceration
733 15th Street, N.W.

Coordinating Center for Education
    in Repression and the Law
1616 Longfellow Street, N.W.
20011

Efforts From Ex-Convicts (EFEC)
1302 New Jersey Avenue, N.W.
20001

Efforts From Ex-Convicts
803 Florida Avenue, N.W.

National Lawyers Guild, D.C.
    Chapter
412 5th Street, N.W., Room 708
20001

National Prisoners Alliance
2325 15th Street, N.W.

National Prisoners Project
1424 6th Street, N.W.

FLORIDA

ACLU of Florida
556 W. Flagler Street
Miami, Florida 33130

American Friends Service Committee
27 1st Street N.
St. Petersburg, Florida 33701

American Friends Service Committee
3005 Bird Avenue
Coconut Grove, Miami, Florida
33133

Gainesville Legal Collective
115 S. Main Street
Gainesville, Florida

GEORGIA

ACLU of Georgia
88 Walton Street
Atlanta, Georgia 30303

ACLU Southern Regional Office
5 Forsyth Street, N.W.
Atlanta, Georgia 30303

Center for Correctional Reform
15 Peachtree Street, Suite 902
Atlanta, Georgia 30303

Legal Assistance to Inmates
Emory University School of Law
Atlanta, Georgia 30322

National Lawyers Guild
815 Myrtle Street
Atlanta, Georgia 30308

Prison Legal Group
P.O. Box 1932
Athens, Georgia 30601

HAWAII

ACLU of Hawaii
235 Queen Street, Suite 410
Honolulu, Hawaii 96813

John Howard Association of Hawaii,
    Inc.
200 North Vineyard Boulevard,
Suite 102
Honolulu, Hawaii 96817

IDAHO

Boise Valley ACLU
1300 N. 23rd Street
Boise, Idaho 83702

East Idaho ACLU
2810 Holly Place
Idaho Falls, Idaho 83401

ILLINOIS

Chicago

ACLU of Illinois
6 S. Clark Street
60603

The Administration of Criminal
  Justice and Prison Reform
  Committee of the Young
  Lawyers Section of the
  American Bar Association
1155 E. 60th Street
60637

Alliance to End Repression
22 E. Van Buren
60605

American Friends Service Committee
407 S. Dearborn
60605

Associated Urban Ministries
  Presbytery of Chicago
1210 E. 62nd Street
60637

Chicago Connections
21 E. Van Buren
60605

Con/tact
537 S. Dearborn Street
60605

Cook County Special Bail Project
22 E. Van Buren
60605

Medical Committee for Human
  Rights
2251 W. Taylor Street
60612

National Lawyers Guild
21 E. Van Buren
60605

Carbondale

People's Law Office
1215 W. Sycamore

Elgin

Prison Release Ministry, United
  Methodist Men
Northern Illinois Conference of
  the Methodist Church
1932 Lin-Lor Lane
60120

Urbana

Radical Clearinghouse
Room 293, Illini Union
University of Illinois

INDIANA

The Church Federation of Greater
  Indianapolis
1100 W. 42nd Street
Indianapolis, Indiana 46208

EXCEL in Indiana
15 E. Washington Street, Suite 915
Indianapolis, Indiana 46204

Indiana CLU
609 Thomas Bldg.
15 E. Washington Street
Indianapolis, Indiana 46204

PACE/Public Action in Correctional
  Effort
1433 N. Meridian, Suite 211
Indianapolis, Indiana 46202

IOWA

American Friends Service Committee
4211 Grand Avenue
Des Moines, Iowa 50312

Church of the New Song
Box 2001
Iowa City, Iowa 52240

Iowa CLU
1101 Walnut Street
Des Moines, Iowa 50309

KANSAS

Kansas CLU
1138 Amidon
Wichita, Kansas 67203

Kansas Media Project
Box 3366, Jayhawk Station
Lawrence, Kansas 66044

Seven Step Foundation
Box 635
Topeka, Kansas 66601

KENTUCKY

Kentucky CLU
205 South 4th Street, Room 302
Louisville, Kentucky 40202

Southern Conference Educational
    Fund
3210 West Broadway
Louisville, Kentucky 40211

LOUISIANA

ACLU of Louisiana
606 Common Street, Room 302
New Orleans, Louisiana 70130

Community Service Center
4000 Magazine Street
New Orleans, Louisiana 70115

Community Service Center
P.O. Box 30102
New Orleans, Louisiana 70190

MAINE

Maine CLU
142 High Street, Room 411
Portland, Maine 04101

MARYLAND

ACLU of Maryland
1231 N. Calvert Street
Baltimore, Maryland 21202

American Friends Service Committee
319 E. 25th Street
Baltimore, Maryland 21218

Efforts From Ex-Convicts in
    Montgomery County
500 Gilscott Place
Rockville, Maryland 20850

The Prisoners Aid Association of
    Maryland
109 Old Town Bank Building
Gay Street at Fallsway
Baltimore, Maryland 21202

MASSACHUSETTS

Amherst

Martin Luther King Jr. Social Action
    Counsel
207 Hampshire House, University of
    Massachusetts
01002

Boston

Civil Liberties Union of
    Massachusetts
3 Joy Street, Room 4
02108

Massachusetts Council of Churches
14 Beacon Street
02108

Paulist Center
5 Park Street
02108

Cambridge

American Friends Service Committee
48 Inman Street
02138

Coalition to Fight Political
Repression
P.O. Box 31
02140

Libra
1145 Massachusetts Avenue
02138

National Lawyers Guild
595 Massachusetts Avenue
02139

Red Prison Movement at Law
Commune
698 Massachusetts Avenue
02139

Roxbury

Prison Committee
8 Warren Street
02119

MICHIGAN

ACLU of Michigan
808 Washington Boulevard Bldg.
234 State Street
Detroit, Michigan 48226

American Friends Service Committee
1414 Hill Street
Ann Arbor, Michigan 48104

MINNESOTA

Minneapolis

American Friends Service Committee
807 S.E. 4th Street
55414

Efforts From Ex-Convicts
2127 Riverside Avenue
55404

HIRE (Helping Industry Recruit
Ex-Offenders)
1931 Nicolett Avenue
55403

Joint Religious Legislative
Committee
122 West Franklin
55404

Minnesota CLU
628 Central Avenue, N.E.
55413

Minnesota Connections Collective
1427 Washington Avenue South
55404

Murton Foundation for Criminal
Justice, Inc.
314 Social Science Tower
University of Minnesota
55455

MISSISSIPPI

ACLU of Mississippi
128½ N. Gallatin Street
Jackson, Mississippi 39201

MISSOURI

ACLU of Eastern Missouri
8011 Clayton Road, Suite 216
St. Louis, Missouri 63117

ACLU of Western Missouri
5123 Truman Road
Kansas City, Missouri 64127

American Friends Service Committee
7184 Manchester
St. Louis, Missouri 63143

Citizens Lobby for Penal Reform
P.O. Box 13726
Kansas City, Missouri 64199

MONTANA

ACLU of Montana
2715 Louise Lane
Billings, Montana 59801

NEBRASKA

Nebraska CLU
302 N. 22nd Street, Apt. 606
Omaha, Nebraska 68102

NEVADA

ACLU of Nevada
P.O. Box 8947
Reno, Nevada 89507

NEW HAMPSHIRE

New Hampshire CLU
3 Pleasant Street, Room 7
Concord, New Hampshire 03301

NEW JERSEY

ACLU of New Jersey
45 Academy Street, Room 203
Newark, New Jersey 07102

NEW YORK

Binghamton

Probe
66 Chenango Street
13901

Buffalo

Attica Defense Committee
P.O. Box 74
Bidwell Station
14222

National Prison Project of the
    ACLU
SUNY/AB Law School
77 West Eagle
14202

New York

American Friends Service Committee
15 Rutherford Place
10003

Center for Constitutional Rights
588 Ninth Avenue
10036

Church Women United
Room 10 F
777 United Nations Plaza
10017

Committee for Public Justice
22 E. 40th Street
10016

Committee of the Professions
133 W. 72nd Street, Room 402
10023

Department of Church and Society
Division for Mission in North
    America
Lutheran Church in America
231 Madison Avenue
10016

Fortune Society
29 E. 22nd Street
10010

Lower Eastside Action Project, Inc.
540 E. 13th Street
10009

NAACP Legal Defense Fund, Inc.
10 Columbus Circle, Suite 2030
10019

National Committee for the Defense
    of Political Prisoners
P.O. Box 1184, Harlem
10027

National Conference of Black .
    Lawyers
112 W. 120th Street
10027

National Emergency Civil Liberties
  Committee
25 E. 26th Street
10010

National Lawyers Guild
23 Cornelia Street
10014

New York Civil Liberties Union
84 Fifth Avenue, Suite 300
10011

Osborne Association
114 E. 30th Street
10016

Quaker Committee on Social
  Rehabilitation Inc.
135 Christopher Street
10014

Task Force on Justice
New York Presbytery, U.P.C.,
  U.S.A.
7 W. 11th Street
10011

Women's Prison Association
110 Second Avenue
10003

NORTH CAROLINA

ACLU of North Carolina
P.O. Box 3094
Greensboro, North Carolina 27402

American Friends Service Committee
1818 S. Main Street
High Point, North Carolina 27260

Jobs for Ex-Offenders
c/o State Department of Corrections
831 W. Morgan Street
Raleigh, North Carolina 27603

NORTH DAKOTA

Red River Valley ACLU
Box 5502
Fargo, North Dakota
58102

Ward County ACLU
c/o Carl Cavelage
Political Science Division
Minot State College
Minot, North Dakota 58701

OHIO

ACLU of Ohio
203 E. Broad Street, Suite 200
Columbus, Ohio 43215

American Friends Service Committee
915 Salem Avenue
Dayton, Ohio 45406

Cincinnati Chapter ACLU
1717 Section Road
Cincinnati, Ohio 45237

Concerned Convicts of America
1560 E. 21st Street
Cleveland, Ohio 44114

Greater Cleveland Chapter ACLU
2108 Payne Avenue, Room 825
Cleveland, Ohio

Prisoner Support Group
Antioch College
Yellow Springs, Ohio 45387

The 7th Step Foundation
133 E. Market Street
Akron, Ohio 44308

OKLAHOMA

Oklahoma CLU
200 N.W. 36th Street
Oklahoma City, Oklahoma 73118

OREGON

ACLU of Oregon
309 Senator Bldg.
732 S.W. Third Street
Portland, Oregon 97204

American Friends Service Committee
4312 S.E. Stark Street
Portland, Oregon 97215

National Lawyers Guild
P.O. Box 14763
Portland, Oregon 97214

National Prisoners Alliance
215 S.E. 9th Street
Portland, Oregon 97214

PENNSYLVANIA

Philadelphia

ACLU of Pennsylvania
260 S. 15th Street
19102

American Friends Service Committee
National Office
160 N. 15th Street
19102

Community Assistance for Prisoners
2513 N. 30th Street
19132

Imprisoned Citizens Union
P.O. Box 4731
19134

National Lawyers Guild
1307 Sansom Street
19107

Pennsylvania Prison Society
311 S. Juniper Street
19107

Pennsylvania Program for Women
    and Girl Offenders
1530 Chestnut Street, Suite 711
19102

People's Bail Fund
1411 Walnut Street, Suite 1201
19102

Prisoners' Rights Council
1 N. 13th Street
13th Floor
19107

Media

Friends Suburban Project
P.O. Box 54
19063
(jail and prison sub-project of
Meeting for Social Concerns,
Philadelphia Yearly Meeting of
Friends)

Pittsburgh

ACLU (Pittsburgh Chapter)
c/o John Flanigan
508 H. Laurance Hall
Point Park College
15222

American Friends Service Committee
Pittsburgh Pretrial Justice Program
1300 Fifth Avenue
15219

Community Release Agency
1100 Lawyers Bldg.
15219

Grubstake Rehabilitation Center
2400 E. Carson Street
15203

RHODE ISLAND

Rhode Island CLU
84 Shaw Avenue
Cranston, Rhode Island 02905

Rhode Island Coalition on Prison
    Reform
P.O. Box 1347, Annex Station
Providence, Rhode Island 02901

SOUTH CAROLINA

ACLU of South Carolina
2016½ Green Street, Room 3
Columbia, South Carolina 29205

SOUTH DAKOTA

South Dakota ACLU
2212 Crestwood Road
Sioux Falls, South Dakota 57105

TENNESSEE

ACLU of Tennessee
P.O. Box 91
Knoxville, Tennessee 37901

TEXAS

American Friends Service Committee
4717 Crawford Street
Houston, Texas 77004

American Friends Service Committee
318 W. Houston, Room 328
San Antonio, Texas 78205

Prisoners Aid Center
1207 21st Street
Huntsville, Texas 77340

Texas CLU
1711 H. Sherry Street
Arlington, Texas 76010

Texas CLU
600 W. Seventh
Austin, Texas 78701

Texas CLU
905 Richmond
Houston, Texas 77006

Texas CLU
P.O. Box 9262
San Antonio, Texas 78204

Texas Jail & Prison Coalition
1701 E. 19th Street
Austin, Texas 78702

UTAH

ACLU of Utah
P.O. Box 8012
Salt Lake City, Utah 84108

VERMONT

Vermont CLU
26 State Street
Montpelier, Vermont 05602

VIRGINIA

ACLU of Virginia
10 S. 10th Street
Insurance Bldg.
Richmond, Virginia

ACLU Post-Conviction Assistance
    Project
P.O. Box 3322
University Station
Charlottesville, Virginia 22903

Penal Reform Institute
P.O. Box 234
110 N. Royal Street
Alexandria, Virginia 22313

WASHINGTON

ACLU of Washington
2101 Smith Tower
Seattle, Washington 98104

Administration of Criminal Justice
    & Prison Reform Committee of
    the Young Lawyers Section of
    the ABA
Prison Law Reporter
15th Floor, Hoge Bldg.
Seattle, Washington 98104

American Friends Service Committee
814 N.E. 40th Street
Seattle, Washington 98105

Inside-Out
106 21st Street East
Seattle, Washington 98102

Job Therapy, Inc.
150 John Street
Seattle, Washington 98101

National Lawyers Guild
P.O. Box 263
Seattle, Washington 98111

President, Resident Government
Council Washington State
Penitentiary
P.O. Box 520
Walla Walla, Washington 99362

Steilacoom Prisoners' Support House
P.O. Box 918
Steilacoom, Washington 98388

WEST VIRGINIA

West Virginia CLU
537 Fifth Avenue
Huntington, West Virginia 25701

WISCONSIN

Correctional Service Federation
526 W. Wisconsin Avenue
Milwaukee, Wisconsin 53203

Wisconsin CLU
1840 N. Farwell Avenue
Room 1, Lower Level
Milwaukee, Wisconsin 53202

Wisconsin Correctional Service
436 W. Wisconsin Avenue, 5th floor
Milwaukee, Wisconsin 53203

NOTES

page 4, line 35
"the prison as a formal or complex organization"
>Lawrence Hazelrigg, ed.: *Prison Within Society* (New York: Doubleday & Company; 1968), p. ix.

page 6, line 5
"The authors of the Attica Commission Report"
>*Attica*, The Official Report of the New York State Special Commission on Attica (New York: Bantam Books, Inc.; 1972), p. 18.

page 7, line 3
"The viewpoint of many an old-time guard"
>U.S., Congress, House, Select Committee on Crime, *American Prisons in Turmoil,* hearings, 92nd Cong., 1st sess., November 29–December 3, 1971 (Washington, D.C.: U.S. Government Printing Office; 1972), p. 301.

page 7, line 19
"Fay Stender in her preface to *Maximum Security*"
>Eve Pell, ed.: *Maximum Security: Letters* (New York: E. P. Dutton & Co., Inc.; 1972), p. 13.

page 7, line 29
"The inmates of prison are not irretrievable"
>Eugene Victor Debs: *Walls and Bars* (Chicago: Socialist Party; 1927), pp. 19, 25.

page 8, line 13
"a much lower moral level than the average"
>Bertrand Russell: *The Autobiography of Bertrand Russell 1914–1944* (Boston: Little, Brown and Company; 1968), pp. 30–2.

page 9, line 2
"Dr. Allan Berman"
From a paper, "MMPI Characteristics of Correctional Officers," presented to the Eastern Psychological Association Meeting, New York City, April 16, 1971. See also Detroit *News,* September 20, 1971.

page 9, footnote, line 6
"the San Francisco *Examiner*"
San Francisco *Examiner,* December 17, 1972.

page 9, footnote, line 11
"the Sacramento *Press Journal*"
Sacramento *Press Journal,* February 12, 1973.

page 10, line 26
"An item in the April 1972 *Grapevine*"
G. Norton Jameson, ed., in *The Grapevine* (April 1972) (Sioux Falls, S.D.: American Association of Wardens and Superintendents).

page 12, line 25
"Director's Rule Book, I decided not to bother"
State of California, Department of Corrections: *Rules of the Director of Corrections and of the Wardens and Superintendents* (Sacramento, rev. edn. 1967).

page 13, line 34
"We are men"
The New Yorker (September 25, 1971).

CHAPTER 3, 101 YEARS OF PRISON REFORM

page 32, line 9
"the prisoner has the advantage"
David J. Rothman: *Discovery of the Asylum* (Boston: Little, Brown and Company; 1971), pp. 84–5, quoting from James B. Finley: *Memorials of Prison Life* (Cincinnati, Ohio, 1851), pp. 41–2.

page 32, line 32
"From this volume"
American Correctional Association: *Congress of Corrections Proceedings,* 1870. Reports of proceedings issued by Association under its earlier names: from 1874 to 1907, the National Prison Association; from 1908 to 1954, the American Prison Association. All proceedings will be found catalogued under the American Correctional Association.

page 33, line 3
"Hard-headed wardens"
Blake McKelvey: *American Prisons* (Chicago: Univ. of Chicago Press; 1936), p. 71.

page 35, line 20
"we may be satisfied, we may be content"
> American Correctional Association: *Congress of Corrections Proceedings,* 1966.

page 38, line 4
"I did it to protect the inmates"
> *The New York Times,* February 28, 1971, p. 26.

page 38, line 5
"he later testified"
> U.S., Congress, House, Select Committee on Crime, *American Prisons in Turmoil,* hearings, 92nd Cong., 1st sess., November 29–December 3, 1971 (Washington, D.C.: U.S. Government Printing Office; 1972), Part I, pp. 342–3.

page 40, line 20
"Correctional Officer Training"
> Allen E. Tullos: "The Alabama Prison System: Recent History, Conditions, and Recommendations" (Civil Liberties Union of Alabama, March 1973), unpubl.

page 43, line 26
"in *Crime and Delinquency*"
> Paul W. Keve: *Crime and Delinquency,* Book Reviews (October 1970), pp. 443–4.

CHAPTER 4, THE CRIMINAL TYPE

page 46, line 7
"the seductions of the Evil One"
> E. H. Sutherland: *Principles of Criminology* (Chicago: Lippincott; 1934), p. 43.

page 47, line 12
"Thieves have mobile hands and face"
> Marvin E. Wolfgang: "Cesare Lombroso," in *Pioneers in Criminology,* Hermann Mannheim, ed. (London: Stevens & Sons, Ltd.; 1960), pp. 168–225.

page 47, line 23
"to check up on Lombroso's findings"
> Harry Barnes and Negley K. Teeters: *New Horizons in Criminology,* 3rd edn. (Englewood Cliffs, N.J.: Prentice-Hall; 1959), p. 127.

page 48, line 2
"Studies published in the thirties by Gustav Aschaffenburg"

G. Aschaffenburg: "Kriminalanthropologie und Kriminalbiologie," *Handwoerterbuch der Kriminologie* (1933–6).

page 48, line 8
"in the forties came the gland men"
  New Horizons in Criminology, p. 133.

page 48, line 22
"examples of the fallacy of false cause"
  Barnes and Teeters: *New Horizons*, p. 129.

page 49, line 7
"Studies made by clinical psychologists of prison populations"
  Barnes and Teeters: *New Horizons*, p. 7.

page 49, line 22
"Bernard Shaw points out"
  George Bernard Shaw: *The Crime of Imprisonment* (New York: The Philosophical Library; 1946), pp. 105–6.

page 49, line 35
"looks like a criminal behind bars"
  Eugene Victor Debs: *Walls and Bars* (Chicago: Socialist Party; 1927), p. 53.

page 50, line 9
"a speaker at the American Prison Congress said"
  American Correctional Association, *Congress of Corrections Proceedings*, 1870.

page 51, line 3
"the centuries of hereditary hate back of them"
  J. E. Brown: "The Increase of Crime in the United States," *The Independent* (1907), pp. 832–3. Quoted in Theodore R. Sarbin: *The Myth of the Criminal Type* (Connecticut: Wesleyan Univ. Press; 1969).

page 51, line 7
"*The Nature and Future of the Urban Crisis*"
  Edward C. Banfield: *The Unheavenly City* (Boston: Little, Brown; 1970), pp. 45–62.

page 51, line 21
"a feeble, attenuated sense of self"
  Ibid., p. 53.

page 51, line 23
"The lower-class individual lives in"
  Ibid., p. 62.

page 52, line 4
"these areas also have the highest crime rate"
> Ramsey Clark: *Crime in America* (New York: Simon and Schuster; 1970), p. 59.

page 52, line 20
"17 percent to burglary"
> James Wallerstein and C. J. Wylie: "Our Law-abiding Law-breakers," *Probation* (1947), quoted in *Struggle for Justice*, A Report on Crime and Punishment in America, Prepared for the American Friends Service Committee (New York: Hill & Wang; 1971), p. 107.

page 53, line 6
"police are conditioned to perceive some classes of persons"
> Sarbin: *The Myth of the Criminal Type*, p. 8.

page 53, line 14
"The President's Crime Commission"
> *The Challenge of Crime in a Free Society*, A Report by the President's Commission on Law Enforcement and Administration of Justice (Washington, D.C.: U.S. Government Printing Office; 1967), p. 79.

page 54, line 9
"bails and fines of the participants"
> *Struggle for Justice*, p. 130.

page 54, line 10
"The President's Crime Commission Report notes"
> *The Challenge of Crime in a Free Society*, p. 44.

page 54, line 24
"underlined by Professor Donald Taft"
> Barnes and Teeters: *New Horizons*, p. 169, quoting Donald Taft, from *Criminology*, 3rd edn. (New York: Macmillan; 1956).

page 56, line 24
"by focusing on the criminal mind of the child"
> Robert C. Maynard: "Testing Children for Criminal Bent," San Francisco *Chronicle*, April 6, 1970.

CHAPTER 5, WHAT COUNTS AS CRIME?

page 58, line 2
"For release Monday p.m. June 22, 1970"
> Charles McCabe: "The Uncrime Wave," San Francisco *Chronicle*, September 22, 1971.

page 61, line 4
"about 15 per cent in the same period"
> *The Challenge of Crime in a Free Society,* A Report by the President's
> Commission on Law Enforcement and Administration of Justice (Wash-
> ington, D.C.: U.S. Government Printing Office; 1967), p. 23.

page 61, line 6
"Norval Morris and Gordon Hawkins say"
> Norval Morris and Gordon Hawkins: *The Honest Politician's Guide
> to Crime Control* (Chicago: Univ. of Chicago Press; 1970), p. 56.

page 61, line 13
"the President's Crime Commission Report"
> *The Challenge of Crime in a Free Society,* p. 39.

page 61, line 16
"two-thirds of rape victims"
> Ibid., p. 40.

page 61, line 28
"by 1964, 8,000"
> Albert D. Biderman: "Social Indicators and Goals," from *Social In-
> dicators,* Raymond A. Bauer, ed. (Cambridge, Mass.: M.I.T. Press;
> 1966), p. 125.

page 61, line 33
"Albert D. Biderman made these observations"
> Ibid., p. 118.

page 62, line 23
" 'crime' has increased"
> Improving Criminal Statistics. American Statistical Association Con-
> ference.

page 63, line 28
"a spokesman explained to the press"
> San Francisco *Chronicle,* January 7, 1972, p. 6.

page 64, line 15
"The Blacksville No. 1 coal mine"
> San Francisco *Chronicle,* July 26, 1972, p. 5.

page 64, line 18
"The Sunshine Mining Co. in Kellogg, Idaho"
> San Francisco *Chronicle,* May 13, 1972.

page 64, line 20
"Lockheed Shipbuilding and Construction Co."
> Los Angeles *Times,* July 20, 1971, p. 1.

page 64, line 27
"from 8 to 15 percent of all food"
> Harry Barnes and Negley K. Teeters: *New Horizons in Criminology,*
> 3rd edn. (Englewood Cliffs, N.J.: Prentice-Hall; 1959), p. 45.

page 64, line 35
"As George Bernard Shaw put it"
> George Bernard Shaw: *The Crime of Imprisonment* (New York: The
> Philosophical Library; 1946), pp. 69–70.

page 65, line 7
"The Commission estimates"
> *The Challenge of Crime in a Free Society,* p. 48.

page 65, line 12
"persons of high status and social repute"
> Ibid., p. 47.

page 65, line 32
"The question"
> Ibid., p. 99.

page 66, line 5
"Polls cited by the Kerner Commission"
> *Report of the National Advisory Commission on Civil Disorders*
> (New York: Bantam Books; 1968), p. 302.

page 66, line 16
"Professor Reiss assembled and trained 36 observers"
> Norman Johnston, Leonard Savitz, and Marvin E. Wolfgang, eds.:
> *The Sociology of Punishment and Correction,* 2nd edn. (New York:
> John Wiley and Sons; 1970), pp. 57–65.

page 66, footnote, line 11
" 'inaccurate' and 'misleading' "
> *The New York Times,* November 28, 1971.

page 68, line 34
"Among the Knapp Commission's revelations"
> *Newsweek* (November 8, 1971), pp. 77–8.

page 69, line 25
"in the archives of government statistics"
> Phillip Buell and Paul Takagi: "Code 984: Death by Police Inter-
> vention," unpubl.

page 69, footnote, line 1
"According to *The New York Times*"
  The New York Times, August 22, 1971.

page 70, line 27
"killed in the line of duty"
  The New York Times, July 25, 1971.

page 70, line 32
"killed by police in that city than any other"
  San Francisco *Chronicle*, March 29, 1972.

page 71, line 1
"the Chicago Patrolmen's Association responded"
  Sacramento *Bee*, March 29, 1972.

page 72, line 4
"thirty-three in 1790 to almost 600 by mid-twentieth century"
  Herbert A. Bloch and Gilbert Geis: *Man, Crime, and Society* (New
  York: Random House; 1962), p. 65.

page 72, line 7
"were not then criminal violations"
  Harry Barnes and Negley K. Teeters: *New Horizons in Criminology*,
  3rd edn. (Englewood Cliffs, N.J.: Prentice-Hall; 1959), p. 74.

page 72, line 13
"since the Puritans first came over"
  Peter Barton Hutt: "Perspectives on the Report of the President's Crime
  Commission—the Problem of Drunkenness," *Notre Dame Lawyer*,
  857–64 (1968).

page 75, line 1
"in *I Chose Prison*"
  James V. Bennett: *I Chose Prison* (New York: Alfred A. Knopf;
  1970), pp. 177–8.

page 75, line 9
"In *An Eye for an Eye*"
  H. Jack Griswold, Mike Misenheimer, Art Powers, Ed Tromanhauser:
  An Eye for an Eye (New York: Holt, Rinehart and Winston; 1970),
  p. 82.

page 75, line 15
"the federal Bureau of Prisons"
  The New York Times, September 27, 1972.

page 75, line 33
"Lesley Oelsner"
> *The New York Times,* September 27, 1972.

page 77, line 12
"full understanding of what the plea"
> *Boykin v. Alabama* 395 U.S. 246 (1969).

page 77, line 29
"According to Gregory J. Hobbs, Jr."
> Gregory J. Hobbs, Jr.: "Judicial Supervision over California Plea
> Bargaining: Regulating the Trade," 59 *California Law Review* 962
> (1971).

page 78, line 3
"In *The Honest Politician's Guide to Crime Control*"
> Morris and Hawkins: *The Honest Politician's Guide to Crime Control*,
> p. 141.

CHAPTER 6, THE INDETERMINATE SENTENCE

page 79, line 6
"and reformation of criminals"
> American Correctional Association: *Congress of Corrections Pro-
> ceedings,* 1870, p. 6.

page 80, line 24
"As adopted unanimously by the 1870 Congress"
> Ibid.

page 81, line 4
"only the indeterminate sentence will be used"
> Ramsey Clark: *Crime in America* (New York: Simon and Schuster;
> 1970), p. 222.

page 82, line 25
"at the 1930 prison congress"
> American Correctional Association: *Congress of Corrections Pro-
> ceedings,* 1930.

page 83, line 26
"Declaration of the 1870 Prison Congress"
> American Correctional Association: *Congress of Corrections Proceed-
> ings,* 1870.

page 84, line 8
"1915 congress of the American Prison Association"
>American Correctional Association: *Congress of Corrections Proceedings,* 1915.

page 84, line 29
"Mr. Butler's point at the 1937 congress"
>American Correctional Association: *Congress of Corrections Proceedings,* 1915.

page 85, line 28
"In his book *I Chose Prison*"
>Bennett: *I Chose Prison,* pp. 187–9.

page 86, line 24
"the California Youth and Adult Corrections Agency"
>California Youth and Adult Corrections Agency (27), p. 71, quoted in *Deterrent Effects of Criminal Sanctions,* Progress Report of the Assembly Committee on Criminal Procedure (Sacramento, May 1968).

page 88, line 17
"An official version of procedures"
>Everett M. Porter: "State Imprisonment and Parole," in *California Criminal Law Practice* (California: Continuing Education of the Bar; 1969), pp. 445–612.

page 92, line 29
"in the *California Law Review*"
>Hobbs, Jr.: "Judicial Supervision over California Plea-Bargaining: Regulating the Trade," 59 *California Law Review* 962 (1971).

page 93, line 30
"the Progress Report"
>*Deterrent Effects of Criminal Sanctions.*

CHAPTER 7, TREATMENT

page 95, line 6
"American Prison Association"
>American Correctional Association: *Congress of Corrections Proceedings,* 1870.

page 96, line 2
"at the 1874 Congress"
>American Correctional Association: *Congress of Corrections Proceedings,* 1874.

page 96, line 10
"equipment and inadequate preparation"
> Karl Menninger: *The Crime of Punishment* (New York: Viking Compass edn.; 1969), p. 19.

page 96, line 11
"Most people who commit serious crimes"
> Ramsey Clark: *Crime in America* (New York: Simon and Schuster; 1970), p. 59.

page 96, line 23
"defined and disguised as treatment"
> Thomas S. Szasz: *Law, Liberty, and Psychiatry* (New York: Macmillan; 1963), p. 108.

page 96, line 26
"The bulk of our criminals"
> Harry Barnes and Negley K. Teeters: *New Horizons in Criminology*, 3rd edn. (Englewood Cliffs, N.J.: Prentice-Hall; 1959), p. 7.

page 98, line 29
"unstinted praise on these achievements"
> Menninger: *The Crime of Punishment*, pp. 231–2.

page 99, line 21
"as John Irwin puts it in *The Felon*"
> John Irwin: *The Felon* (Englewood Cliffs, N.J.: Prentice-Hall; 1970), p. 53.

page 100, line 2
"written in the fifties by Norman Fenton"
> Norman Fenton: *Treatment in Prison: How the Family Can Help* (Sacramento: State of California; 1959).

page 100, line 27
"entitled 'Psychiatry in Prison' "
> Harvey Powelson and Reinhard Bendix: "Psychiatry in Prison," *Psychiatry* Vol. XIV (1951).

page 103, line 12
"1966 study"
> *Deterrent Effects of Criminal Sanctions*, Progress Report of the Assembly Committee on Criminal Procedure (Sacramento, May 1968).

page 108, line 12
"a modern institution that houses about 425"
> *The New York Times Magazine* (September 17, 1972).

page 108, line 19
"the welfare of the patients"
> In the Supreme Court of the United States, October Term, 1971. No. 71–5144. *Edward Lee McNeil v. Director of Patuxent Institution.* On writ of certiorari to the Court of Special Appeals of Maryland. Brief of Respondent. Francis B. Burch, Attorney General of Maryland. April 17, 1972.

page 109, line 13
"an institution like this in our state"
> Ibid.

page 109, line 15
"Patuxent is a progressive step forward"
> *The New York Times Magazine* (September 17, 1972).

page 109, line 17
"Montgomery Circuit Court"
> *McCray v. Maryland*, Misc. Pet. No. 4363 (Montgomery City, Md., Cir. Ct., Nov. 11, 1971) (excerpted in 40 U.S. L.W. 2307), *appeal docketed*, No. 45 (Md., Sept. Term, 1972).

page 111, line 21
"drunkenness was offered at his trial"
> E. Barrett Prettyman, Jr.: "The Indeterminate Sentence and the Right to Treatment," 2 *American Criminal Law Review* 7 (1972).

page 112, line 27
"The U.S. Supreme Court thought otherwise"
> 407 U.S. 245 (1972).

page 113, line 28
"told the Washington *Post*"
> Washington *Post*, June 22, 1962.

page 114, line 14
"The behavior changing process involves"
> Rehabilitation Research Foundation: *The Draper E & D Project*, Final Report to U.S. Department of Labor Manpower Administration and HEW, Office of Education, Vol. I (Sept. 1, 1964–August 31, 1968), p. 31.

page 114, line 19
"In a frank talk ponderously entitled"
> American Correctional Association: *Congress of Corrections Proceedings*, 1964.

page 116, line 17
"that lowest of mortal creatures—the stoolpigeon"
Eugene Victor Debs: *Walls and Bars* (Chicago: Socialist Party; 1927), pp. 135–6.

CHAPTER 8, CLOCKWORK ORANGE

page 119, line 7
"California Prison, Parole and Probation System"
Technical Supplement #2, *The California Prison, Parole and Probation System,* A Special Report to the Assembly (Sacramento), p. 45.

page 120, line 20
"forecast a decade ago"
Edgar H. Schein: "Man Against Man: Brainwashing," *Corrective Psychiatry and Journal of Social Change,* Vol. 8, No. 2 (2nd quarter, 1962).

page 124, line 21
"operations memorandum from the bureau to staff"
Bureau of Prisons Operations Memorandum, Washington, D.C., 7300.128, October 25, 1972.

page 125, line 2
"Tom Wicker of *The New York Times*"
The New York Times, December 31, 1972, and January 2, 1973.

page 125, line 17
"an article in *Psychology Today*"
James V. McConnell: "Criminals Can Be Brainwashed—Now," *Psychology Today* (April 1970).

page 127, line 22
"1970, when *Medical World News*"
"Scaring the Devil Out," *Medical World News* (October 9, 1970).

page 127, line 30
"Anectine therapy program at Vacaville, California"
Arthur L. Mattocks and Charles C. Jew: "Assessment of an Aversive 'Contract' Program with Extreme Acting-out Criminal Offenders" (undated), unpubl.

page 128, line 10
"sensations of suffocation and drowning"
San Francisco *Chronicle* (This World), October 18, 1970, and Los Angeles *Times,* September 9, 1970.

page 129, line 6
"neurosurgery would be performed"
Letter from R. K. Procunier, California Director of Corrections, to
Robert L. Lawson, Executive Officer, California Council on Criminal
Justice, September 8, 1971.

page 129, line 12
"anyone who wants such assistance"
San Francisco *Chronicle*, December 31, 1971.

page 130, line 7
"in some patients appear to be irreversible"
1970 *Physicians Desk Reference*, 24th edn. (Oradell, N.J.: Medical
Economics; 1969).

page 130, line 20
"what will the prisons of 2000 A.D. be like"
James V. Bennett: *I Chose Prison* (New York: Alfred A. Knopf; 1970),
p. 226.

page 130, line 23
"in *The Crime of Punishment*"
Karl Menninger: *The Crime of Punishment* (New York: Viking
Compass edn.; 1969), pp. 276-7.

page 131, line 16
"1972 by LEAA reports"
Peter C. Buffan: *Homosexuality in Prisons* (U.S. Department of Justice,
Law Enforcement Assistance Administration, National Institute of
Law Enforcement and Criminal Justice, PR 72-3, February 1972).

page 131, line 27
"the California Department of Corrections *Research Review*"
Robert M. Dickover, ed.: *Annual Research Review, 1971* (Sacramento:
State of California, Human Relations Agency, Department of Corrections; 1971).

page 132, line 31
"the American Justice Institute"
Robert E. Doran: "Prison Adjustment Center Study" (LEAA Grant
N170-037, American Justice Institute, September 1971), unpubl.

page 134, line 22
"Robert E. Doran describes"
Ibid.

page 135, line 1
"a congressional subcommittee"
> U.S., Congress, House, Subcommittee No. 3 of the Committee on the
> Judiciary, *Corrections,* hearings, 92nd Cong., 1st sess., October 25,
> 1971 (Washington, D.C.: U.S. Government Printing Office; 1971),
> Part II, pp. 72–7, 32.

CHAPTER 9, CHEAPER THAN CHIMPANZEES

page 140, line 1
"I hope the chimpanzees don't come to hear of this"
> M. H. Pappworth: *Human Guinea Pigs* (Boston: Beacon Press; 1968),
> p. 64.

page 140, line 29
"In 1963, *Time* Magazine"
> Ibid., pp. 65–6.

page 141, line 5
"In July 1969"
> *The New York Times,* July 29, 1969.

page 144, line 27
"University of California Department of Criminology"
> Martin Miller: unpubl. paper.

page 145, line 11
"reports of serious adverse effects"
> Washington *Post,* July 24, 1966.

page 146, line 1
"*Journal of the American Medical Association*"
> Robert E. Hodges and William B. Bean: "The Use of Prisoners for
> Medical Research," *Journal of the American Medical Association,* Vol.
> 202, no. 6 (November 6, 1967).

page 150, line 17
"prisoners as subjects in medical experiments"
> "Ethics Governing the Service of Prisoners as Subjects of Medical
> Experiments," Report of a Committee Appointed by Governor Dwight
> H. Green of Illinois, *Journal of the American Medical Association,* Vol.
> 136, No. 7 (February 14, 1948), pp. 447–58.

page 151, line 13
"prison experiments in Alabama"
> U.S., Senate, Subcommittee on Monopoly of the Select Committee on

Small Business, *Competitive Problems in the Drug Industry: Present Status of Competition in the Pharmaceutical Industry,* Part 14, hearings, 91st Cong., 1st sess., June 19, August 7 and 12, 1969 (Washington, D.C.: U.S. Government Printing Office, 1969), p. 5689.

page 153, line 14
"Policy on Protection of Human Subjects"
DHEW Publication No. (NIH) 72–102 (Washington, D.C.: U.S. Government Printing Office; 1971).

page 155, line 2
"Phil Stanford, writing in *The New York Times Magazine*"
The New York Times Magazine (September 17, 1972).

page 156, line 24
"According to *Business Week*"
Business Week (June 27, 1964).

page 157, line 6
"use of the device here involved"
Calvin Sims et al. v. Parke Davis & Co. et al. D.C., 334 F. Supp. 774 (1971).

page 161, line 34
"The California constitution specifically prohibits"
California Constitution, article 10, section 1.

page 165, line 1
"annual *Research Review*"
Robert M. Dickover, ed.: *Annual Research Review, 1971* (Sacramento: State of California, Human Relations Agency, Department of Corrections; 1971).

page 166, line 26
"After the trial, Andrew C. Ivy"
Alexander Mitscherlich et al.: *Doctors of Infamy: The Story of the Nazi Medical Crimes* (New York: Henry Schuman; 1949).

CHAPTER 10, THE PRISON BUSINESS

page 170, line 7
"Ramsey Clark chides us for spending"
Ramsey Clark: *Crime in America* (New York: Simon and Schuster; 1970), pp. 123, 216.

page 170, line 33
"the effort was slowed by a tight budget"
  The New York Times, September 27, 1971.

page 171, line 1
"in 1971 the New York State prison budget"
  A Review of Various Aspects of the New York State Correctional Program, A Report to the New York State Legislature by the Senate Finance Minority, Samuel L. Greenberg, Chairman (August 29, 1971), unpubl.

page 171, line 15
"before Attica erupted *The New York Times*"
  The New York Times, September 27, 1971.

page 171, line 32
"emergency allocation of $4 million"
  The New York Times, September 28, 1971.

page 173, line 10
"fiscal years 1964–5 to 1972–3"
  Table I, Population and Cost Growth, 1959–73. Source: *Analysis of the Budget Bill: 1968–9 through 1972–3 additions* (Sacramento: Office of the Legislative Analyst).

page 174, line 27
"sets about program budgeting"
  Memorandum to Mr. R. K. Procunier, Director of Corrections, from Marie Vida Ryan, Senior Statistician, Administrative Information and Statistics Section. Subject: 1972 Legislative Bills: Computation Cost of Proposed Bills Which Involve *Death Penalty*, January 20, 1972.

page 177, line 13
"in the Folsom work strike"
  Eve Pell, ed.: *Maximum Security: Letters* (New York: E. P. Dutton & Co., Inc.; 1972), p. 209.

page 179, line 25
"released that year was $563,005.70"
  Letter to author from Philip Guthrie, August 7, 1972.

page 181, line 1
"the Federal prison system"
  U.S., Congress, House, Select Committee on Crime, *American Prisons in Turmoil*, hearings, 92nd Cong., 1st sess., November 29–December 3, 1971 (Washington, D.C.: U.S. Government Printing Office; 1972), Part I, pp. 277–99.

page 183, line 1
"Center for Democratic Studies"
  The Center Magazine, Vol. III, No. 3 (May/June 1971), p. 10.

page 183, line 26
"When pressures for reform"
  Struggle for Justice (New York: Hill and Wang; 1971), p. 172.

CHAPTER 11, EMPLOYMENT AND WELFARE

page 189, line 26
"departmental directive to the institutions"
  California Department of Corrections Administrative Manual, "Inmate
  Pay Plan," BA-XXXVII-01, 02, 06.

page 191, line 14
"Inmates do all the maintenance work"
  U.S., Congress, House, Subcommittee No. 3 of the Committee on the
  Judiciary, *Corrections*, hearings, 92nd Cong., 1st sess., October 25,
  1971 (Washington, D.C.: U.S. Government Printing Office, 1971),
  Part II, p. 6.

page 194, line 3
"succinctly set forth in a 1969 report"
  Assembly Office of Research, California Legislature: *Report on the
  Economic Status and Rehabilitative Value of California Correctional
  Industries* (Sacramento, February 1969).

page 194, line 18
"the National Institute for Public Health"
  Ralph K. Schwitzgebel: "Crime and Delinquency Issues: A Monograph
  Series," *Public Health Service Publication No. 2067* (February 1971).

page 194, line 22
"the 1965 Congress of the American Correctional Association"
  American Correctional Association: *Congress of Corrections Proceedings*, 1965.

page 195, line 4
"from 1828 to 1833 netted over $25,000 in profits"
  Richard Singer: "Bringing the Constitution to Prison: Substantive
  Due Process and the Eighth Amendment," 39 *Cincinnati Law Review*
  650 (1971).

page 195, line 18
"at the 1870 prison congress"
  American Correctional Association: *Congress of Corrections Proceedings*, 1870.

page 195, line 24
"the 1870 Declaration of Principles of the American Prison Association"
Ibid.

page 196, line 11
"the purpose of the proposed prison industries corporation"
James V. Bennett: *I Chose Prison* (New York: Alfred A. Knopf; 1970),
pp. 88–9.

page 196, line 25
"the most profitable line of business in the country"
Federal Prison Industries, Inc., Board of Directors *Annual Report
1970*, to the Congress of the United States. See also Ben H. Bagdikian:
The Shame of the Prisons (New York: Pocket Books; 1972), p. 20.

page 197, line 27
"The enemy is inmate idleness, so you put him to work"
Jack Waugh: "Prisons: Changing a System That Doesn't Work," *The
Christian Science Monitor,* December 16, 1971.

page 198, line 12
"Mark Lane, published in *The Black Panther*"
Mark Lane: "Excerpts from an Interview with Huey by Mark Lane,"
reprinted from the Los Angeles *Free Press. The Black Panther,* August
1, 1970.

page 198, line 26
"Both systems [contract labor and prison industry]"
Interview with author. See also *Justice Magazine* (May 1972).

page 199, line 3
"For example, the Director's Rules"
State of California Department of Corrections: *Rules of the Director
of Corrections and of the Wardens and Superintendents.*

page 202, line 5
"for the Director's Rules"
State of California Department of Corrections: *Rules of the Director
of Corrections and of the Wardens and Superintendents.*

page 203, line 3
"and a net of 13 percent"
Memorandum to Mr. R. K. Procunier, Director of Corrections, from
A. R. Todd, Deputy Director, Management Services Division, April 29,
1970. Subject: Inmate Welfare Fund Survey (Sacramento, California).

page 204, line 10
"as unconstitutional by the California Supreme Court in 1971"
> In re *van Geldern*, 5 C. 3d 832 (1971).

page 205, line 8
"charges, amounting to some $40,000 a year"
> Memorandum from Robin Lamson, California Assembly Office of Research, to Assemblyman Willie Brown, March 9, 1972.

page 206, line 19
"recreational and entertainment items for inmates"
> Letter from Philip D. Guthrie, Information Officer, California Department of Corrections, to Ms. Barbara Johns, August 12, 1969.

page 208, line 14
"as James V. Bennett put it"
> James V. Bennett: "Maryland's Prisoner Work Release Program: A Study and Evaluation," prepared for Governor J. M. Tawes, July 1966, p. 23. Quoted in Tim Fitzharris: "Work Release in Perspective," Doctoral Dissertation (School of Criminology, University of California, Berkeley, 1971).

page 210, line 18
"are enthusiastic about work furlough"
> Ibid.

page 212, line 13
"*Pitts v. Reagan*"
> *Pitts v. Reagan*, 14 C.A. 3d 112 (1971).

page 214, line 13
"Tim Findley, writing in the San Francisco *Chronicle*"
> San Francisco *Chronicle*, February 2, 1973.

CHAPTER 12, PAROLE

page 216, epigraph
"Justice Hugo Black"
> Justice Hugo Black, quoted in Robert J. Minton, Jr., ed.: *Inside Prison American Style* (New York: Random House; 1971), pp. 214–15.

page 216, line 5
"any of the same 200,000 individuals"
> H. Jack Griswold, Mike Misenheimer, Art Powers, Ed Tromanhauser: *An Eye for an Eye* (New York: Holt, Rinehart and Winston; 1970), p. 203.

page 216, line 9
"prescribed path to eventual freedom"
  Corrections, the President's Commission on Law Enforcement and the
  Administration of Justice, Task Force Report, 1967.

page 217, line 19
"They don't want to lose you"
  Minton: *Inside Prison American Style*, p. 255.

page 218, line 5
"The first time I started across the street, I remember"
  John Irwin: *The Felon* (Englewood Cliffs, N.J.: Prentice-Hall, Inc.;
  1970), p. 115.

page 218, line 12
"the President's Crime Commission Report"
  The Challenge of Crime in a Free Society, A Report by the President's
  Commission on Law Enforcement and the Administration of Justice
  (Washington, D.C.: U.S. Government Printing Office; 1967), p. 165.

page 218, line 17
"former U.S. Senator Charles E. Goodell"
  Testimony of Charles E. Goodell and Andrew von Hirsch before Sub-
  committee No. 3 of the House Judiciary Committee on H.R. 13118,
  April 26, 1972.

page 218, line 22
"tend to conflict"
  Testimony of Goodell and von Hirsch.

page 219, line 29
"get permission before suing for divorce"
  For parole conditions see Ralph K. Schwitzgebel: "Crime and Delinquency Issues: A Monograph Series," *Public Health Service Publication No. 2067* (February 1971).

page 220, line 20
"the California parole system"
  Nuttall: "The Protection of Human Rights," unpubl.

page 221, line 2
"conducted by James O. Robison and Paul Takagi"
  Paul Takagi and James Robison: "The Parole Violator: An Organizational Reject," *Journal of Research in Crime and Delinquency* (January
  1969).

page 222, line 2
"would have been made by random selection"
Testimony of Goodell and von Hirsch.

page 222, line 35
"legend that two-thirds return to prison"
Norval Morris and Gordon Hawkins: *The Honest Politician's Guide to Crime Control* (Chicago: Univ. of Chicago Press; 1970), p. 117.

page 223, line 4
"80 percent of all felonies are committed by repea. ʔrs"
Ramsey Clark: *Crime in America* (New York: Simon and Schuster; 1970), p. 215.

page 223, line 8
"estimates that among adult offenders 35 to 45 percent"
Corrections, Task Force Report, 1967.

page 223, line 19
"male parolees released in 1969"
David Greenberg: "How Dangerous Is the Ex-Convict?" (Committee for the Study of Incarceration, November 1972), unpubl.

page 224, line 9
"rules in the 'contract' "
Christopher Nuttall: "The Protection of Human Rights in the Rehabilitation of Prisoners," unpubl.

page 225, line 19
"Goodell and Hirsch told the House Judiciary Committee"
Testimony of Goodell and von Hirsch.

page 225, line 35
"at New York State University"
American Correctional Association: *Congress of Corrections Proceedings*, 1970.

page 226, line 5
"published by the Public Health Service"
Schwitzgebel: "Crime and Delinquency Issues: A Monograph Series."

page 227, line 1
"*Transactions on Aerospace and Electronic Systems*"
Joseph Meyer, in *Transactions on Aerospace and Electronic Systems*, (January 1971).

page 227, line 18
"within a broad view of the issue"
Schwitzgebel: "Crime and Delinquency Issues: A Monograph Series."

CHAPTER 13, PRISON PROTEST

page 228, epigraph
"It used to be"
> U.S., Congress, House, Subcommittee No. 3 of the Committee on the Judiciary, *Corrections,* hearings, 92nd Cong., 1st sess., October 25, 1971 (Washington, D.C.: U.S. Government Printing Office; 1971), Part II, p. 5.

page 229, line 6
"In his book *Violence Behind Bars* Vernon Fox"
> Vernon Fox: *Violence Behind Bars* (New York: Vantage Press; 1956), pp. 1–33.

page 230, line 5
"During the past 2½ years"
> American Correctional Association: *Congress of Corrections Proceedings, 1953.*

page 230, line 18
"clearly, the perception of riot causes"
> American Correctional Association: *Congress of Corrections Proceedings, 1960.*

page 230, line 29
"his colleagues in the American Prison Association"
> American Correctional Association: *Congress of Corrections Proceedings, 1913.*

page 231, line 8
"Warden R. W. Meier of McNeil Island Federal Penitentiary"
> American Correctional Association: *Congress of Corrections Proceedings, 1969.*

page 231, line 18
"question by Congressman Charles B. Rangel"
> U.S., Congress, House, Select Committee on Crime, *American Prisons in Turmoil,* hearings, 92nd Cong., 1st sess., November 29–December 3, 1971 (Washington, D.C.: U.S. Government Printing Office; 1972), Part I, pp. 347, 367.

page 233, line 19
"by 1968 *The Outlaw*"
> *The Outlaw,* July 1, 1968.

page 235, line 24
"The Tombs demands of August 1970"
>   *Struggle for Justice* (New York: Hill and Wang; 1971), pp. 2–3.

page 235, line 34
"new manifesto was issued containing this language"
>   Herman Badillo and Milton Haynes: *A Bill of No Rights: Attica and
>   the American Prison System* (New York: Outerbridge and Lazard, Inc.;
>   1972), pp. 27–9.

page 237, line 30
"closing of access roads would be prudent"
>   Unpubl. paper given to author by Associate Warden Park.

page 238, line 18
"This modest publication"
>   *Grapevine*, Vol. 4, no. 1 (January 31, 1971), to Vol. 4, no. 12 (Decem-
>   ber 29, 1972).

page 245, line 4
"Senator Thomas J. Dodd's committee"
>   U.S., Congress, Committee on Judiciary, Subcommittee to Investigate
>   Juvenile Delinquency, *Juvenile Delinquency,* hearings, 91st Cong.
>   (Washington: U.S. Government Printing Office; 1971), Part 20.

CHAPTER 14, THE LAWLESSNESS OF CORRECTIONS

page 248, epigraph
"I would like to say one thing"
>   U.S., Congress, House, Select Committee on Crime, *American Prisons
>   in Turmoil,* hearings, 92nd Cong., 1st sess., November 29–December
>   3, 1971 (Washington, D.C.: U.S. Government Printing Office; 1972),
>   Part I, p. 238.

page 249, line 5
"According to an 1871 case"
>   *Ruffin v. Commonwealth*, 62 Va. (21 Gratt.) 790, 796 (1871).

page 249, line 17
"with the ordinary prison rules or regulations"
>   *Banning v. Looney*, 213 F.2d. 771 (1954).

page 249, line 20
"the management of disciplinary rules of such institutions"
>   *Sutton v. Settle*, 302 F.2d. 286, 288 (1962).

page 250, line 11
"As stated in the Director's Rules"
> State of California Department of Corrections: *Rules of Director of Corrections and of the Wardens and Superintendents* (Sacramento, Calif.), revised 1967.

page 251, line 17
"by a San Quentin guard for *Correctional Review*"
> Sidney Ten-Eyck: "The Correctional Officer's Job," *Correctional Review* (Department of Corrections, Youth and Adult Corrections Agency, February 1963).

page 252, footnote, line 1
"decision of Judge Zirpoli in *Clutchette v. Procunier*"
> *Clutchette v. Procunier*, 328 F. Supp. 767 (N.D. Cal. 1971).

page 259, line 21
"Hirschkop's operation"
> Philip J. Hirschkop and Michael A. Millemann: "The Unconstitutionality of Prison Life," 55 *Virginia Law Review* 795 (1969).

page 260, line 13
"may amount to cruel and unusual punishment"
> *Holt v. Sarver*, 309 F. Supp. 362 (E.D. Ark. 1970).

page 260, line 30
"earned good time credit may be revoked"
> *Sostre v. McGinnis* 442 F.2d. 178 (2d Cir. 1971).

page 261, line 15
"the state penal system"
> *Landman v. Royster* 333 F. Supp. 621 (E.D. Va. 1971).

page 262, line 17
"in the *Buffalo Law Review*"
> Fred Cohen: "The Discovery of Prison Reform," 21 *Buffalo Law Review* 855 (1972).

page 262, line 27
"the case of *Clutchette v. Procunier*"
> *Clutchette v. Procunier*.

page 263, line 6
"punitive segregation"
> David F. Greenberg and Fay Stender: "The Prison as a Lawless Agency," 21 *Buffalo Law Review* 799, 811 (1972).

page 264, line 16
"Again in 1966 a U.S. district court"
    Jordan v. Fitzharris, 257 F. Supp. 674 (N.D. Calif. 1960).

page 264, line 33
"Leading Edge of the Law"
    Published by Bancroft Whitney Co., 301 Brannan St., San Francisco,
    Calif.

page 265, line 18
"New York State Special Commission on Attica"
    Attica, The Official Report of the New York State Special Commission
    on Attica (New York: Bantam Books, Inc.; 1972), pp. 451–2.

page 265, line 27
"Second Circuit Court of Appeals"
    Herman Badillo and Milton Haynes: *A Bill of No Rights: Attica and
    the American Prison System* (New York: Outerbridge and Lazard;
    1972), pp. 27–9.

page 266, line 28
"writes Professor Cohen"
    Cohen: "The Discovery of Prison Reform."

page 267, line 10
    Fortune Society v. McGinnis 319 F. Supp. 901, 905 (1970).

page 267, line 21
"*v. Brewer*"
    Morrissey v. Brewer, 443 F.2d 942 (1972).

page 268, line 5
"Professor Fred Cohen points out"
    Fred Cohen: "A Comment on Morrissey v. Brewer," 8 *Criminal Law
    Bulletin* 616 (1972).

page 268, line 23
"gains of prison litigation"
    Cohen: "The Discovery of Prison Reform."

CHAPTER 15, REFORM OR ABOLITION?

page 270, epigraph
"if any person is addressing himself"
    George Bernard Shaw: *The Crime of Imprisonment* (New York: The
    Philosophical Library; 1946), p. 13.

page 270, line 4
"the authors of *Struggle for Justice*"
Struggle for Justice (New York: Hill and Wang; 1971), p. 8.

page 271, line 11
"Declaration of Principles"
American Correctional Association: *Congress of Corrections Proceedings*, 1870.

page 271, line 20
"Wickersham Commission"
U.S. National Commission on Law Observance and Enforcement: *Reports* (Washington, D.C.: U.S. Government Printing Office; 1931).

page 271, line 31
"Skip now to *The Challenge of Crime in a Free Society*"
The Challenge of Crime in a Free Society, A Report by the President's Commission on Law Enforcement and the Administration of Justice (Washington, D.C.: U.S. Government Printing Office; 1967), pp. 159–185.

page 272, line 18
"of the American Prison Association"
American Correctional Association: *Congress of Corrections Proceedings*, 1870.

page 273, line 3
"Dr. Frank Tannenbaum, a pioneer student of prison"
Harry Barnes and Negley K. Teeters: *New Horizons in Criminology*, 3rd edn. (Englewood Cliffs, N.J.: Prentice-Hall; 1959), p. 585, quoting Frank Tannenbaum, *Wall Shadows* (New York: Oxford University Press; 1948), p. 11.

page 273, line 8
"prison mail censorship case"
Morales v. Schmidt 340 F. Supp. 544 (1972).

page 273, line 16
"I also agree with the authors of *Struggle for Justice*"
Struggle for Justice, pp. 23–4.

page 273, line 35
"a headline in the San Francisco *Chronicle*"
San Francisco *Chronicle*, November 22, 1971.

page 274, line 7
"his book *Crime in America*"
Ramsey Clark: *Crime in America* (New York: Simon and Schuster; 1970), pp. 215, 224–5.

page 274, line 28
"a guest editorial in *Saturday Review*"
> Arthur Waskow: " ' . . . I Am Not Free,' " *Saturday Review* (January 8, 1972).

page 276, line 15
"deputy attorney general of Washington, D.C., describes the process"
> Center for the Study of Democratic Institutions: *The Center Magazine*, Vol. III, no. 3 (May/June 1971), p. 10.

page 277, line 2
"or .05 percent, was for murder"
> Barnes and Teeters: *New Horizons in Criminology*, p. 319.

page 277, line 11
"Of those convicted of sex offenses"
> Herbert A. Bloch and Gilbert Geis: *Man, Crime, and Society* (New York: Random House; 1962), p. 290.

page 277, line 23
"a lower record of recidivism"
> Barnes and Teeters: *New Horizons in Criminology*, p. 102.

page 278, line 13
"Charles Howe of the San Francisco *Chronicle*"
> San Francisco *Chronicle*, January 22, 1973.

page 279, line 6
"in the United States than there are today"
> Edward M. Brecher and the eds. of Consumer Reports: *Licit and Illicit Drugs* (Boston: Little, Brown & Company; 1973). See also Peter Steinfels and Robert M. Veatch in *New York Times Book Review* (February 4, 1973).

page 280, line 23
"California Assembly Committee on Criminal Procedure"
> *Deterrent Effects of Criminal Sanctions*, Progress Report of the Assembly Committee on Criminal Procedure (Sacramento, May 1968).

page 281, line 34
"incarcerated until his sentence expired"
> American Bar Association Project on Minimum Standards for Criminal Justice, Standard Relating to Sentencing Alternatives and Procedures 59, quoted in Ronald L. Goldfarb and Linda R. Singer: *After Conviction* (New York: Simon and Schuster; 1973), p. 180.

page 284, line 16
"an unpublished working paper"
> Patricia Ebener, Susan Steward, and Andrew von Hirsch, The Committee for the Study of Incarceration: "Alternatives to Incarceration: Current Programs" (November 20, 1972), unpubl.

page 285, line 27
"exhaustive study *After Conviction*"
> Goldfarb and Singer: *After Conviction*, pp. 179–80.

page 286, line 33
"the American Friends Service Committee in February 1973"
> Minutes, American Friends Service Committee meeting, First Unitarian Church, San Francisco, California, February 1973.

page 287, line 24
"In contrast are the views of L. H. Fudge"
> Memorandum from L. H. Fudge, Associate Superintendent—Camps, North Coast Conservation Center. Subject: In-Service Training Recommendations, November 4, 1970.

page 288, line 22
"two kinds of political prisoners"
> Fred Hiestand and Jim Smith: "Of Panthers and Prisons: An Interview with Huey P. Newton," 29 *National Lawyers Guild Practitioner* 57 (1972).

page 289, line 21
"As the authors of *Struggle for Justice*"
> *Struggle for Justice*, p. 16.

page 289, line 27
"writing in the *Criminal Law Bulletin*"
> Samuel Jordan: "Prison Reform: In Whose Interest?" 7 *Criminal Law Bulletin* 779–87 (1971).

page 292, line 21
"Attorney General John N. Mitchell announced"
> John N. Mitchell: "New Doors, Not Old Walls," Address to the National Conference on Corrections, Williamsburg, Virginia, December 6, 1971 (Washington, D.C.: Department of Justice; 1971).

page 293, line 20
"by the authors of *Struggle for Justice*"
> *Struggle for Justice*, pp. 158, 169.

page 294, line 26
"the Annual Chief Justice Earl Warren Conference"
Annual Chief Justice Earl Warren Conference on Advocacy in the
United States: *A Program for Prison Reform. The Final Report,* June
9–10, 1972 (The Roscoe Pound–American Trial Lawyers Foundation,
20 Garden Street, Cambridge, Mass. 02138).

INDEX

A NOTE ON THE TYPE

The text of this book was set on the Linotype in Times Roman, a type face designed by Stanley Morison for *The Times* (London) and first introduced by that newspaper in 1932.

Among typographers and designers of the twentieth century, Stanley Morison has been a strong forming influence, as typographical adviser to the English Monotype Corporation, as a director of two distinguished English publishing houses, and as a writer of sensibility, erudition, and keen practical sense.

The book was composed, printed, and bound by The Haddon Craftsmen, Inc., Scranton, Pennsylvania.

Typography and binding design by Earl Tidwell.